In *The Offering*, Judy Powell tells the story of Barkley Moore, one of God's choice servants. In so doing, she records the remarkable history of Oneida Baptist Institute and a significant part of the mission work of the people known as Kentucky Baptists.

Barkley Moore was a father-figure to thousands of children, many of whom had no father. One paragraph sufficiently illustrates what Moore meant to his students and the need for his story to be told:

> "Mr. Moore you are the nearest to a father I've had." I am a little startled. The boy goes on to relate to me a conversation that he had with me once in the laundry room as he washed his clothes. I don't remember that particular conversation, but the boy said, "You'll never know just how much that meant to me." I don't tell him that I don't remember. He cries some more. We never know when we are saying something that sticks with someone a lifetime.

Thanks to Judy Powell, many of Moore's words will now stick with me for a lifetime. More importantly, Moore's life dedicated to humbly serving Christ and preparing the next generation to serve Christ, can challenge and inspire generations to come.

I am praying the Lord will use *The Offering* to stir us to make of our lives the kind of fragrant offering to Christ that surely was the life of Barkley Moore.

Paul H. Chitwood, Ph.D.
Executive Director-Treasurer, Kentucky Bap

D1608097

Barkley Moore was a remarkable man—a visionary who worked tirelessly to serve the Lord and the school he loved. I did not know Dr. Moore personally but he has come to life for me through the pages of *The Offering*. I arrived in Kentucky in September 1999 to begin serving as Executive Director-Treasurer of Kentucky Woman's Missionary Union. I quickly learned about Oneida Baptist Institute and began to hear stories about Barkley Moore. On visits to Oneida, I have been impressed by the facilities, the working farm, and the stories of students whose lives have been changed "for time and eternity." But through reading *The Offering*, I have not only learned about the history of Oneida, but can now appreciate the significant impact of Barkley Moore and why people remember him so fondly.

The vision of Dr. Moore to work with students who need an Oneida education, to welcome students from around the world, and to share the gospel continues to this day. *The Offering* not only conveys the life story of Barkley Moore, but introduces the Oneida experience. Kentucky Baptist support of Oneida through the Cooperative Program and the Barkley Moore Offering are vital to continue the mission of this great school.

Above all, pray for Oneida! Pray for the faculty and students. Pray for a host of volunteers and all of the donations they bring. Pray for students who are struggling academically and need the special help of Oneida. Pray for students from around the world who want to attend school in the United States and somehow find Oneida. Most are not Christians when they arrive.

Who would ever dream of the impact of a school nestled in the mountains of Eastern Kentucky to touch the world? Barkley Moore had traveled far and wide through the Peace Corps, but came home to Kentucky with the world on his heart. His life offering was well-pleasing to God.

Joy Bolton
Executive Director-Treasurer, Kentucky Woman's Missionary Union

At a time when the United States of America was being viewed nationally and internationally as the "Ugly America", Barkley was seen by the national media such as the New York Times and others, as the "Beautiful American" who put service above self. I read several national publications and even saw Barkley on Robert Schuller's national TV program as the "Beautiful American" and justifiably so. Barkley made the world a far, far better place because he graced us with his presence as an outstanding Christian in word and deed. This book is a "must-read."

For everyone who remembers Barkley, the book brings back so many memories. For those who did not have an opportunity to know him, the book gives you a glimpse of the person who made this world a better place for so many.

Dr. Jim Taylor
President, University of the Cumberlands, Williamsburg, Kentucky

Very detailed and is presented with a literary style that brings "life" to "facts", which is what Mr. Moore's life did for the missionary message of the Scripture. A great narrative of a man's life that is almost too great to be believed by the common reader.

Reverend Steve May
Former teacher at Oneida Baptist Institute

Alabama Campers on Mission have done volunteer work at Oneida since the mid-nineties. The first year was right after Dr. Moore died so the Alabama COMers did not meet him; but they met "his people". To be a part of the Oneida project each year is the highlight of the year for Alabama Campers on Mission. When we talk about Dr. Moore's "people" we are saying people who know how to welcome a group, and how to make a group feel like they are really needed. Oneida from the very beginning has always treated the Alabama COMers like they were the best group they had ever had, and allowed us to "really see" the ministry of the institute - a way to touch a lot of young people's lives.

The school is always well prepared for our team, which some years have numbered in the sixties, and the opportunities to help are so varied that regardless of the talents/skills of our group there seems to be something that everyone can do. We have more people who want to help at Oneida than in any other single project. Everything our group does for Oneida seems to be a "you can do it" and "a good job, thanks!" It seems that the "Volunteer" tradition that Dr. Moore instilled in Oneida lives on!

Steve Stephens
Alabama Baptist State Board of Missions, Men's Ministry/Brotherhood Consultant, Royal Ambassador Consultant, SBOM Liaison for Campers on Missions, SBOM Liaison for Agriculture & Vet Fellowship

Oneida Baptist Institute has been a special name to me since my high school days when our schools played each other in basketball. In October 1985 I had the privilege of visiting the campus for the first time when a group of ladies from our church took a donation of clothing. We met with President Barkley Moore, who gave us a tour of the campus and shared stories and history of the school. It is a trip I have never forgotten. You could just feel his love for the school and compassion for the students. Serving with the Kentucky Baptist Convention, I have had many opportunities to be on the OBI campus for meetings and conferences and have worked closely with each president since Dr. Moore to help place short-term volunteer teams and missionaries to serve there. OBI is a unique place. The students are literally from "across the street" and "around the world." They get a first-class education, experience love from faculty and staff, and, most of all, hear the message of Jesus.

Teresa Parrett
Missions Mobilization Coordinator, Kentucky Baptist Convention

What the Media had to say in 1971

The National Observer: When you meet a guy like Barkley, says his friend John Newton, "It makes you realize that there really is a Supreme Being, a force for good in the world. There's got to be *somebody* that could create a person like him. You just can't believe in *nothing* when you're around Barkley.

The National Observer: Barkley Moore: A beautiful American...a Peace Corps volunteer who couldn't come home. "Don't talk about principles...get out and live them."

The Christian Science Monitor: Barkley Moore's concept of a revolutionary is one "who changes the life of people for the better".

The Chicago Sun-Times: If the fabric of Barkley Moore's life could be ripped into a thousand pieces, each would be a good deed.

Focus—Chicago Today: He's the Lawrence of Iran.

The New York Times: Barkley Moore thinks that it is important to "love people" and as a Peace Corps member he demonstrated that belief by staying at his overseas post longer than any of the other 37,000 volunteers. [This story by Tom Seppy of the Associated Press was carried in approximately 100 newspapers.]

After His Death

Dr. Moore has shown generations of young people that hard work, devotion to community, and service to God are the most honorable and everlasting pursuits.
U.S. House of Representatives
Representative Harold "Hal" Rogers
January 26, 1994

The most prominent glory of a country is in its great men—a nation's spirit—and its success will depend on its willingness to learn from their example. In life we shall find many men that are great, and some men that are good, but very few men that are both great and good...
A resolution... in loving memory and honor of Barkley Moore.
Senators Blevins, Huff, Berger, Borders, Boswell, Buford, Casebler, Kafoglls, Karem, Kelly, Lackey, Leeper, Moore, Pendleton, Rand, Rogers, Saunders, Shaughnessy, Smith and D. Williams
Kentucky State Senate Regular Session, January 26,1994

Mr. President, Barkley Moore had a motto he referred to when he described [Oneida]. He said, "You don't have to be anybody to get here, but you're going to be somebody before you leave." Barkley Moore was someone who gave to others throughout his entire life and his absence will be felt by all whose lives he touched.

The Senate of the United States
Senator Mitch McConnell
Congressional Record, *February 1,1994*

In many ways, Barkley Moore was the Albert Schweitzer of eastern Kentucky...He was one of the finest servants Kentucky Baptists have ever produced. His life was consumed with taking care of and strengthening Oneida Baptist Institute...All Kentucky Baptists owe him a debt of gratitude and will miss him greatly.

Reverend Bob Browning, President Kentucky Baptist Convention, January 27, 1994

Barkley was a man of "deep" faith. Many of us like to think that we are people of faith, but Barkley was one who truly put complete trust in God. He was deeply convinced, that if we always insist on having tangible evidence that something could be done, there was no faith. Our faith is shown, if we are willing to launch out into the deep without a life preserver in sight. Our faith is shown, if we are willing to penetrate the darkness trusting that He will be a "light unto our path." Buildings have been built, equipment purchased, programs developed, teachers hired and students accepted on scholarship simply trusting that the Owner of "the cattle upon a thousand hills" is easily able to meet our needs.

Dr. W.F. Underwood, President Oneida Baptist Institute, 1994-2012
Barkley Moore: A Compilation of thoughts and Memories by Friends and Acquaintances, (Dr. Joel A. Rackley, Compiler, 1999)

Barkley Moore, President, Oneida Baptist Institute, 1972-1994.

The Offering

Barkley Moore—A Life for Time and Eternity

Judy Ratliff Powell

CROSSBOOKS
PUBLISHING

CrossBooks™
A Division of LifeWay
1663 Liberty Drive
Bloomington, IN 47403
www.crossbooks.com
Phone: 1-866-879-0502

First published by CrossBooks 05/23/2014

ISBN: 978-1-4627-3751-2 (sc)
ISBN: 978-1-4627-3750-5 (hc)
ISBN: 978-1-4627-3752-9 (e)

Library of Congress Control Number: 2014909323

Printed in the United States of America.

This book is printed on acid-free paper.

Photo credit for Chapel Steeple
image to Rebekah Hasty Travis

Dedicated
to
Barkley Moore's mother
Mrs. Evelyn Moore
and
Every member of the Oneida family
Past, present, and future
and
Every member of Barkley Moore's Iranian family

Contents

Acknowledgements

There are so many without whom this book could not have been written, so many to whom I owe a debt of gratitude.

First, I must say "Thank you" to Rev. Larry Gritton, Jr., Oneida Baptist Institute's current president, for endorsing and supporting the publication of *The Offering*. President Gritton clearly sees the importance of Oneida's students knowing their roots and keeping the rich heritage of faith and values handed down by our forefathers—for Time and Eternity.

Dr. Conley Powell, astronautical engineer, college professor, my husband, and my editor—a native of Clay County, and a graduate of the Institute. I owe Conley my deepest gratitude and love.

Ms. Myrtle Webb Cooke, former student and Oneida Alumni Director, who loaned personal letters and spent many hours correcting errors and editing my first feeble attempt at writing *The Offering*.

Ms. Amanda Roberts, current Oneida Alumni Director and "Keeper of the Dreams" for proof reading the manuscript and helping find photos.

Rebekah Hasty Travis' *Chapel Steeple* (2006) photograph was perfect for the cover of the book. Mary Ratliff Schuck, my daughter, took the author photo. Thank you both.

My schoolteacher sister, Frances Cobb, who listened to me read every chapter as it was written and Joyce Sullivan, my friend, who traveled extensively with me while I was doing research.

Mr. Shannon H. Wilson, Head, Special Collections & Archives, Berea College, and Ms. Wanda Hendrix, Interlibrary Loan Librarian, Decatur, Alabama Public Library.

Dr. Todd Deaton, Editor of the *Western Recorder*, for access to archived articles written by Barkley Moore.

Mrs. Peggy Smith, one of Barkley's best friends, loaned personal letters from Barkley to her family, read the manuscript each time it was altered, and encouraged me to keep at it.

Mr. John Monday, Ms. Denise Spencer, Ms. Tamara Cochran, Mr. Jerry Pierce, Oneida staff members.

Gloria Bowling, Barkley's sister, who loaned family pictures and helped me with family history, without whom I would never have begun to write *The Offering*.

To Barkley Moore, "Thanks." You wrote the story of your own life in words and deeds, right down to the last detail. May all who read your words be resolved to keep the faith, knowing that " ...in all things, we are more than conquerors through him that loved us." (*Romans* 8: 37)

Foreword

Larry A. Gritton, Jr.
President, Oneida Baptist Institute

As I read the words written by Judy Ratliff Powell in the book you are about to read, my heart was moved. Her words on the following pages brought Dr. Barkley Moore and his legacy back to life. For those who knew Dr. Moore, this book will move you and remind you what a privilege it was to know him. For those who did not know Dr. Moore, this book will serve as a wonderful lesson on the history of Oneida Baptist Institute and the mark that he left on his beloved school.

As I currently am privileged to serve as Oneida's twelfth president, I often find myself thinking of Dr. Moore. I am a plain and simple person, especially when it comes to decorative things. There are very few pictures in my office, but one of those few includes Dr. Moore. I often ask myself the following types of questions: What would Dr. Moore do in this situation? Would Dr. Moore allow this to happen? What would Dr. Moore think of this decision? I can picture him sitting in the same office in which I now sit. I can hear, feel, and see him all over this campus. He loved the Lord. He loved Oneida. He loved people and he loved me and every other student and staff member who ever passed through this little campus in the hills of southeastern Kentucky.

I have had the privilege of personally knowing a few great people in my life, and Dr. Barkley Moore was most definitely one of those great people. As I grew up as a faculty kid at Oneida, Barkley Moore was not only the intimidating and passionate man at the helm of my school, but he was also a part of my family. His late night visits and meals, stories about Oneida's history, discussion with my parents about school issues and challenges are indelible images seared on the Oneida Baptist Institute portion of my brain. Even as a child, I knew that whenever I was in the presence of Dr. Moore I was indeed in the presence of greatness. To know Barkley Moore was to know greatness.

I have also had the privilege of knowing a few passionate people in my life, and Dr. Barkley Moore was most definitely one of those passionate people. You did not have to be around Dr. Moore very long to find out what he was passionate about. Just as the psalmist talked of his cup running over, so did Dr. Moore's cup of passion for the school he so loved. As a matter of fact, his cup overflowed and spilled onto everyone in his life. He was passionate about the Lord, the school that he loved, and her people. As he quickly and emphatically moved across the Oneida campus giving tours and talking about his school, it was often amusing to watch the tour groups, young and old, struggle to keep up with this passionate man and hear what he was saying. His passion for serving the Lord and others was astounding. To know Barkley Moore was to know passion.

Oh the tales I have heard Dr. Moore tell. He could tell the story of most any student on the Oneida campus and often did just that to anyone who would listen. One of the stories Dr. Moore seemed to enjoy telling about me was one involving my birth. Just after my birth in Corbin, Kentucky my father brought his basketball team to the hospital to see me. They were returning home from a game and of course Dr. Moore was with the team. Dr. Moore would later tell the story over and over of how these large basketball players convinced the nurse that they were my older brothers and that they needed to see me. Everyone who had ever been a part of this school was family to Dr. Moore.

Basketball was a huge part of my Oneida experience, but knowing Dr. Moore was an even bigger part of that experience. In March of 1993, my Oneida basketball playing experience came to a close as we were defeated by Corbin High School in the regional tournament at Bell County High School. As I sat in the shower area of the locker room and wept like a child the first person on the scene to comfort me was my coach, who also happened to be my father. Dr. Moore soon followed with his own support. His words were comforting and his care for me as a young man meant so much. He knew I wanted to travel with the Kentucky Baptists Sports Crusaders that summer, and that the trip to China would be far more expensive than my family could ever afford. As I cried that night in the locker room Dr. Moore said, "I am going to pay for your trip to China". That trip cost $2500 and Dr. Moore wrote me a personal check for the trip. In the fall of 1993, Dr. Moore had me speak in Chapel to the current student body about my trip. Even as an 18-year-old kid, I could clearly see how proud he was of me and what I had learned on that trip. That trip and my subsequent mission trips had such a major role in making me who I would become, and Dr. Moore had a major part in that. In the summer of 1994 I would return to China, and the Lord used that trip to teach me lessons about trusting Him that I still carry with me today. Had Dr. Moore not sent me on that first China trip in 1993, I am sure I would not have gone in 1994. Dr. Moore's generosity was spurred by his love for Oneida and a young man who had grown up at Oneida. Dr. Moore's generosity changed my life.

Like any other family, Oneida had her share of problems during Dr. Moore's tenure as president. With the Lord's help Dr. Moore, like any good father would, led his Oneida family through some difficult times. Each of the thousand upon thousand family members who have passed through this little place we call Oneida could probably tell you their own Dr. Moore stories. I could tell you story after story about my encounters with this great man named Glen Barkley Moore.

Dr. Barkley Moore lived, ate, breathed, and slept Oneida Baptist Institute. Now two decades removed from Dr. Moore's death people tied to Oneida still talk about the man known as "Barkley". While I am sure he had some, I am not sure what Dr. Moore's interests were outside of Oneida. He always seemed to be here, and even when he wasn't here he was promoting his beloved school to anyone and everyone who would listen.

What was it that made Barkley Moore great? What was it that made him so passionate about Oneida Baptist Institute? Was it his super intelligence? Was it his time spent in the Peace Corps? Was it his ability to believe in both God and people? Was it his ability to forgive and give people second, third, and fourth chances to succeed? Was it his heart for all things related to service to Christ and Oneida Baptist Institute? While all these things were surely part of what made Dr. Moore great and passionate, I believe what really set him apart from most leaders was his faith. His faith could move mountains. He built buildings when there was no money. He accepted kids who had seemingly had no hope. He exercised a faith the likes of which I have never seen in any other person.

Dr. Moore exercised tremendous faith in the Lord and the creation made in His image. Dr. Moore often said, "God made them, Jesus died for them, and we have a bed for them." Both young people and adults who passed through Oneida during the Barkley Moore era experienced and saw that faith and love firsthand. It is one thing to profess to love the Lord and people, but it is quite another to show it through our daily actions.

As you read this book, it is my prayer that the Lord will not only impress upon you the greatness and passion of Dr. Barkley Moore, but that even more so he will impress upon you His own greatness and passion for you, his creation. Dr. Moore was a great and passionate man, but it is our Lord and Savior, Jesus Christ, who created and inspired him to be whom and what he was in and for the Kingdom of God. The Lord used Dr. Moore to touch so many lives, and I pray He uses this book to touch yours.

Introduction

William W. Marshall
Executive Director of the Kentucky Baptist Convention
1983-1997

The state of Kentucky has had its share of our nation's notable leaders in its past, including Abraham Lincoln, Daniel Boone, and Henry Clay. Biographers have kept such leaders "alive" for future generations to gain a richer understanding of the person and the leader-characteristics evident in the subject. The reader is about to embark on author Judy Powell's enticing biographical journey through the life of one of Kentucky's most remarkable leaders of the 20th century. His name is Dr. Barkley Moore, a former president of the Oneida Baptist Institute, Kentucky's oldest boarding school. His most famous words were: "You don't have to be anybody to come here, but you are going to be somebody when you leave". Read about this unique school on Face book! He is the most singularly dedicated and achieving Christian I have known, growing the struggling school to 600 students and a 4 million dollar annual budget.

Moore furthered his education from a "mountain boy" to a degree from The University of Kentucky and two additional years in the UK law school, to a six-and-a-half-year Peace Corps assignment in Iran, to the Director of the little mountain school from which he graduated. He held multiple honorary degrees. Powell will lead the reader sensitively through the incessant and often painful struggles of a school which faced closure almost every year of his presidency. This charismatic and gifted man refused to believe that what he dreamed for the school could not be accomplished. His faith in God that donors and volunteers would come through was unquenchable. An accomplished speaker, he had a remarkable ability to move donors and audiences with real-live stories of the "victories" God was achieving through the school. Listening to him speak, audiences would laugh and cry almost at the same time. Unfortunately, his lungs had been damaged by some unknown agent while he was a Peace Corps volunteer in Iran. He had known this for years and should have slowed down, taken care of himself. However, he chose to continue on, using himself up for his boys and girls at Oneida. When he contracted pneumonia, it unexpectedly proved fatal. Everyone was stunned. He was only 52. When the dreadful news reached the public, it was said that "the mountains cried!"

The author's extensive research of school minutes, documents, letters etc. assures the reader an authenticity found in her gifted writing. Judy Powell was a volunteer and student at the school and knew him well. This is a biographical history worthy of the read and exciting enough that the reader won't want to put it down!

Prologue

Stories

I was born to John and Bessie Teague in 1944, deep in the Cumberland Mountains in east Tennessee, a mountain range in the southeastern section of the vast mountain range known as the Appalachian Mountains that extends all the way through parts of Canada to its southern tip in Alabama. In one of my fondest memories of early childhood, I recall that winter had come to our mountain cove, and masses of glittering icicles hung like ornaments from the eaves of our weathered tin roof. From where I stood on tiptoes looking out, the world was a frosty, glittering wonderland. In the distance the snow-covered peaks of the Cumberlands rose like castles in some faraway magical kingdom. The deep verdant green of the hemlock forest, draped in blankets of white, lay quietly below as if to pay homage to the stately castles. The brilliant rays of dawn created prisms of sparkling diamonds on the frosted window pane through which I viewed the scene before me. It was Sunday morning and soon my daydreaming would be interrupted by Mother's call to come help in the kitchen. Thanks to my father, who had risen long before sun-up to stoke the fire that he had banked the night before, our plank cottage was toasty warm. Soon our family would be going to church.

Through the mists of the years I still see those pristine peaks. Those were wonderful times. Our family was poor, but I didn't know it because we were rich in the beauty that surrounded us.

That was before the deep coal mines were shut down. That was before the 50s, before the absentee landholders found a new, easier way

1

in strip mining to make money in the coal that lay in veins just under the surface of our rich soil, before they raped our mountains and robbed us of our way of life. Those greedy land barons had discovered a bounty too easy to harvest. The quietness of our lives, the sacredness of work tilling the land, the natural beauty surrounding us were shot through with the blasts of that harvesting.

It was also a time before coal lost its dominant position in the world as a source of energy. That was before our world was replaced with the helplessness of unemployment that drove mountaineers north to Ohio and Michigan and left in its place a people largely uneducated and dependent upon welfare. Harry M. Caudill, in *Night Comes to the Cumberlands* (1962) described it so well. We who were descendants of those fiercely independent, moonshining, feuding, uneducated mountaineers were to be left facing the deepest, blackest night of a forsaken people.

We had known how to carve a simple life on the edges of hills and along the valleys and creeks flowing through those deep primeval forests, filled with thickets of laurel, hemlock, tulip poplar, southern paw paw, honeysuckle. We didn't know how to be take advantage of the richest mineral wealth in the world lying under our soil. That was left to wealthy politicians.

There were so many wounds, wounds to the roads that wound around the valleys and over the high hills surrounding my home. Worse were the wounds left by dynamite charges that blasted the beauty of my sacred, magical mountains into the scarred desolate world that the Cumberlands had become. Worst were the wounds to the soul, wounds that crippled the spirit, wounds that others gave a name that connoted poverty with a place—Appalachia! This ugly tragedy tore my world apart. As the stripping drew closer, we had to leave our home on that lush tableland. We moved into Clairfield, a mining community.

Although we were now indeed poor, I defined my life by the heroic Christian mothers who kept our families going and food on the table, by fathers who had dug coal deep inside those mountains, risking their lives for their families, and by the missionaries whose stories I had heard in Sunbeams or sitting at my mother's side in the Woman's Missionary

Union meetings that she faithfully attended. I so wanted to help our families, to become a missionary. I was sure God had called me to do so, but I needed a good education.

It was in a church in a neighboring village that I first heard of Oneida. Mrs. Maude Dance spoke that night about the Oneida Baptist Institute, where she taught. From the moment she began, I was inspired and overjoyed. I would go to Oneida. I could barely wait for the service to end.

When I expressed my desire to Mrs. Dance, she graciously agreed to speak to Mrs. Chester Sparks, Mai Mai to all who knew her, the president's wife and dean of the Institute. Mom's eyes brimmed with tears at the thought of my going away from home, but she too was filled with hope that her daughter would be a missionary, so she tried to hide her tears from me. I was so excited that I tried not to notice as she quietly brushed them away. I was so excited that I didn't hear Mrs. Dance say I should send for an application!

So it was that I came to Oneida Baptist Institute on a cold, rainy Sunday in January, with school to begin the next morning. I arrived at Oneida wearing one of my best homemade dresses, with two "pokes" (what we in East Tennessee call paper bags) filled with all my clothes, but no sheets, towels, soap, money. My mom asked for Mrs. Sparks, who appeared shortly. "I've brought you my daughter" was all Mom could say through her tears. An understanding formed between two women's hearts. Mai Mai had expected to hear from me, but I didn't find that out until years later. She acted as though I was fully expected, took me in, explaining that "God works in mysterious ways his wonders to perform"—took on the task my mother couldn't fulfill, my education.

I remember how beautiful the campus looked to me. The plank homes in our mining village clung to the hillsides. They were connected to the other homes by the rutted road, the railroad, or the dirt paths that twisted through our community. Here the stately Classic Revival buildings that made up the campus were connected to the other buildings by clean swept sidewalks. They looked like magnificent mansions to me. Our weathered plank homes had linoleum floors. Here were old wood floors, oiled and shined. My small window looked across the valley to a coal tipple atop another hill. Dusty trucks lined up to drop their loads of coal into the shaft of the spindly-legged tipple that dropped the coal onto an endless conveyor belt that dropped the black gold down a chute into coal cars—the songs of birds drowned out. Here lofty windows looked out over stately old trees, birds sang at daybreak—twittered the day through. Coming from a coal mining camp, I was in paradise!

My love of beauty was given wings in that wonderful place, my sense of awe, of God's greatness, His protection, His love. A peace hovered over me, around me, and in me. When I got homesick, Mai Mai took me to her home, Anderson Hall, and introduced me to Miss Mary Nancy Wilson, a teacher who also lived there. Miss Wilson soon became my mentor, and a lifelong friendship began.

Many were the times in that winter and the following two and half years until I graduated, that she would stir together home-made snow cream from fresh-fallen snow, or bake delicious cookies and brownies to share with me and others, or pop corn, and on special occasions pour the most divine caramel syrup I've ever tasted on the freshly popped corn and roll it into popcorn balls.

I could go on, the scholarship to the University of Kentucky, the Institute trustee and later president of Kentucky Baptist Woman's Missionary Union, Mrs. Encil Deen, who obtained the funding, who took me in as her daughter, who now, at 107, is still Mom to me. She calls me her "coal miner's daughter". I could tell you how Mrs. Elwood Moore, Barkley Moore's mother, now nearing 100, also took me in, and remains to this day my special mom. Because of my mother's faith in God, in Mrs. Dance, in Mai Mai, I became rich in friendship. All of these dear women, and dozens more, became family to me. I am blessed beyond measure because of the dedication of those leaders, teachers, mentors who loved me and others like me and gave the offering of their lives for us. I tenderly recall them today. I am deeply indebted to Oneida Baptist Institute for being there when I needed a place away from home to get an education, for giving me a home and the start of my journey toward a meaningful life.

I did get the opportunity to be a summer missionary in Whitley, Claiborne, and Bell Counties while in high school and my first years of college. I would go on to become an interior designer and a writer. The memories of my treasured mountains and Oneida are always at the heart of who and what I am.

The sad truth for many of us in the mountains at that time is that there was no way to make a living in our mountain communities. An education was the only liberating door open to the world beyond. Oneida helped to open that door. Today, the Appalachia I knew as a teenager has vastly changed. There is hope that the damages done to the mountains can be reclaimed. A 1977 law requires a coal company to post bond to pay for reclamation by state or Federal government, should the company fail to do the reclamation. President John F. Kennedy appointed an Appalachian Regional Commission, which has overseen the expenditure of more than fifteen billion dollars in aid to the region.

The transportation system has been vastly improved. It has opened the door to the world, and the world has found our beautiful mountains. Today tourism is a major industry. The arts and crafts community, folk festivals, story telling, drama, music, capture the spirit and imagination of visitors from around the world. Major colleges and universities such as Berea College, Lincoln Memorial University, and the University of the Cumberlands have blazed the way toward enlightenment and freedom from poverty. There is hope for every young person to have a meaningful life, to live a significant life, right there in our beautiful mountains.

It has been my privilege to write the story of a great leader of the mountains—Glenn Barkley Moore—who took upon himself the unnamed hopes and dreams of children like me, not just from Appalachia but the world over. Yes, the lowest income levels in the nation are still to be found in Appalachia, and Clay County is at the bottom of the list but many of the brightest young minds of our country have and are coming from Appalachia, from families that were steeped in the rich heritage of faith, hard work, of getting an education to better themselves.

This is the same region that produced Abraham Lincoln; Harry M. Caudill, author, lawyer, legislator, environmentalist; Jesse Stuart, Poet Laureate of the state of Kentucky; Bert Combs, Governor of Kentucky;

Grace Moore, world-renowned opera singer, actress; Jean Ritchie, folk musician, singer, and songwriter; Hal Rogers, Congressman; and Barkley Moore—the Lawrence—the Albert Schweitzer of the mountains—now gone too soon! This is the setting of the story you are about to read. There may well be unspoiled children up those hollows and in mining communities who still view the world as our ancestors did, who when given the opportunity for an education will go out and set the world ablaze with their raw courage, genius, determination and commitment to God and family.

However, Oneida is not just about mountain boys and girls, in my day nor today. In 1993 Barkley Moore wrote: "NEARLY ONE MILLION BOYS AND GIRLS IN THE UNITED STATES ARE 'DROPPING OUT' EVERY YEAR before ever getting a high school diploma." Today it is over three million every year and growing daily. Barkley Moore saw this oncoming avalanche—felt it in the lives of those who came to Oneida from a world that didn't care. The students then and now come from the far corners of the globe, from every state in the Union and twenty-seven foreign countries. They came then and they come now from every stratum of society, from Ghanaian nobility to welfare families.

This is the story of a man who loved children, of the school he loved and the heritage he left to its students. It is the story of a man who stood as staunchly for his students as Mother Teresa did for the poor of Calcutta, as ably as Albert Schweitzer for his native Africans in need of medical attention, as faithfully as George Mueller for his orphans in England. Barkley Moore took his stand for the Oneida School, for the young men and women who came there, in need of an education and in need of a Savior as if their lives depended on him. It didn't matter if they were from Appalachia, Chicago, New York, Taiwan, Iran, or Korea. He saw their needs as one—saw the possibility of greatness in every one.

This is a true story, although it sounds like a fable. The Oneida Baptist Institute still stands. Its students are living proof of who and what he did. They went out to become great educators, scientists, doctors, business men and women, musicians, and artists. Many of Barkley Moore's students are back at Oneida today. President Larry

Allen Gritton, Jr., one of the brightest, is leading the way toward the future. The students still come from around the world, the cause of Christian education more needed today than ever, the possibilities in the lives of those there today as rich as the hope of the rising star over the fields outside Galilee over two thousand years ago.

Homecoming, September, 1960

I had been at Oneida well over a semester, but it was Homecoming, September, 1960 before I first realized who he was, the young man who always seemed to be in such a hurry as he strode back and forth across campus. I had seen him more than once from the windows of my dorm room that looked out over the lovely buildings on the east side of Oneida Institute. Most of the time there was a group of older students with him—Myrtle Webb, Brenda Baker, and others I didn't know. Once I had seen him walking briskly across campus, in the wee hours of the early morning. The setting moon's rays were beginning to wane and the sun's first rays were peeking over Little Bullskin's hills as he walked away from Marvin Hall, the building that housed the administration offices, classrooms, and chapel of the school perched on a knoll at the center of the village. He was clearly on a mission, with stacks of papers tucked under his arms.

The students, alumni, the administrative staff, president of the Institute, board of trustees, teachers, much of the village of Oneida, as well as friends and family had gathered in D. Chester Sparks Hall on that hot September day to celebrate Homecoming. Seated on the stage were President Chester Sparks, and his wife Mai Mai, who was Dean; Principal David Jackson, the song leader, Golden Hensley; and the young gentleman I had seen hurrying around campus. Principal David Jackson welcomed all the guests; then Brother Sparks walked to the podium. His slow Clay County drawl gathered us all closer. He had much to say. We listened. He was Papa Sparks to so many in that gym—young men and women who had decided to follow the Lord and walk in His footsteps. He finished his admonitions, and introduced the young man to us. He walked over to him and put an arm on his shoulder, as if he were his son. Clearly, he was very proud of him. If we students didn't know it before, we were to learn that this was Barkley Moore, a 1958 graduate of Oneida and a student at the University of Kentucky, in Lexington. Brother Sparks proudly told us that this former student spent most of his free time on weekends and his summer breaks at Oneida, helping out around the school—that he was extremely active in the Oneida Alumni Association and was the editor of the *Oneida Alumnus*. It would become very clear that, at the very least, he was already a Royal Ambassador on mission to little Oneida Baptist Institute. When he rose to speak, the whole room hushed, waiting expectantly to hear what the serious five-foot-nine nineteen-year-old with the sharp brown eyes and the black crew-cut had to say. With the entire student body, leaders, and alumni looking on, he stepped to the podium, and with his entire being launched into his talk.

His piercing eyes bored into our souls. *What is Oneida Institute?* His words poured out as if they were a part of him, not a speech written to be delivered. He was the embodiment of the past—the present—the future of Oneida Institute. Through his words, the former presidents of the Institute stepped out of the pages of time. They commanded, demanded our attention! The chiseled, square-boned, somber Lincoln-like figure of a man—founder, James Anderson Burns, the gracious, beautiful, brilliant business woman—Sylvia Russell, the brilliant English professor—Dr. Saul Hounchell.

What is Oneida Institute?

Dr. Saul Hounchell, a graduate and former president of Oneida, would tell us: "First of all, Oneida Institute is J.A. Burns, his lifetime of labor and service, of sowing and reaping, of suffering and rejoicing. Then it is all the friends near and far, living and dead, who have shared, and all those who have worked at the school, from the first faculty to the present one, all the student bodies who have attended through the decades and gone out over the world. Oneida is a Christian Institution doing an outstanding work in Christian evangelism and education, in developing Christian character and personality…unless it were that it would be worse than nothing, presented and supported as it is, and would have no right to existence. The friends who give money to Oneida give it on that basis, and with it give their prayers and a part of themselves. So every student who shares in these benefits accepts an obligation, whether he understands it or not, to be fine and worthy and most of them measure up. And every teacher and worker, each on the same level as every other, if he belongs on the staff of Oneida, has set at the Master's feet and got up to follow Him, knowing the full requirements of discipleship." "Whosoever will come after me, let him deny himself and take up his cross and follow me. For whosoever will save his life shall lose it: and whosoever shall lose his life for my sake and the Gospel's, the same shall save it."

Oneida's founder, Burns of the Mountains, would tell us that Oneida was "first a vision: then, a hope: then a prayer: then a determination to build." Mrs. Sylvia W. Russell, President Associate of Oneida 1921-28, when asked, "What is Oneida?" would reply: "There is that intangible, indescribable, inexpressible something, which pervades this Institution—something not to be found in any other."

What Is Oneida Institute?

Do you have the vision of Oneida in your soul? Oneida Institute is more than some old buildings. Oneida Institute is more than an institution that often has to make do with what it has, rather than what it should have. Every step forward, through the years, though taken with complete trust has been accomplished only through struggle and sacrifice. There never has been an easy year and should never be. One has but to know the history of Oneida Institute to understand that faith and prayer are the most powerful forces within human reach. Day after day, year in and year out, right down to the present hour. God's care, manifested through his people, has kept the work of Oneida going and growing.

But always at the inevitable cost of precious human life and sacrifice. The way of Christian sacrifice is the way of great achievement.

What Is Oneida Institute?

Oneida Institute is people. It was founded to help people. The great emphasis at Oneida has been and should be on individual development…mentally, physically, socially, spiritually: on Christian character: on high ideals of service: on the dignity of labor: and the necessity of all of these for human happiness. This is as it should be, as it has been, and as it will ever remain as long as this school remains Oneida Institute. Take this emphasis out of Oneida Institute and Oneida Institute is dead. But as long as this emphasis is maintained, as long as we remain true to the principles and purposes on which the school was founded and has served these sixty years, as long as the world stands in need of Christian character and of education, so long will Oneida meet a need, accomplish a glorious purpose…so long will it live and serve.

What Is Oneida Institute?

Oneida Institute is an ideal. It was founded on love and cemented by faith. Our founder, James Anderson Burns, said: "A loving heart with a throb for suffering humanity makes the hardest yoke easy, the heaviest burden light, the longest day short, and the hottest sun set too soon." This is the secret of Oneida. This is the mark of a real Christian, "A loving heart with a throb for suffering humanity." And faith? Faith founded Oneida Institute, and faith sustains this school even unto this very moment. The faith that it took to begin this work with only seventeen months of formal education, not one cent of money, no roads, forty miles from the nearest railroad, a virtual wilderness. Think of the faith it has taken in those periods of our history when it seemed we were sinking beneath the waves. The Apostle Peter was in a similar situation once. The Lord told Peter to walk. With that command Oneida, has survived. And then there is the faith it takes today to begin each year knowing that well over $100,000 must be obtained somewhere, and that it will take a little more next year.

Oneida Institute today is important. Why? Oneida is important because it is dealing with two most important things in this world, the souls and minds of men. Every school deals with the mind of men, but there are few schools which, like Oneida, deal with the soul as well. If ever there was a need for educated people and for strong Christian character, today is the day. Christian education gives hope to the hopeless, power to the weak, and ambition to follow the ray of hope and exercise the power given.

The influence of Oneida today extends into the Governor's Mansion, has extended into the very halls of the Congress of the United States, into the State legislature, into numerous public offices, into hundreds of classrooms influencing thousands of young lives, into operating rooms, into numerous business establishments, into thousands of homes where new generations are coming. A shaper of the destinies of the world could well be influenced by Oneida.

Recalling the great souls who have written chapters of the Oneida Story, recalling these, I say, if I may paraphrase the eulogy of Mr. Burns delivered by that great Presbyterian educator Dr. Elmer Gabbard, "We must keep faith with them! They leave an inescapable responsibility in the hands of the leaders, the students, the people of Oneida, the alumni, all the people of the mountains, and friends of them and their work everywhere. Their spirit will live to inspire us when difficulties and handicaps stand in the way. On this Institution and all the friends of the mountains waits the fulfillment of their dreams, their hopes, their struggles, their lives. Oneida Institute's heritage, its goals, its needs should be a ringing challenge to action for every student, every friend, every teacher, every member of the administration, and to every alumnus."

When I think of Oneida, I am reminded of a wonderful little poem that goes like this:

> *Master, where shall I work today?*
> *And my love flows warm and free,*
> *He pointed me out a tiny spot,*
> *And said, "Tend that for me."*

I answered, "Oh, no, Lord! Not there
Not that little place for me.
Why, no matter how well work was done,
No one would ever see."
Then the words He spoke, it was not stern
He answered me tenderly,
"Ah little one, art thou working for them
or Me?
Nazareth was a little place,
And so was Galilee."
Stanley Singleton

What Is Oneida Institute?

Oneida Institute is our Nazareth, our Galilee.
Oneida Mountaineer, August 1961 (A speech given by Barkley Moore, Homecoming, 1960)

If there had been an altar call, an army of us would have been on our knees, ready to follow the Lord. Perhaps that was why he didn't give such a call. We would have responded before we were ready or fully understood that to which he was calling us. Golden Hensley stepped back to the podium, lifted his hands to worship in song. We sang, as was the custom for these occasions:

Oneida Fair

Thy hills protect on every side, Oneida Fair, Oneida Fair,
Refreshing streams around thee glide. Oneida Fair, Oneida Fair.
A thousand flow'rs each spring appear,
and tuneful songbirds charm the ear,
Bright shines the sun from heavens clear, Oneida Fair, Oneida Fair.
Oh scene of school days passed too soon, Oneida Fair, Oneida Fair.
We owe to thee how many a boon, Oneida Fair, Oneida Fair.
Those hours of work, of sport, of glee,

Will linger long in memory, Oneida Fair, Oneida Fair.
To add new luster to thy name, Oneida Fair, Oneida Fair.
Shall ever be thy children's aim, Oneida Fair, Oneida Fair.
In hearts as steadfast as thy hills, in souls as gen'rous as thy rills,
We'll onward go and fear no ill, Oneida Fair, Oneida Fair.
May God above shine down on thee, Oneida Fair, Oneida Fair.
And fill our souls with serenity, Oneida Fair, Oneida Fair.
Let Jesus live in all of us, Teaching honor, love and trust,
Holy Spirit, abide with us, Oneida Fair, Oneida Fair.
Evelyn Carter (heir to Carter Ink fortune), 1913, New York

Beloved Bible teacher Brother Melvin Davidson, who had lost an arm many years before when he worked as a logger, walked to the lectern to lead us in prayer. We held hands as we sang *Blest Be the Tie That Binds*. That ended the service. There were tears of love and pride for our dear Oneida school, and tears of love for the Christ who had come to Galilee, swelling in more eyes than mine as we quietly hugged our friends, and teachers hugged as many of us as they could embrace.

By the time this speech was given, Barkley Moore had already given his "where I came from" speech in glowing detail to the fascinated audiences who listened to his "Oneida Story", which he told with rapid-fire zeal to Woman's Missionary Union and church groups around Kentucky. If you pressed him further, you would hear his heart throb— his passion for hurting boys and girls—not only of the mountains, but in every state in the union and around the world—their desperate needs—right then and there. The questions then turned—on you— how can you help with these great needs? But before we get that far, let's ask him where he came from. It will appear that you've asked the wrong question.

First, you will hear the story of Oneida in a nutshell:

The story of Oneida is the story of a man, a great man. The life of James Anderson Burns mirrors that of humanity. Oneida Institute is the lengthened shadow, a continuing affirmation of his life and labors.

Achieving first regional and then national fame as a reformed feudist, teacher, preacher, lecturer, and educator, "Burns of the Mountains" became one of the unique men of the first quarter of the twentieth century. Oneida Institute, now a boarding school for children grades 6-12, reflects that uniqueness even to this day.

My family was closely associated with Mr. Burns years before the founding of Oneida. He shared a room with my grandfather George Ponder in my great-grandfather's home at Rader's Creek. There my great-grandparents and Mr. Burns were members of the Pleasant Run Baptist church. Great-grandfather was a school trustee and hired Mr. Burns to teach several school terms. Later, William DeKalb Ponder served on Oneida's early board of trustees. He had moved his family to Oneida so his children could attend the new Oneida School. Known as "Bill", he built a large sawmill and shop on the South Fork of the Kentucky River, across from the mouth of Bullskin Creek, in the new village. He sawed most of the lumber for Oneida's earliest buildings, donating much of it. Many other families also moved to Oneida, building on land owned originally by the Widow, Martha Hogg, with the same idea my great-grandfather had. They wanted an education for their children, and Oneida was a quality school from the beginning. Most of those early homes were built with lumber from his mill.

"Bill" Ponder was born in November 1848. He married Mary Luvica "Vicey" Buttrey, whose parents were German and spoke with a strong accent. My grandfather George Lafayette Ponder (1875-1951) was their only son. He married Lucy Hensley (1878-1954) in 1900. Both my grandparents briefly attended Oneida, as did all their seven children including their youngest daughter, Evelyn, my mother.

Squire Hensley, the father of my grandmother Lucy Hensley Ponder, was on Oneida's first board of trustees. He gave an early cash donation matching the $50 donated by his brother, "Big Henry" Hensley. Great-grandfather Squire Hensley was born in 1830, died at the age of 87 in 1917, and is buried one mile west of Oneida on land that he owned. Three generations of his descendants are now buried around him. My great-grandmother was Alabama Gilbert

(1851-1896). Five years a widower, at the age of 71, Squire married Paralee Gilbert. It is said he approached her on his horse and said, "I'm a man of few words. I have heard of you. If you want to be my wife, climb up behind me and we'll get married!" She did and they did.

Six generations of my family have lived and died within seven miles of Oneida School. I am a mountaineer and an Oneidian by heritage, training, and choice for I was born in Detroit, Michigan, on August 8, 1941. Most of my formative years and all but one and one half years of my pre-university education were at Oneida. Excerpt from a speech given by Barkley Moore on many occasions. (Transcript in Mountain Rising among other places.)

Barkley gave his heart to God when he was nine. Like Samuel, he had heard the Lord calling. Like Hannah, Barkley's mother sensed her boy would be used by God. She had encouraged him to listen to God—had taken him to the Lord's House. She had talked freely about the Savior to him. Many a mother who loves the Lord is gifted by God to see into her child's heart. Barkley's mother saw sparks of great compassion and faith in his heart. Pastor Lyn Claybrook saw them too. The day he baptized Barkley, he said prophetically to her, "Mrs. Evelyn, I know one thing for sure, the Lord didn't give this great understanding to Barkley to be used in some lesser way than to serve the Lord—Barkley will do the Lord's work."

While still a child, Barkley had seen his five-year-old brother George run over by a drunken driver and killed. From that time forward, he seemed to grasp God's love and compassion for the broken-hearted— His purpose in sending His Son. From that time forward, he understood that time is a possession to be prized. He often quoted from Ecclesiastes:

To everything there is a season, and a time to every purpose under the heaven: a time to be born, and a time to die; a time to plant, and a time to pluck up that which is planted; a time to kill, and a time to heal; a time to break down, and a time to build up; a time to weep, and a time to laugh; a time to mourn, and a time to dance; a time to cast away stones, and a time to gather stones together; a time to embrace, and a time to refrain from embracing; a time to get, and a time to lose; a time to keep, and a time to cast away; a time to rend, and a time to sew; a time to keep silence, and a time to speak; a time to love, and a time to hate; a time of war, and a time of peace. (*Ecclesiastes* 3:1-10)

Because time is so valuable, even as a child Barkley determined to use it wisely. He graduated from high school at age sixteen. By age twenty he had graduated from the University of Kentucky, combining his studies with volunteering at Oneida. After graduating, he continued his studies in the UK law school. But, with the needs of Oneida heavy on his heart, he left after two years to become assistant to Institute President David Jackson. Two years later, he was at a crossroads. In an article in the *Oneida Mountaineer*, May, 1964, he wrote:

> For seventeen of my twenty-two years of life, I have deeply loved Oneida Institute as student, friend, alumnus and these past two years, as a worker in the school.
>
> During my student days at Oneida and while away at college, I wrote more than a score of articles for the *MOUNTAINEER*. During the past two years I have been privileged to edit this paper and have written nearly every article. It has been a lot of hard work, a lot of fun, and there have been great rewards. In this closing article of the last number I shall be writing, I find that words of farewell come less easily than any that have gone before.
>
> Life is full of endings and beginnings. They are the sign-posts that mark our earthly journey. I have come to a crossroad. As many a traveler, I have suffered that momentary doubt as to which road to take. I look behind to see from whence I have come. I peer ahead to try to see what lies in the Future.

Rich and Full Years

> For the past two years I have been privileged to serve Oneida Institute as a member of the working force. I have always considered work at Oneida a privilege, I so consider it today. These years have

been rich and full, even in the disappointments that attend any kind of work, the culmination of many years in which I have eaten, slept, worked and thought little else but Oneida Institute.

Until about six months ago, I never had the least doubt but that I was where the Lord wanted me to be, in the place He had prepared me to serve. But, then, there were other promptings. I fought. I resisted. I could hardly bear the thought that, perhaps, my work at Oneida was done…the months had passed so quickly…that there was a call to service in another place. I tried to push the thought from my mind over many weeks. I prayed that it not be so. But as the weeks and months passed, I became convinced that He was calling me elsewhere. If I would be true to such a call, I would have to leave the place that I have always loved, and will ever love, above all places on earth. I finally gave in.

I Believe

So, recent days have been spent in saying "goodbye" to those places and people whom I have known and loved in all my years of memory. My feelings concerning Oneida Institute are those which I have had or so many years. I BELIEVE in Oneida Institute, its past and its present. I BELIEVE in its FUTURE. The Lord's work is eternal, and I firmly believe Oneida to be the Lord's work. I believe that Oneida is worthy of the support of all who love Him, and are concerned with the minds and souls of today's boys and girls, tomorrow's men and women.

Oneida had given me much, taught me much. The most important lesson learned, the one for which I am most grateful, is the lesson of concern for the needs of others. This concern led me from law school to Oneida two years ago and now, it seems, that I am being led 5,000 miles from Oneida to a village in Iran, to a people, to a work.

I volunteered some months ago for Peace Corps service, and said I was willing to go anywhere in the world where I could do a useful work if I were found to be qualified. I did not ask for an assignment to Iran, but, in my heart, that is where I hoped to go because of the

Persian students we have had at Oneida since 1953. My room-mate for three years at Oneida was an Iranian boy, the first of many Persian students we have since had, and I was inspired with his desire to prepare himself for service to his people. I never dreamed that one day I would have an opportunity to work in his land among his people, as he is now doing in such a wonderful way.

God's Will or Coincidence?

What led Monoutchehr to Oneida? How did we happen to be assigned as room-mates? What led to the many Persian contacts I have since had, the friends made? So my appointment to the Peace Corps came and it said "Iran". The appointment could as well have been to any of the other sixty-four countries where Peace Corpsmen serve. Is my assignment to work in ancient Persia the Lord's doing or is all this mere coincidence?

I did not understand why I had to leave Oneida. Today, I can understand a little better. Perhaps, in His time, all things will be made clear.

A Plea

You, Oneida's friends, have been wonderful to Oneida these past two years and all the years which have gone before. I commend this work to you.

Peace Corps Training Center
Utah State University, Logan, Utah
August 8, 1964

Barkley Moore and thirty-four of his fellow trainees were assembling a sizeable pile of rocks. One group dug small pits, lined them with the rocks, and had their fire pits ready for cooking. A second group collected wood for the fires. The third group dug a four-foot pit for their garbage. The fourth group dug a latrine. They would soon have a fire going. Up since 5:30 AM, they would be found boiling tea (*cha*) over their fire, and preparing eggs (*totemorgs*) over the open flames. By 10:00 AM he and a fellow volunteer would begin a hike high into the Utah mountains to a sheep camp. Thus would begin an intense six-week training camp that would "select out" more than half of the number who had made the grade to be in the program in the first place; only one in six applying had even been considered prospects for the training. These had made it so far.

Not all of them would make it overseas. The intense training included: Iranian studies, language study five hours a day, learning to write in Farsi, and learning to make bricks and the molds for the bricks. Barkley described it: "I have spent many hours, jumping straight up and down, barefoot in a pit as we mixed the clay mud to a good consistency for bricks." They were getting good practical experience for the sort of thing they would do in Iran.

Finally, on September 9, one by one, they filed by to receive a white envelope, which each opened very slowly, to get the news, good or bad. For eight it was crushing. For him it was good news; he would be going to Iran.

The next day he would leave by plane for Denver, Colorado, spend the night, arrive in Lexington, Kentucky on Friday, go to a cookout in Georgetown on Saturday, and on to Oneida on Sunday. After just a few days at home, he would fly to Washington, D.C. the following weekend, then on to New York. He would board a plane in New York City at 6:30 PM on September 23, making stops in Frankfurt and Munich, Germany; Istanbul, Turkey; Beirut, Lebanon; and finally Tehran.

With a final *hodahafez* (may God bless you), he stepped on board! He had been on the plane twenty hours when he saw the twinkling lights of Tehran come into view. It was 4:30 PM Kentucky time. It was shortly after midnight in Tehran. He had arrived in his new country!

The first city he saw in Iran was Tehran, a city of more than two million people, the largest city in southwest Asia. Little more than a

sleepy, oversized village a generation ago, it sprawled in every direction. Tehran is located in a vast horseshoe-shaped valley surrounded by glinting hills that almost look metallic. The city's skyline was dwarfed by the snow-capped ridge of the Alborz Mountains and the towering 19,000-foot volcanic peak of Mt. Damavand. A low range of hills separated the city from lush green forests to the north. Looking out the door of his hotel with its modern plumbing facilities that first morning, he saw a woman washing clothes in the *jube* before the hotel. A *jube* is an open, water-filled ditch that runs through the streets. Only two cities in Iran had pure drinking water: Tehran and Shiraz. Tehran had 100,000 automobiles and 20,000 taxis whose drivers raced one another, paid little attention to traffic lights, and shook their fists at each other. There were so many hazards that none of the Peace Corps volunteers were ever allowed to drive. He saw men dressed in western business suits alongside men wearing flowing robes and turbans. Most older women were in the traditional *chador*. Many of the younger women were in western attire. There were twelve-foot walls around all the houses, and all the gates were locked tight at night. Along the streets were little shop-like markets—many selling fruits, vegetables, some shoes, some clothes, with very few modern supermarkets.
Letters from Iran, 1972 (paraphrased)

One of the very first places he wanted to visit was an orphanage. He got one of the top men to go with him. Soon he was having quite a time. He was taken to the courtyard where children aged two to twelve gazed at him shyly. He quickly had them giggling and laughing by asking their names, ages, and making appropriate comments. A little girl sang for him. He responded in Farsi with a few lines from one of their favorite songs, *Baroon Barune*, which brought delighted smiles to all their faces. He had begun writing love letters to their hearts! And they had captivated him.

After days of orientation, thinking he would be leaving for his city the following day, he saw the regional officer of the Peace Corps walking toward him. Barkley was a bit taken aback when he was asked if he could be ready to go in two hours but he answered, "Yes, where is it?" The officer said, "The Turkoman area, near the Russian border, about eight hours by jeep. Very few of the people there speak Farsi. You will have to learn Turkoman, also. Oh, yes, you will be alone and, perhaps, the first American that most of the people will have seen." The Turkoman until just a few years ago had moved about with their herds, doing very little farming. Numbering nearly 50,000 people, speaking their own language, they were a strongly independent people. They refused to learn to speak Farsi and did not marry outside their own people. They are famous for their horses... perhaps the finest in the world. When Barkley had volunteered for the Peace Corps, he was prepared for anything, willing to tackle anything. And here it was!

The road Barkley was to take to Gonbad from Tehran went through Sari onward through the heart of the Turkoman area to finally arrive in Gonbad. They would go by jeep. They left just before dark. Traveling through the night, he saw little of the scenery, and it was just as well! They pitched and rolled over the road through the dark. Barkley was sure he was going to the end of the earth. He held on for dear life!

They climbed higher and higher into the mountains until there was snow on the road itself. They passed behind Mt. Damavand, which was 19,000 feet high, and on to Sari. From Sari the road on which he traveled through the night was one of the engineering feats of the world. It was literally carved out of the side of the mountain. There were at least 20 long tunnels through various mountain ranges. The whole road was one long curve through which they barreled just as if there were no curves. On each side of the road mountains towered thousands of feet high. Some 400 to 500 feet below the road there was a river that flowed through the valley.

Late in the night they made their descent into Gonbad. It had been like riding a bucking horse for eight hours. When he finally arrived, a Persian rug was placed on the floor in one of the two rooms in a very small house. He promptly went to sleep in a strange land, in a city of 40,000 souls, with a family he had never met.

The next day he saw that he was in a beautiful section of Iran. There were great plains enclosed by beautiful tree-covered mountains; the peaks of some couldn't be seen for the clouds.

The Ghrierlys, who were his host family, lived in a small compound. Their part of it was two rooms with a very small room in between. There was another apartment of the same size on the opposite side; both were enclosed by a courtyard with a twelve-foot-high wall and a securely locked gate. There was no furniture except one small table and six metal chairs. The floors were covered with inexpensive Persian rugs.

Letters from Iran, 1972 (paraphrased)

He had come to his place of service. Yes, he would labor there, where no one else would go, "far from the madding crowd." He would tend their children, open for them the door of knowledge, open the windows of the world for them to see what lay beyond. He could have been climbing up some hollow in Appalachia, for he knew these children had the same hopes and dreams as all other children. Though they were poor, uneducated, they were beautiful and full of promise to him. That is a story in itself. Those ancient people would forever be a part of him, imbedded in his heart and mind. They would be to him a treasure he would draw on, return to, turn over like leaves of gold on a fine autumn day. He would be to them a friend, a father, a brother—their Barkley. When he had to leave them, his departure would make a "thousand eyes cry".

His time there would be the most beautiful, painful, joyful, sorrowful journey he would ever take. It would be a journey through the desert, over vast mountains, to mud brick huts perched on mountainsides, to sheepherders on lonely grassy heights, to villages that stood on those vast mountains, lost in time. No one cared that their hungry hearts and minds longed to see the other side of those towering, forbidding mountains. He would live alongside those proud Turkoman—eat the same food—be exposed to the same hardships and dangers.

Those years of service would define for him what true suffering, hopelessness, and heartache meant. He would take under his wing those children living in a culture as old as the shepherds, herding and tending their sheep, trapped in a world that had left them behind. But before he would go he would have helped them build libraries, for he would have convinced the wealthy that they should be responsible for their neighbors, get involved, share their wealth. He, speaking on their behalf, would have helped them acquire thousands of books. He would have helped them to build schools where their children could be educated; he would have shown them how to do it, working alongside them. He would have shown them the beautiful hardworking American with his sleeves rolled up, demonstrating the spirit that has made America great. He would have stayed longer than any volunteer serving in the Peace Corps at the time.

Finally, six and a half years later, he would have to leave them on their own, but they would know for themselves the rewards of working together, from the richest landowner or politician to the governor of the province. His name would be written in the history books but, more importantly, his name would be written on their hearts. He would draw them to himself out of a heart of love. With actions he would show them the Galilean, who had walked deserts just like theirs, who had climbed mountains just as steep as theirs, who had known every sorrow they knew, been just as downtrodden—He who had left Heaven on their behalf. And all these things they would desperately need to know in the years ahead!

Barkley would make the prayer of Saint Francis of Assisi his own each day while he was there.

Lord, make me an instrument of thy peace;
Where there is hatred, let me sow love;
Where there is injury, pardon;
Where there is doubt, faith
Where there is despair, hope;
Where there is darkness, light; and
Where there is sadness, joy.

Divine Master,
Grant that I may not so much seek to be
Consoled as to console;
To be understood as to understand;
To be loved as to love;
For it is in giving that we receive;
It is in pardoning that we are pardoned;
And it is in dying that we are born to eternal life.
Saint Francis of Assisi

And in doing the deeds of that prayer, he would attract the attention of the world to his beloved Gonbad. As he prepared to leave Iran, he shared his heart with his best friends, Bill Gene and Peggy Smith, back home.

Tabriz, Iran
October 13, 1970
Dear Bill and Peggy and children,

I finally left Gonbad about ten days ago amid unforgettable scenes. My last days were filled with love and tears and gifts. They made me an Honorary Citizen, gave me many gifts and hundreds turned out to say good by not only in Gonbad but in many other places along the road. The other night in Tehran more than forty were at the bus station (about 500 to 600 in Gonbad) as I left for here on my way to Turkey. In the group was Ardy (last name omitted for security reasons) with whom I had spent a wonderful four hours in my last night in Tehran. I hadn't seen him since that first night six years ago for he had been in the Iranian Embassy in London five years. He is a very mature person and I was quite impressed by his thinking and he has a very distinguished grey around the ears and temples at the age of 30. He told me his father grayed very early also.

So I am staying here a few days with some of my former students now here in the University and using the time to do some letter-writing and then on to Turkey by bus where I will probably be nearly a week as I have many former students and friends there. Then on to

Europe by the Orient Express and perhaps to Scandinavia and plan to stay in London about a week as I have some friends there. Then to the States by ship. Those are my tentative plans. So I hope to see you before Christmas. If you would care to give me a quick letter and I hope you do, you can catch me on the way at this address:

Barkley Moore

c/o J.E.B. Gray

77 Primrose Mansions

Prince of Wales Drive

London S.W. 11, England

I know Shari has grown a lot and red-haired Barkley must be a very big boy now. Tell him the fellow he's named for will be along soon…also that he got to meet the daughter of the man he was named for the last day in Tehran. I had tea with Mrs. Douglas MacArthur II, wife of the Ambassador. Her husband is a nephew of the General and she is the daughter of the late Senator Barkley. Of course that was a thrill for me getting to talk with her and she told me some personal stories about him and her upbringing and all.

I'll sign off for now. Did you get to the Oneida Homecoming? Haven't heard any details of that but understand that Dr. Hounchell was to have been the speaker. Wish I could have been there. Is Pig still the Coach? That was too sad about Joe Barnes.

Hope all is well with you and looking forward to seeing more of you than we've been able to for six years. Did I hear a groan?

Love,

Barkley

He slipped the letter into the post. He was on his way home!

In order to know Barkley Moore fully, you would have had to follow him for the next year and a half as he crisscrossed America, to the delight of millions who heard or saw him on live television, or read about him in front-page stories, or walked with him in marches across the greatest cities of America, in rallies for the cause of peace and goodwill toward children the world over. You would have had to have seen him, dressed in his best Sears Roebuck suit, tie askew, shoes worn but polished, as he captivated everyone from the high and mighty to the everyday ordinary American, as he spoke of his boys and girls in his Kentucky drawl.

You would have had to hear the stories told by great and powerful leaders, such as the head of the Peace Corps, Sargent Shriver; by ambassadors; by statesmen. Presidents wrote to him. The story of the "beautiful American", "the legend of the Peace Corps", was told by Associated Press on three separate occasions, and by lead reporters for the *New York Times*, the *Chicago Tribune*, the *Christian Science Monitor*, the *National Observer*, the *Boston Globe*. He was interviewed on the *Today Show*. He was on *What's My Line?* He spoke in the great churches of the time. He was the featured guest on a Sunday broadcast from the Crystal Cathedral with Dr. Robert Schuler, who wrote a special chapter about him in one of his inspirational books. In 1971 his alma mater, the University of Kentucky, bestowed on him that institution's most prestigious award, the Sullivan Award, for humanitarian service rendered to poor and needy children in Iran. He was the youngest person ever to receive the award. He mesmerized people everywhere he went across the country. He could have headed for the House of Representatives, the Senate, or even the Presidency of the United States!

1972-73

Year 1

I am a firm believer that there is a purpose in all things.
—Barkley Moore

During the last week of July, 1972, Barkley was on a speaking trip for the Peace Corps in St. Louis, Missouri when a call—the Call—came from Oneida Institute. His dear alma mater in the Kentucky mountains was in a crisis. That was a call he would have taken from anywhere in the world, wherever he might have found himself. The president had resigned. Would he come as interim president for one year? There was only one answer for Barkley and that was a resounding "Yes". All the glamour in the world meant nothing to him; it was a small offering for him to leave it all behind, but could he give up his job with ACTION immediately and expect to be able to come back in a year? He needed to give this some thought. He loved his job representing the Peace Corps and didn't want to jeopardize his potential future. One year! Why had they asked him to come for just one year? He understood he was young for the job. However, it was his Oneida and clearly the school was in trouble. Being a man of action, he didn't dawdle around, twiddling his thumbs. He was on the phone to ACTION headquarters. Yes, they would release him and look forward to his return. With that settled, he could wholeheartedly say "Yes". He raced to the airport where he got a plane ticket to Lexington, Kentucky.

In a letter posted on August 22 from ACTION headquarters in Washington D.C., he received the following acknowledgement:

Dear Barkley:

　　I want to take this opportunity to again thank you and commend you for the outstanding contributions you have made to Peace Corps and ACTION. You are already missed at ACTION, but I can well understand your desire to help out at Oneida Institute. I know your enthusiasm and ability will give a tremendous boost to the school. Best of luck for the coming year. We all look forward to your return to ACTION.

Joe Blatchford

And in longhand, "Stay in touch!"

On the plane trip to Lexington, he began to formulate his plans for getting the school ready for its seventy-second academic year. He was fired up, ready to take action, but in his heart he felt he couldn't do this job alone. While he hadn't said it to the chairman of the board of trustees, he had said it to God. He needed a strong team beside him. He knew one person he wanted to ask to join him. But, while he was confident that he could persuade this person to come, he wanted it to be God's will. He wouldn't push or pull on her emotions to leave her comfortable and beautiful apartment in the historic home on W. John Fitch Street in Bardstown, Kentucky—the home she shared with two gracious ladies—the home with the grand staircase he had climbed many a time—the home where they had sat in rocking chairs on the front porch, shaded by ancient trees and facing toward the historic square of the bustling tourist town, home of Stephen Foster.

As the plane sped through the clear blue sky high over Missouri, he fondly recalled all the wonderful meals she and other friends from Elizabethtown and Georgetown had shared at the quaint Boone Tavern on Sundays years ago. What would the Smiths, Colemans, Bodens, Morgans, and especially Miss Martha Bain think of his dragging their dear friend, Mary Nancy Wilson, back to Oneida? How could he ask her to leave her church home, First Baptist, just a few blocks from her home—an easy walk for a lady who didn't drive? How could he ask her to leave this pristine, carefree life for one he knew would offer no leisure time and precious little luxury? She must be willing on her own and see it as God's will for her life.

She was indeed at Bardstown, ready to begin another year as guidance counselor for the school system there. She had worked with him when he was at Oneida as assistant to the president. She had a master's from Peabody, was the embodiment of the excellence and dedication for which Oneida stood, and was known far and wide for her persistence in helping young men and women. Miss Wilson's friendship had passed the test of time. She loved him as if he were her own dear son, but she would also hold him accountable, as if that could ever be needed, to the standards, academic, moral, and spiritual, of the leader of a Christian school. She rose at 4:00 AM every morning, got on her knees by her bed, and besought the Lord in prayer. She ended every day in the same manner. She was humble, not seeking the applause of man, but she was powerful in prayer and faith, and her influence on young people and her love for young people were priceless.

Although her hair had long since turned gray, she still had a sparkle in her blue eyes, loved basketball, and listened to her former student Cliff Hagan's games every time he played for the Saint Louis Hawks. She was a wonderful cook, brilliant conversationalist, witty, and a lady with gracious Southern manners. He longed to have his beloved friend beside him. She would be his strong right arm. But would she come? He knew he would need her wise counsel in the days ahead if he were to lead Oneida. He called her as soon as the plane landed.

He had always sought out the wisdom of those older in the Lord and drawn heavily on their counsel. He must have one other saint of the Lord—the Rev. D. Chester Sparks, who would be eighty years old in January. Mai Mai, his dear wife, had died several years before. That call went out as well.

Both Nancy Wilson and Brother Sparks were thrilled that he was coming back, and, yes, they too would come. Brother Sparks was to be his sounding board. His years of experience in the ministry and as past president of Oneida Institute would be invaluable. He would name Brother Sparks President Emeritus. Miss Wilson would take her place as guidance counselor and be his right arm in ministering to the needs of the students.

And there were still three other people who mattered most in the world to him—his mom, dad, and sister Gloria. But he didn't have to ask them. He knew they would be overjoyed to know he would be in Kentucky again. They would be nearer than they had been in eight and a half years. Lexington, Kentucky was just two hours away from Oneida, not that he would have time to go there, but they could come to him. He was deeply loved by all of these and it gave him solace and contentment in the deepest recesses of his heart. Yes, he would leave the path of fame and fortune didn't matter to him.

Finally, the thought that had been hovering just out of reach, gently tugging at his soul made its way through to his heart first and then his head! He had a place to bring his boys left behind in Iran by necessity when he came home from the Peace Corps. He had his own school— with all the resources necessary to care for them. His thoughts settled into a deep peace.

So it began. With a burning vision in his soul, Barkley Moore, now thirty-one, had the burden of Oneida Institute fully on his shoulders. He was to join the ranks of James Anderson Burns, Sylvia Russell, and the others who had labored before him. He himself had said, "There never has been an easy year and should never be." He was full of faith, ready to take that step, knowing that hardship lay ahead, knowing the school right at that moment had a $29,000 deficit, but also knowing in his heart that the Master whom he served was in charge and would lead the school and him through these perilous times.

He had but to keep faith and to keep his eye on the Savior. He had put the Lord first in his life and Oneida Institute was his Galilee. How could the Lord let him down, when he would be answering the Master's divine call to a divine work? He must keep faith with James Anderson Burns and all those who had gone before him. He hoped and expected that teachers, students, friends of Oneida, alumni, all the people of the mountains, and all those who would become friends would step up to their responsibilities, and together they would be victorious, because they would be dealing with the minds and souls of young people.

In the dewy mist settling in over the Bullskin Mountains at evensong, the crisp fragrance of sumac, pussy willows, spicy yarrow, deep red dogwoods, brilliant yellow sugar maples, golden oaks, and purple sycamores filled the dusk with the promise of a glorious fall day tomorrow in the little village of Oneida. This was the day for which God had been preparing Glenn Barkley Moore since his first breath. Tomorrow he would be given the gavel first wielded by James Anderson Burns. Tomorrow he would officially offer all that he held in his hands, all that he was or would become, to the mission for which he was born. He hurried across the campus toward Anderson Hall, former home of James Anderson Burns and all the succeeding presidents of Oneida Institute, where he would spend the night, as he still had much preparation for tomorrow.

Most everyone in the little village of Oneida was praying for him—trustees, friends, and faculty of the school. Seeing his well-known figure as he had moved around in the community and on campus earlier in the day had brought smiles and joy to the hearts of those who were so relieved to see his presence in their midst again after nearly eight years. Their beloved son had come home, and it was just in the nick of time. Their precious school was in desperate financial need, on the brink of closing, and many wondered whether the school would even open in just a few days.

They knew it was "for such a time as this" that Barkley Moore had offered his life years before. They all knew what their beloved Barkley Moore, at the peak of a successful career in the Peace Corps, knew in his heart. It was time to come home! It was time to pick up the mantle that God had placed on his shoulders with the call. This was his "Galilee" and he knew it—loved it.

Barkley Moore had one month to be ready to open for school, the seventy-second year of Oneida Institute. But that was just the half of it. The bills had to be paid and there had to be a way to get them paid.

The board of trustees met with him immediately. They wanted him to know they were fully behind him in any way he thought they should move forward. The very first objective was to get the school in the black as soon as possible. Another was to broaden the base of Oneida supporters. The present ones were under a tremendous weight as the cost of everything had gone up over the years while the support base had stayed basically the same. The board knew they must find more people to help carry the load.

The trustees sent out a letter just one week later to all the friends of Oneida whose names were on the current mailing list, putting their full support behind him in this endeavor and asking for continuing support.

School enrollment had been down to 103 the previous year and that just wouldn't do. A campaign to get the students who needed Oneida was launched with a new blue and white brochure (blue and white are the school's colors), sent to every prospective student in the county and beyond. Barkley himself was up and down every hollow as much as he could possibly be away from the office. When he was in the office, he was on the phone talking to pastors all over Kentucky, asking for their support and, of course, asking if any of their church families needed a place for a child to go to school. When he wasn't in the office, or climbing up some hillside recruiting students, he was showing folks around the campus, giving tours of buildings and talking of things to come. Just days before the school's opening, he said, "We are going to have many more students it seems than we could dare hope for just three weeks ago."

Like a young father, Barkley Moore was so glowingly proud of his boys and girls—students from the mountains and beyond—students from many states in the U.S., students from other countries—that he could almost make others envious of his children. Nothing was too good for them and none of them had so little to offer mankind that he wouldn't lay down his life for them. He believed in them that much. He loved them that much. Just as he had done in Gonbad, he worked every day on their behalf. And in the middle of everything he started the letters to his boys about coming to America, and officially began the long journey through the proper embassies and channels that would allow this to happen.

On August 28, to a friend and supporter of the school he confided:

> I have had the most difficult month of my life...when I got the call from my alma mater here in the Kentucky mountains, I bowed to their decision and hastened here. What a month it has been! But God has been blessing...and I have pulled together a staff unlike any in the school's 72-year history in terms of their academic qualifications, Christian dedication and all.

This wasn't meant as a boast. He had called on every educator he knew personally. He had pled when pleading was necessary, and at last enough had answered the call to undertake this mission.

As the school opened its doors on September 1, pastors, parents, friends, and teachers of these boys and girls poured onto campus and stayed until 183 were registered and enrolled, exactly eighty more than the year before. He paused to think that he too would soon be bringing his very own boys from Gonbad, Iran to their new home in America. How full his heart was! The hot rays of the sun that September day reflected the warmth of joy that flooded over the campus. No one thought to fuss or lose his temper in the heat. Their hearts were beating to the tune of a different day—a new day rising over the mountains!

Homecoming was the next day, the largest in the history of the school, with 275 at the Homecoming banquet and around 500 there for one or more of the events of Homecoming weekend.

On September 8, Barkley wrote to an elderly lady in Cincinnati, Ohio, a longtime friend of the school, who had missed Homecoming but had sent a wonderful letter and a $25 gift:

> Homecoming was so beautiful…and such a marvelous spirit. People slipped me around $5,500 before it was over…and, of course, that was very encouraging. We will start planning for you to be here next Homecoming. I will send a car for you…that is if I am still here. Whether I will be here or not will depend on how I feel about things by the end of the year, and how the Board feels. It was a terrible situation to have walked into. However, school opened yesterday with nearly double last year's enrollment. Also we have the best qualified staff in Oneida history: 10 Masters degrees (4 last year), two near Masters, two Bachelor of Divinity degrees, one mechanical engineer and of course, I have studied law two years. They are a wonderful dedicated group of people working at a base salary of $4,000 a year, room and board.
>
> I am enclosing a copy of our new brochure, and we'll be keeping in touch. I hope I will be able to be in the Cincinnati area sometime before long. If so, I shall certainly be visiting with you. God bless you in a special way, for your friendship is a special blessing to me.

The board had asked for everyone to send his name and address, along with the names and addresses of anyone he knew that might be philanthropically inclined, with a promise of a follow-up by Barkley personally. The letters started to pour in, and between September and Christmas Barkley had responded with personal letters that he typed himself to well over 650 friends and would-be friends of the school—and not short letters, most were single-spaced and filled at least one or two pages. Someone who contributed a dollar received the same warm letter as someone who sent hundreds. Many were three-page letters. He took very seriously this commitment. The letters were warm, caring and always ended with: "I want you to plan to COME AND VISIT." To many he made the offer to send a car to meet them at the airport in Lexington.

Barkley reached out with his own list of names—those whom he had met while in the Peace Corps and ACTION, friends from affluent, prestigious parts of the country, and even many out of the country. That was a very large list indeed, with hundreds of names on it, and he asked all of them for the names of friends who might be interested. By Christmas, letters had gone out to thirty-two states: Tennessee, Kentucky, Ohio, Washington, Pennsylvania, New York, Maryland, Florida, Texas, California, Wisconsin, Mississippi, Arizona, Vermont, Michigan, Kansas Rhode Island, Iowa, Connecticut, Indiana, Oklahoma, New Jersey, Massachusetts, Arkansas, Georgia, Alabama, Virginia, West Virginia, North Carolina, South Carolina, Illinois—and several foreign countries, including Iran, Turkey, Germany, France, and England.

To his pastor at National Baptist Memorial Church in Washington, he sent a long letter. It said, in part:

> Everything has happened so fast that I haven't even had time to get back to Washington to close my apartment and get my clothes. I'm still wearing what I had in my suitcase when I left Washington on that trip. There has simply been so much to do here that I haven't dared leave…
>
> I am sending you some materials which I trust you will read carefully. If we can be of service to any of National's young people, or

any boys or girls in the area who need/and/or desire a Christian high school education (grades 9-12), just call on us. We are here to serve.

Barkley's photographic memory stunned many who had met him briefly many years before. He never forgot a date or any details about a person. He got addresses from almost everyone he ever met and somehow got them filed away for future reference. If you were ever connected to the school, he remembered your aunts, uncles, cousins and friends, as well as the dates you were there.

To a friend in Louisville, Kentucky, regarding a speaking engagement and other matters, he wrote:

> Your letter came day before yesterday, and I can't tell you how it lifted my spirit that day. I will be delighted to speak to your WMU group…I am accepting every speaking engagement I get, THAT IS MOST IMPORTANT for Oneida's story must be TOLD and 'how can they know if they have not heard?'. I'm leaving no stone unturned. Among other things, I've got feelers out to Colonel Sanders of Kentucky Chicken fame. We may not get anywhere but we will have tried.

To a lady in New York, Barkley wrote:

> As worthy as our students are, as dedicated and prepared is our staff, still the work would not be possible without the help, the prayers, the concern of our FRIENDS, people like yourself. I recall writing acknowledgements of your generosity when I was here working ten years ago. If my memory is not playing tricks on me (and I have been away several years…my memory may not be what it was), you are one of the most faithful friends of this work spanning many, many years…further it seems to me that another member of your family was also very much interested in Oneida, but I may be wrong there. Can you help me refresh my memory?

He went on to ask her for names of friends of hers who might help. He ended by asking:

Have you ever visited here? We would be so happy to have you as a guest. You should see our mountains just now as the leaves begin to change into autumn's golden colors. God bless you for you have blessed lives at ONEIDA.

He was grieved in October when the postal service dropped the school's mailing permit for a period of time until the old list was gone over.

We have removed more than 600 duplicates, dead, and wrong addresses from the mailing list and have worked desperately hard (with still much to do) to get our mailings into compliance with law and postal regulation.

A Time to Build Up

That mailing list positively had to be up and running, and every one breathed a sigh of relief when it was—just in the nick of time. The mailing permit was barely restored when a lifetime friend of the school offered to give $40,000 if the school could raise $60,000 by Christmas Day. There were more than 10,000 mostly new names on the list. On November 3, Barkley wrote friends Vesta and Lucy:

It is late Friday evening and we are thinking of you. Many of the students and staff have been with me all evening. We have been working for days and will be days more as get out a letter to nearly 10,000 people…most of whom have never heard or helped Oneida before. But we are sowing new seed in our drive for the $60,000 we MUST raise by Christmas Day. If we succeed in raising that amount, a friend will give us $40,000. Think of that! And what it will mean for Oneida. What a fitting way to celebrate His birth.

In about a week or ten days, I will probably be writing a special letter to the old and faithful contributing friends or the School. In the last analysis, I'm sure they will be the ones to carry us over the top. But I thought it was time to break new ground too.

Many of our students and staff are away tonight for our first ball game of the season. They should be getting back soon.

We are working very hard, and God is blessing in different ways. There is a good spirit among the students and staff, in the community and church, and God always blesses such a spirit.

So glad to have been able to talk with you by phone last week, and to find you both in such good spirits and doing so well. That's it for now from Oneida.

Barkley and the trustees were ecstatic. They desperately needed the funds this would provide to get them in the black and do some things that really needed to be done for the coming semester. A formal letter was drafted, to be sent to over 10,000 now on the new mailing list, and Barkley was working furiously to update the old list. On Monday before Thanksgiving the letter was mailed.

Dear Friend of Young People:

A longtime friend of our School has offered us a $40,000 gift IF we can raise $60,000 by CHRISTMAS DAY. Without your help, many boys and girls may lose the opportunity they need NOW. Oneida Institute, in 73 years time, has NEVER turned a needy boy or girl away. PLEASE help us keep this record intact. Today, more than half of our students are on full tuition scholarship and others are given free room and board and even clothing, each according to NEED.

Our students are prepared not just for college, but to LIVE a full life. They are taught: (1) to STUDY and more than 60% go on to college; (2) to work as each one does 11 and one half hours a week and many work eight hours a day during the summer months as we raise and process our own food…potatoes, corn, beans, tomatoes, beef, pork, etc; (3) to WORSHIP God without which we feel life has no ultimate meaning, and (4) to PLAY in a wholesome way.

The business world presents its attractive appeals in bond, stocks, real estate, etc. and the investor anticipates a goodly return. HOWEVER Oneida offers the opportunity to invest in PEOPLE… the Christian education of young men and women. An investment in youth is not only in good manhood and womanhood but a hardheaded venture that fosters a strong economy and a more stable nation. Refine the tastes of people, elevate their standards, increase their learning, and enable the person to "find" himself, and you have potentially increased sales in most all commodities needed and used by man.

We hope that YOU, blessed as you have been in life with material possessions, and appreciative of eternal values, will call to mind the MASTER'S commendation of those remembering Him in the ministry to the needy…"Inasmuch as ye have done it unto one of the least of these, my brethren, YE have done it unto ME"

Doing so are you ready to aid by financial assistance ONE of our boys or girls in securing the all-around mental, moral and physical training Oneida provides? Five hundred dollars (500) a year allows the School to teach, feed and house a worthy person whose potential is beyond measure or price.

Oneida is a non-profit institution and all contributions area tax deductible. For the blessings in life you have enjoyed, are you grateful? Will you express your gratitude by INVESTING IN A GIRL OR BOY TODAY? What you do may make the DIFFERENCE. The difference may be a life salvaged, a "dropout" or potential "dropout" off the streets, prepared for service. That ONE might even find the cure for cancer. He may save your life. Who knows?

The personal letters continued daily—whenever Barkley could work them into a hectic daily schedule that by now was also seeing him go on many speaking engagements. He carried his typewriter with him if he was to be gone overnight. Many nights in the hours between midnight and daylight he could be found pecking away. On Thanksgiving it was no different.

Dear Mr. Smith,

On this Thanksgiving Day, it is with a heart filled with thanksgiving that I sit down to write you. We are grateful for your most generous $100 contribution toward our $60,000 goal. Many other friends are responding and we are increasing our efforts. We must not fail our boys and girls. We know them. We work with them. We believe in them, believe that theirs can be lives of great usefulness.

Working with our students are a number of highly trained and dedicated people that God has led to this work: in this group are nine Masters degrees, two near Masters, two Bachelor of Divinity degrees and a mechanical engineer. Their base pay is $4,000 a year. In this number is Mary Nancy Wilson, who was there in Owensboro for thirteen years, and was a member of First Baptist. Do you remember her? This wonderful soul is back with us at Oneida this year after an eight year absence.

But blessed as we are with students and staff, we feel especially blessed in the wonderful people who make possible this work with their gifts. We get no tax funds…we depend on the $25, $50, $100 gifts of people like you. Without such gifts and such friend this work of 73 years duration would end.

So, I thank you, not only as Oneida's president, but as one who was privileged to grow up in the school, to graduate from it fourteen years ago.

God bless you and yours for having made ours a brighter Thanksgiving at Oneida.

To another dear friend he wrote, also on Thanksgiving Day:

Many friends are responding and we are increasing our efforts. Sometimes I have my doubts that we can make it…but, then, I cling to the faith that God will surely bless such great effort for such a worthy cause.

I was away all last week in the Kentucky Baptist Convention. Of course that was a very important meeting, and it was a time of intensive activity for me. Then I was in Chicago for three speeches and also spoke at the University of Louisville. Last night I spoke here in the county at the county-wide Thanksgiving Service which was broadcast over the radio. There are a number of other speaking engagements coming up, and soon we will have gotten out 15,000 letters. Most of these I have been sending to people who had never heard of Oneida, trying to win new friends, break new ground…but most will fall on barren soil for now, but am seed-sowing for later. I will be getting out a letter to the traditional supporters of the School around December 1st. telling them of results to date, and appealing to them to take us "over the top". Don't know if this "holding in reserve" has been the best strategy or not, but trust it will prove so.

Hope you all are having a good Thanksgiving as you have helped brighten our Thanksgiving, with your friendship, at Oneida.

On November 30, Barkley wrote:

I have been working very, very hard on the fundraising effort, and we are still some distance from the goal. We must not fail there… aside from what we raise, that $40,000 gift can be mighty helpful. There just aren't enough hours in the day.

On the same day he wrote to one of the trustees:

We have been getting a number of contributions, and some larger ones too. There have been about four (1,000) or (more) contributions to date. You know the anxiety that accompanies this work…I'm sure you watched your dad over many years…particularly when you wonder if you are going to make it moneywise sometimes. There are days when it seems that all the world has forgotten and deserted. You know I am grateful for all you have given in the past, for the time you spend in Oneida's behalf in Board meetings and such…grateful for this gift. Of course, you know too that we trust God will continue to bless you, and that you'll be able to make many more gifts to Oneida's work in the future!

In the middle of all this, the second board meeting was so poorly attended that if one fewer had shown up, there wouldn't have been a quorum. He wrote letters to each of them, encouraging them and thanking the ones who came the month before.

An uplifting note came from a near relative in Crossville, Tennessee: "I watched you with Hugh Downs on the *Today Show*—never dreaming you are my cousin 'removed' and I was proud you are a Clay Countian."

On December 5, after he returned from a speaking engagement in Kentucky and Ohio, he found a letter containing a check for $1085.72. He replied:

> Thank you very, very much. I showed your gift to our former President, Rev. D. Chester Sparks, who served here fourteen years… that dear man who will be eighty years old next month, who kept the faith here for so long, said, 'God bless his heart.' Really, our words are inadequate to express how we feel, and how much your gift means. We are now less than $20,000 short of our goal, and only twenty more days in which to raise the remaining sum. We are redoubling our efforts. We must not fail our boys and girls.

On December 14, he got a letter with $1,000 from a neighbor in Oneida. It said, "If you can get ten people to agree to pick up the balance needed the day before Christmas I will be one of them…so, line them up!"

On December 15, Barkley wrote to a man in Manchester:

> This is a call from Macedonia. Come over and help us…help us in this work with many boys and girls. I understand that you remember the Lord and His work through Baptists very generously every year. I wonder if you might remember Him through Oneida this year before Christmas Day.

To another Clay Countian he wrote:

> So, having done all we can in other places, I am looking to some of the people in Clay County to help us. If you can help us, we will be most grateful. We trust that the Lord has blessed you this year, and that you will be able to make this birthday gift to Him, and a Christmas gift for 'even the least of these' at ONEIDA.

On September 18, he wrote to a Chicagoan:

> You will be surprised to get a letter from a perfect stranger. But, I have known your sister-in-law in Somerset for many, many years… and we appreciate her so very much. We are desperately in need of help here at Oneida. I understand that you are a Southern Baptist, concerned, and that the Lord has blessed you. If you feel our cause worthy, and God leads, we would be so very, very grateful for any help you might extend.

On December 20, he wrote to a personal friend in South Carolina:

> I am on the verge of exhaustion, but victory is in sight! I have worked day and night the past several months to do this…have written several thousands of letters, and, at times, feared we might fail. But with four days to go, we are within that many thousand dollars making it—and I feel we are going to do so. That is going to mean so much, be such a boost to our work with these boys and girls.

To a Peace Corps friend he wrote:

> I am on the verge of exhaustion…still have much reorganization to do, but feel that God is blessing our efforts. I am a firm believer that there is a purpose in all things. Having survived two serious earthquakes and cholera epidemic when all about me people died, having been abundantly blessed in so many undertakings, it would be impossible for me to feel otherwise.

A Time for Giving Thanks
Christmas Day Letter

Dear Oneida Friends:

You…and hundreds of others…made a fine Christmas gift to Oneida this year. Ten days before Christmas, it seemed quite likely we would not make our $60,000 goal. But God moved many hearts…and all the gifts totaled together the good sum of $77,781.95…$17,000 more than our goal, and making us eligible for the $40,000 challenge Gift.

What a great God we serve! Thank you for SHARING with Oneida's young people. Because of you and others similarly concerned, we were able to close 1972 by having every back and current bills paid, to pay off a $15,000 note. We will be placing $45,000 in our Endowment Fund (how we need to increase that!) and we have a small surplus in our General Fund. Also, we have increased our library one third in size, and made some greatly needed improvements.

Earlier, today, our students and staff had a special flag raising to commemorate that first day of school so long ago. We thought it fitting to start off 1973 by being hard at work. All those whose faith and gifts have made, and make, Oneida possible were remembered today in speech and prayer. In a particularly moving prayer by one of our teachers, you were remembered.

Thank you! God bless you and those you love! Happy 1973.

The campus was quiet now. A million stars lit the cold night sky above Oneida. The outlines of mountain ridges rose like giant guardians in the distance as Barkley Moore finished his walk around the campus, making sure all was well ere the shades of night closed down on his beloved school. By midnight he was to be found sitting at his desk in the president's office, finally empty of all the people who had been there during the day. His desk was piled high with ledgers, letters, Christmas cards. This hour of the night seemed to be the best for his being able to focus on the details that must be seen to after all the chasing about of the work day.

So it was that the hour ending 1972 found President Moore at his desk laboring over the financial statement for the closing year and reminiscing over how God had so mightily blessed in the closing hours leading up to that Christmas Day just past, when the final moment of the all-out effort to raise that $60,000 had ended so gloriously! On his desk the Bible lay open to *Psalms* 107:8: "Oh, that men would praise the Lord for His goodness, and for His wonderful works to the children of men!"

He would be there until the wee hours, assessing the efforts of the past five months. His body was near exhaustion from the Herculean effort he had put into those months, but he was filled with such hope for the coming year that he was determined to finish the report before New Year's Day. He knew there was much wonderful news in those numbers and he was determined to get the message out to everyone—accurate to the penny if he could. Then they could properly praise the Lord for His goodness to them. He folded the note from Preston Baker, who had graduated from Oneida in 1928, and read again its message: "Barkley, An old saying, 'The darkest of the night is just before dawn.' I hope this is the case with OBI. Best wishes." The school had indeed weathered the darkest night since James Anderson Burns. Dawn was very near when he walked out of the office.

1973-74

Year Two

We have poured our souls into the work this year. There it is. There is what it is all about…sixty- three decisions
—Barkley Moore

Ｔhe first morning of January 1973 was cold, with threatening clouds hanging over the mountains. It was foggy as Barkley looked outside his window, but he was so relieved at having the financial statement finished that his first waking thought was a snatch of the beloved song, *To God Be the Glory, Great Things He Hath Done.*

God had blessed Oneida's work in so many ways the past five months. This was his greatest reassurance, even though he was still faced with many difficulties and anxieties. The generosity of so many fine friends of Oneida gave him proof that the Lord was still in Oneida's work. So even though the sky was promising rain for the day ahead, he could be grateful—would be faithful—in his praise.

That morning he felt the need for a hearty breakfast, so he dressed quickly and, between raindrops, ducked under the shelter of the towering trees as he made his way down the steep road that wound around down the hillside to the road and across the highway coming into Oneida to the kitchen at the girls' dorm, Sparks Hall. One of the cooks prepared him three eggs to go with the sausage and biscuits that were already made. He never drank coffee, but sometimes had a large glass of buttermilk with his meals. Today he had the buttermilk. After quickly eating his breakfast, he headed to the office.

Most of the faculty were still away for the holidays. But all who were still in the office were working furiously. Nancy Wilson had stayed on during the holidays, and she was pecking away at her typewriter. Barkley stopped at the small office next to his to say good morning to her. As he felt the press of work, he stayed just a few moments. As usual, they would confer for brief moments through the day, as the need arose. He set about the task of trying to thank the hundreds who made the fund drive such a success. He thought about how discouraging it had looked for a while and how he had thought they might fail. But right now the most pressing thing on his mind was to thank each and every one, no matter the size of the contribution.

Brother Sparks was turning eighty on Saturday, January 6, and Barkley had already planned a big birthday dinner and celebration starting at 5:30 that evening. By letter and phone, he had invited his family, who were scattered all over, to come and stay at his house, the former home of President Burns, where he and Brother Sparks lived. (He had bought Burns Mansion just after returning to Oneida). He had personally called many of the faculty, trustees, and church family, especially the church at Horse Creek, just thirty minutes away from Oneida, to which Brother Sparks had ministered over the years. He expected quite a crowd.

Still on his desk from last night lay the financial report. He put that aside and felt under the desk pad, where he had gotten into the habit of placing letters, checks, *etc.*—things he must see to personally. There was a special letter he had put aside since Christmas. He opened it and began to read.

It was from the famous Kentucky pastor, archeologist, and acclaimed author of more than thirty books, Darrell C. Richardson, who had written a great story about Barkley for the Southern Baptist Press. It was entitled *A Living Legend*.

Darrel Richardson was the most robust, healthy, full of life, vim-and-vigor person he had ever met. The thought of him drew up the image of a tall, muscular, tanned man dressed for an archeological dig or a safari in Africa.

Not expecting the contents of the letter, he was stunned at what he read! Darrel Richardson had had an encounter with the dark angel of death. He read how his friend had nearly died— should have died— according to all known medical wisdom of the day. He had been struck down with leukemia, given three months to live—and now, just a few months later, was completely healed. Barkley knew something of what his friend had experienced. He paused for a reflective moment. In Iran, he had lived with death all about him, through earthquakes in which thousands died, a cholera epidemic, and a deranged man who nearly killed him.

He could understand that his miracle-working God had protected his friend, even healed him, as he himself had been miraculously protected many times. He believed in miracles. Hadn't they just experienced an awesome miracle at Oneida?

He dashed off a letter, rejoicing with Dr. Richardson. He wrote about the harrowing days that brought him down to the brink of despair and the laying aside of every thing in order to contact more and more people—how during the last few days of the drive the Lord moved many hearts and a great harvest was reaped. He wrote of how one librarian, with volunteers, had been able, even in the midst of all the fund raising, to shelve books given to the school by the truck load— enough to increase the volume by one third! His heart was overflowing with gratitude and it came through in every word and thought he expressed.

While his fingers were flying across the keys, tapping out 100 words a minute—his mind worked on several different projects. This would be the undoing of most, but he thrived on it. In the middle of it all, he answered phone calls, greeted visitors, gave tours.

He delegated tasks to his staff with full confidence the job would be done. They were in the army of the Lord. They couldn't be defeated! Only set forth and victory was theirs.

When he finally trudged up the hill at night, he still had hours to go before he would allow himself to fall into a deep sleep, which would be all too brief. He looked toward the new year and the major tasks that needed to be accomplished. Through the hectic pace of the last five months, repair work had been done only on an emergency basis. He was aware of some things that would be major issues if they weren't taken care of in the very near future.

Long into the wee hours he outlined projects in order of need. Food was the second largest cost in the operation of the school and every day that cost was going up. Oneida's once-thriving farm had fallen onto hard times due to many factors. Its hundreds of prime acres lay in near ruins. Its equipment stood rusting in the fields, with no fences. One lone pitiful sputtering tractor was all they had.

Buying food when they could raise it didn't fit with his philosophy of doing everything the school could do for itself. Oneida boys and girls had always earned their way by helping raise, harvest, and prepare the food. He had to look ahead to the fall and perhaps the largest enrollment in the school's history, and prepare! He realized that the kitchen's freezer space wouldn't be nearly enough. They would need to at least double the space. That might cost thousands!

It was almost like being back in Gonbad as far as the water supply was concerned! They might as well be in the desert, they were so dependent on the weather. If it flooded, and it did at least once or twice each spring, the water supply from Goose Creek was like a mud pie and clogged the filters. If a drought lasted for more than a few weeks, they couldn't pump at all. The whole campus felt it. Already they had experienced near disaster. Teenage girls without water, cooks without water, farm boys stinking from pig manure on their clothes—and teachers all in the same boat and all of them working, eating, studying, living together twenty-four hours a day, seven days a week. This would strike sheer terror in city folks' minds, and a lot of comedy as well, if one really thought about it. Teenage girls even at Oneida are just as temperamental as those in Lexington, Kentucky!

He knew he would have to make those major physical needs the thrust of his work for the coming year. He was willing to lay down his life himself but he also knew he would have to call on every man, woman and child at the school to pick up more of the work themselves. However, to anyone he met, this great burden would be turned into a greater opportunity to make a difference in more lives, a difference for time and for eternity.

There were other needs just as important in his mind. He was certain that by fall, there would be many more students, and more teachers would be needed. And then there were the dreams he had for his boys and girls—yes, they were his greatest concern. They were covered for the present moment with enough teachers but it had been years since the school had had a band, because of the burning of Marvin Hall. He felt his boys and girls deserved to have the advantage of instrumental music and training, as they would elsewhere. But he would have to start from scratch.

When the burden seemed almost too heavy to bear alone, he sat down with Papa Sparks for a father-to-son talk. He unburdened his soul to this saintly old warhorse in the Lord. They sat together, rocking in their simple rocking chairs, before the fading embers of the fire and talked to the Lord. When that prayer meeting among him, Papa Sparks, and the Lord was finished, there was a glow about him in the light of the fire. Maybe it was the settled decision in his heart to do his best and leave the rest to God. He later wrote, "If we were in the black we would praise God; if we are in the red, I am not going to be embarrassed to let friends know it, for I will be conscious of the fact that I have done all I could, and it is not my personal failure." Having made this declaration to himself and God, he knew that he would not have to carry these burdens on his own back, but was casting them all onto the Lord. Whether he encountered failure or success, he would give it to the Lord. With a firm grip on the fear lingering in the back of his mind that any failure the school suffered would be blamed on him, he was ready to begin the new year.

The party for Brother Sparks was a great success. More than 150 people came, even though the weather was bad. Papa immensely enjoyed it. However, about ten days later Barkley had to rush Papa to the hospital, where he had to stay for the next nine days. His lungs were congested—a combination of age and all those cigars—but he came back fit as a fiddle. Barkley moved him down to the campus so he wouldn't have to get up and down the hill during the rest of the winter!

The faculty and he closed out the old year with dinner on New Year's Eve, and a session of prayer and concern for the students. They discussed their strengths and weaknesses, and how they might better help each one. The meeting lasted until nearly 1:00 AM. As he trudged back up the hill toward Burns Mansion, he was tired but felt the Lord's presence beside him.

The opening day of the new year began in a downpour of rain. However, the day before, Sunday, had been clear and all of the buses made it back to campus from London safely, as did all of the students who came by car. (London, Kentucky was the drop-off point for students returning by bus from their homes all over the states.) There were already fifteen new students and more to come. They were all excited to be back as they settled into dorm rooms, unpacking overstuffed luggage.

On the first day of school, students, faculty and staff slogged to classes through the cold rain. At the morning chapel service the students, faculty, and Barkley sang heartily as they stood, warming up with the singing. When Barkley stood to speak, nearly 200 pairs of eyes meet his piercing brown eyes. At times he gripped the podium with both hands, but more frequently his hands rather gently caressed it—depending on the point he was making. While Barkley expected much of his students, there was a tender side as well. There was a little bit of fear and a great deal of respect and awe for him in the students, but they had already discovered that he loved them dearly. However, they didn't want him catching them talking or being inattentive during one of his lectures, as he was apt to walk directly down to the culprit.

By the time chapel ended, the mail was usually on his desk. Opening it was one of his most pleasant tasks. Reading the many letters got him in touch with the supporters of the school and those he knew were praying for him. He gained enough strength many days to endure the long hours ahead. From what he read in a letter that very day, he got a big smile on his face. "You seem to me to really be a 'Living Legend', I hope I can become your friend." It was from a young man whom he had never met. He wrote back that day. There were dozens more. That month alone, scores of letters came in every day in response to the more than 20,000 letters the school had sent out over the past two months.

He answered a couple in Pennsylvania who wrote in response to one of the campaign letters—an honest inquiry about the service the school was performing in the area:

> Many of these are very needy…cannot pay anything, and some of them we are having to help even with clothing…You mentioned Pikeville in your letter and the fine work there: three of the boys who came in are from there, all of them are having to be helped with everything…one had three shirts, one a pair of blue jeans.

To another lady who wanted to help with a scholarship of $50 a month, he wrote:

> I recommend to you a brother and sister, who are both freshmen. Their names are Steve and Sandra. Steve was 16 last Friday. They are among the very finest and neediest students that we have. We help them even with clothing.
>
> Their mother lives right here in Oneida, but we keep the children in our dorms to get them out of their home environment. Their mother gets a small welfare check. There are six children (one born a few months ago), but no father in the home. But a baby appears every so often. But Steve and Sandra (names changed) are very solid children, so wonderfully cooperative, hard-working, helpful to others, good solid citizens. Hopefully with the love and training we can give them that will be so. If you are still of a mind to help in this way, I think these two young people are worthy of help…In any event, we are most grateful for your wonderful friendship and concern for the Lord's work being carried forward at ONEIDA.

As often as he could if he was on campus, he attended the nightly vespers services the students held in the village church. On February 8, Barkley wasn't able to be in the chapel service because of a speaking engagement. David Bausum, a fine student, active in the BSU, led the service. He spoke of death—noted that it was not to be feared by the Christian—testified to his belief in the eternal victory of the Christian over death. The students joined hands in a circle and prayed together as they usually did. They sang *Blest Be the Tie That Binds*. "When we asunder part, it gives us inward pain, but we shall meet again." They left the church in a downpour of rain.

David went back to his dorm. As usual he had his own prayer time before bed. He took out a piece of paper and wrote, "Pray for: Mr. Moore, the President, Mr. Sizemore, the dorm dean, the physics teacher, Oneida's pastor, several other teachers, missions, family, Richard, Bible study, U.S. prisoners of war in Vietnam, several students, several missionaries, his Uncle Fred, self [underlined three times]." He got off his knees and went straight to bed, as he had to be up early. His job was to carry the slop from the kitchen over to the farm. He was so proud of his job.

When he came to Oneida, being a farm boy, he spent a lot of his spare time on the farm. He noticed their old jeep wasn't working. He loved working on vehicles and had helped his dad repair theirs on more than one occasion. It was the natural thing for him to ask if he could work on Oneida's rusting jeep sitting idle on the farm. He went to Mr. Moore, asking for permission to do so, and finally, after Barkley had conferred with David's father, he had been given permission. In no time at all, he had the jeep up and running, and with that he got to drive it back and forth to the farm once a day to deliver slop.

At daybreak came he headed for the farm with his helper. It was still raining and the county's low-water bridge, which they had to cross, was about to be covered. They hurried on, got the slop delivered. On the way back, with the water over the bridge, the right front tire of David's jeep slipped over the edge. Both boys were thrown into the rushing water. One swam to safety. David was lost in the current.

As soon as the word reached Dr. Moore, everyone was alerted, both on campus and in the whole community of Oneida. An all-out search got underway. But as the day dragged on, David wasn't found. A group of teachers went to his dorm room and on the top of his chest found the prayer list lying there as he had left it the night before.

It was be over a month before his body was be found, on March 13, four miles below the spot where he fell into Goose Creek. The day before David's body was found, Barkley wrote to Nell Britton about how stressful it had been, but how beautiful the weather was that day—almost spring like—how the rain had stopped some hours ago. The next day, with the river inexplicably at its lowest since this tragedy began, David's body was found. And the very next day, the river rose again!

Barkley already had speaking engagements scheduled for the next week, but amid spring break, with the students leaving on Friday and the seniors heading for Washington on Saturday, there would be a funeral for David at Oneida, with Barkley officiating. While he was on the speaking engagement in Ohio, he would have to take a train trip over to Maryland for another funeral for David, where he would be speaking again.

Even with all this, he continued writing letters every day. He wrote to the family and talked with them almost daily. He was a tower of strength for everyone around him.

David was the kind of student Oneida was honored to serve. David had earned his own money to come to Oneida, had led several students to the Lord in his short time there, and blessed all those who knew him in many ways. Barkley earnestly asked everyone to pray for the school, for David's parents and family, and for himself.

It was often that Barkley stopped at Miss Wilson's office and just dropped into the extra chair—too beat to move. He drew on her strength—knowing she was praying for him. In that small room, he felt the Lord's presence more than anywhere else in those troubled days. Barkley sorely needed solace from the Lord and he found it there. In the *Mountaineer* the following month he described the funeral.

"On the afternoon of March 21, David's schoolmates and teachers at Oneida assembled in the Oneida Baptist Church at 2:00 PM…" The Oneida memorial service opened with the congregation singing the old hymn *It Is Well With My Soul*. All present rejoiced in the certain knowledge that it *was* well with David's soul.

Rev. D. Chester Sparks, President Emeritus, led in prayer, and the OBI Chorus, under the direction of George Hensley, Class of 1957, sang *Does Jesus Care?* Rev. Carlyle Hounchell, Class of 1930, recalled seeing David going about his daily chores, and spoke of the eternal destiny of the born-again Christian. Oneida pastor Rev. Clyde Shackleford responded with a splendid solo rendering of *How Great Thou Art*, the first hymn that David's mother could recall him singing as a child.

David's family was present in that service. Rev. George Bausum, David's cousin and pastor of the Calvary Baptist Church of Somerset, read some letters of David's and delivered a sermon. Beside Brother and Mrs. Bausum, also representing the family, were Mr. and Mrs. Roy Robertson and daughter Dixie from Virginia.

Barkley read *I Corinthians* 13. David had distributed this scripture in tract form to his schoolmates before his death. The service ended with the chorus singing the joyous *I've Found a Hiding Place*.

In a precious letter from David's parents addressed to "Friends", the Bausums told how the Lord had been in the timing of all that had happened the week of David's death. They were just about an hour from Oneida when they got the news and could come directly to Oneida. Otherwise they would have been in Annapolis, Maryland. Expressing their thankfulness that Tim, the other student, had not been hurt, they affirmed that David "left this world doing what he loved most".

"It sure is a wonderful blessing in knowing that David is in heaven with our Lord and Master. When we think of him, I hope we will examine our lives to see where we could do better. As you know God calls us any time, he does not wait until we are ready."

A Time to Build Up

Almost immediately after the funeral, Barkley left for the airport with his student driver at the wheel. He flew to Ohio to speak, then took a train to Baltimore. One of his friends, Dr. William Irons, on staff with the Department of Social Relations at Johns Hopkins University, whom he had met during the Peace Corps years, picked him up at the station. He not only got him where he needed to be in Annapolis, but picked him up after David's funeral and took him to his home for the night, giving him a small reprieve before he had to plunge back into the speaking tour.

From there he went to Washington, D.C., Texas, South Carolina, Georgia, and finally back to Louisville, where he was a speaker at the

BSU Convention. The speeches came straight from his heart. They always began, "What is Oneida?" He focused on the needs. Faithful to the message of Christ's love, he spoke of the profound need for young people to get an education—and even more important—their need to hear how Christ laid down His life for their very souls. So much was at stake in the lives of these young people—everyone in his hearing must shoulder some of the load. He had stories to tell of students right then and there that needed their help. His audiences must burst into applause or run for cover. Nothing short of their personal help in answering the Macedonian call would do. How could you turn this selfless man's pleas away? How could you turn these children away? Turning a deaf ear was the only option he left you—other than helping him in some way.

He collapsed into a deep sleep the minute he got into the back seat, completely trusting the Lord to keep the driver and him safe—completely confident that this young man would do his best—not take the curves too fast or stop too quickly and awaken him. He slept all the way to Lexington, Kentucky.

So many of the letters Barkley received after such a message were full of kind expressions of support. Some of the letters would contain a dollar, others $10, $20. Average, everyday men and women came to love him and started giving faithfully from their average paychecks. One dear old fellow, from Sun City, California, wrote, "Mr. Moore, I surely do sympathize with you trying to get all the things done that you are called upon to do. Seems to me that you need to be in four or five places at once. I just hope that you do not burn the candle at both ends, as Oneida will need you around for a long time to come."

"What a great joy it would be if my wife and I could find someone who could just clean the slate of all these physical needs at Oneida. We will keep praying and trying because we do understand."

He came home to beautiful weather, with many more friends. To everyone he had met, and to everyone he wrote, he extended a warm welcome to come and visit. After all, he said,

It is beautiful here tonight…forty miles from nowhere…we are having real spring weather, crickets cricking, and frogs croaking, moon hanging low in a clear starlit night. Yes, spring is definitely in the air!

He made the towering mountains—strip mined with huge gashes ripped into their beautiful sides, their majestic peaks torn away—sound like taking a trip to a virtual paradise. To him it was! While others with fine educations fled to the cities, he planted himself right in the midst of his beloved poverty-stricken mountains—filled with poverty-stricken children. He settled in—planting seeds of love for His Master. While others saw only the raw pain of poverty, he saw in every home diamonds that would gleam with just a little polish. He would build up these children—give them educations for time and eternity. When the board of trustees asked him in the March board meeting to stay on indefinitely he had only one answer, YES.

A Time to Reap

By early May, a new farm manager was in place and under his direction the farm was nearly ready for spring planting. They had installed a new fence along the road leading to the farm, and had also installed a new electric fence around eight more acres to keep in the hogs. They had begun laying pipe for the much needed water system that would be ready before school resumed.

When planting season arrived, the fields were plowed and farm workers and Oneida's students, staying over for the summer, were ready to plant. The farm crew planted nine 200-foot rows of peas, thirty-eight rows of sweet corn, ten rows of cucumbers, thirty-five rows of beans, one row of mustard and lettuce, four rows of radishes, three rows of cabbage, one row each of carrots and beets, seven rows of tomatoes, 1500 plants of sweet potatoes, and eighteen bags of potatoes for the school's use. Then, for a cash crop they planted two acres of pepper, eight acres of silage corn, twenty-four acres of feed corn, and twenty-six acres of hay.

Not only was the farm planting done, they had also planted flowers everywhere on campus. In fact, Barkley said, "more than everywhere, we have planted both cannas and scarlet sage".

Barkley wrote to a new friend he had made for Oneida during the campaign:

It is my favorite time of day at Oneida…between sunset and dark, cooling breezes blow among our campus trees after a very hot day, and the woods always look so restfully dark green up Bullskin Creek at this time of day. I take a break, look around, then come back to my desk for the second half of my day. Since I came back here last August, I have not had off a single day, and I put in about 16 hours most days. Sometimes I grow weary, but God is blessing our efforts, and we must keep trying! We have poured our very souls into the work this year, all the staff and myself, and God has been giving the increase…read our last *MOUNTAINEER* again. THERE IT IS. There is what it is all about…read *Outstanding Teenagers, 63 Decisions.*

In the *Outstanding Teenagers* article on the front page was the story about Bruce Davidson and Linda Sizemore, *Why Oneida?* Linda Sizemore is one reason. She has been chosen by the faculty as the "Outstanding Teenage Girl" for the current academic year.

Always smiling, Linda keeps an extremely neat room in the dormitory. Much of the year she arose at 5:00 AM each day to help the cooks prepare breakfast.

Linda is fifteen years old and a freshman. She is a top student academically, and one of the very finest girls we have in every respect.

Linda is one of a long line of Oneidians.

Why Oneida? Bruce Davidson is a reason why.

Bruce, an outstanding member of our basketball team, is outstanding in character also. It is little wonder that the faculty has honored him by selection as "Outstanding Teenage Boy."

What makes Oneida different from a public high school? In one sentence…the difference lies in a concern for the souls of our students as well as their minds and bodies.

That difference was highlighted during the week of May six-eleven. We could not end the school year without making one last effort to reach the souls of many of our students. There were seniors graduating, others who likely would not be back in the fall. Many of these had not 'made it right with God.

A night-long, twelve-hour vigil of prayer on Saturday, May 5, preceded the opening of the revival effort. Students, teachers, people of the community came and went throughout the night in a chain of prayer, Bible reading, and meditation.

Rev. Don Pinson, a twenty three-year-old evangelist from Hazard, did the preaching beginning with the Sunday morning service. Our students were not required to attend the weekday service…this was left voluntary…and the early services saw the church less than half-filled.

But on Wednesday evening there were several decisions. After the service, many remained to sing. Two of our boys who had worked late in the evening on the Farm were passing the church on the way to the Dorm. They joined the singing group in their work-stained clothes with a faint smell of cow manure. As the singing continued, these two boys made professions of faith as did one other.

Those present felt the Spirit of God working in a very real way, and this spirit was felt throughout the remainder of the week. The church was nearly filled for the remaining services.

Services closed Friday evening, May 11 with thirty two having come forward making professions of faith, and thirty one others coming to rededicate their lives. Several of these were adults of the community, these and others the object of prayer for several years.

Fourteen were baptized at the Sunday morning service on May 13, and seven others will be baptized May 20 when relatives and friends can be present, after which the entire church will celebrate the Lord's Supper. The remaining eleven will be baptized in their home churches.

Commitments made, the opportunity to make such commitments, having the privilege, and exercising it, of presenting the gospel of a risen Lord in chapel, in the classroom, and elsewhere- this makes Oneida DIFFERENT.

How can the worth of even one soul be measured?

We only know that the stars, in the clear air of revival nights, reflected the "joy of the presence of the angels of God over one sinner that repented". *Luke* 15:10.

There was not only much rejoicing in heaven the week of May 6-11, but also in the community and school called ONEIDA.
Letters, 1973

The academic year ended on a strong note, with nineteen graduating in a beautiful commencement service. Everyone was still on a mountain top, spiritually, from the revival. A sweet spirit pervaded the campus until the last student departed for the summer.

By the time the school year came to a close, much had been accomplished. Preparations for the fall semester were well under way. Anticipating many more students, perhaps a third more, Barkley had hired five more full-time staff people for the next year. By the time the schedule was made, textbooks had already arrived. Barkley said, "Why, we could start school tomorrow!"

He had a band director coming—a person he considered to be the best possible choice. He was certain the band would become very important as the years went by. He had promised her that as long as he was at Oneida, he would "push, promote, and support it". Always bubbling over when accomplishments had been made. However much he achieved where his school was concerned, he continued to set the goal higher. Would he ever achieve all his dreams?

He wrote to Professor Horton Walker, from Louisville, Kentucky, pleading with him to come to Oneida:

I feel such a keen responsibility as director of the Lord's work here…a work that serves all of Kentucky, reaches out to other states, and foreign lands as well: students this year from six different foreign countries: such a MISSION opportunity. These boys and girls burden my soul (I was once one of their number) for I am concerned for THEIR souls, as well as good training for their minds and bodies. I covet for them the BEST teachers…trained teachers, competent teachers (teachers who know their subject and can discipline a class), God-filled teachers, EXPERIENCED teachers.

As always, Barkley was thinking ahead to the future and dreaming dreams for one more wonderful way to have a celebration. He loved celebrations. Maybe this was something he picked up in Iran, where celebrations were performed with wonderful rituals even among the poorest. He knew the power to elevate life to a higher level that came with celebration. To every letter that he wrote that summer, he added his plans for instituting a Founder's Day, beginning in the fall.

> We want to have a program of inspiration at that time as counterpoint to the Commencement, which is an inspirational time at the end of the year. We want to give incoming students and staff a sense of the heritage and history of Oneida, a day to honor those who have served long and faithfully through Oneida's history. If we can get it worked out, we hope to have our FACULTY AND TRUSTEES march in ACADEMIC PROCESSION on that day, appropriately gowned and hooded, with the colors of their varying degrees. This has never been done in Oneida history. Then we hope to have such an ACADEMIC PROCESSION each Commencement Day.

Barkley already had next year's Commencement speakers lined up: Sargent Shriver of Kennedy and Peace Corps fame was to be the speaker for Commencement, and Dr. Franklin Owen, Executive Director of Kentucky Baptists, would deliver the sermon. Next year would be Oneida's seventy-fifth anniversary.

The mailing list for the *Mountaineer* was now up to 25,000, triple what it had been. Barkley had it in mind to be the primary "house organ" for getting out Oneida's Message. Although not a businessman, he had acquired many of Sylvia Russell's methods, which had proved to be just as successful as Professor Burns' lecturing around the United States.

But they were fast approaching the summer camp season. The twentieth annual Mountain Mission Conference would have hundreds of preachers coming from all over the state. They would occupy every dorm room available in both girls' and boys' dorms. This was one of the most challenging weeks of the summer, feeding, housing, and hosting the conference sessions all over campus. Right on the heels of the conference, there followed the G.A. camp.

School was back in session with the largest enrollment ever, 258 boys and girls, seventy-five more than last year, and double the number from just two years before. Many of the physical projects were finished that he had foreseen back in January. The water system had cost $4,000 and would eliminate shortages that they had periodically suffered. A new $5,000 walk-in freezer in which to store food produced on the farm was in place. Also, a new twelve-passenger van had been purchased for the students whom the school bused in from the mouths of hollows for miles around. Many of those students still had to walk as far as three miles to get to where the bus would pick them up. And although he got a $2,000 discount, the van still cost $3,500.

Another thing Barkley had done over the summer was to raise funds with which to endow the Oneida cemetery. It lay high on the mountain ridge coming into Oneida, overlooking the school. Many of Oneida's greats, including James Anderson Burns, were buried there. Now, it could be maintained.

Homecoming was a great day with a splendid outdoor pageant in the evening—generous giving and pledges on the part of the alumni. Around 1,000 gathered, many more than in any previous year—so many that the banquet overflowed from the dining hall onto the lawn. Founder's Day was celebrated in colorful and inspirational fashion, with academic procession and all! At Homecoming, one of the 1913 graduates who had attended Oneida on full scholarship presented the school a $50,000 gift for the Endowment Fund. Barkley wrote about it all in every letter that went out, ending each letter with this verse. "Truly cast thy bread upon the waters and it shall return after many days." And a warm, "Thank you for writing, and God bless you and yours and we trust you will remember us in your prayers and the work that is ONEIDA."

On September 16 Barkley was up and ready to leave at 6:00 AM for a week in Washington, Philadelphia and New York. He had been away many days during the summer as well, speaking around Kentucky for the Mission Focus Week for Kentucky Baptist. But he was still accepting any speaking engagement he could get.

By October he had $25,000 worth of bills on his desk, and precious little money with which to pay them. He worked all the harder. In answer to a letter to one of his Peace Corps buddies who was off to a tennis tournament, he wrote:

> It is always good to hear from people, and I feel that the more people one is in somewhat regular contact with, the more friends one has, life is a little richer. I vicariously enjoyed reading of your tennis playing! I just wish I had time to do something like that—or anything. But I must really keep my nose to the wheel to keep this place going, and it seems everything I have ever been engaged in has taken me completely, body and soul. But the Lord has blessed richly and I can't, don't complain. We can't have or do everything...
>
> I am exercising faith...and working as though it is all up to us, and praying as though it is all up to the Lord... Two things we ask you to do for us... (One) remember to tell others of the work here, thereby helping to win some new friends...and send us names that we could add to our mailing list; your name will not be used (Two) Do remember to PRAY for us daily. It really helps.

On November 22 he wrote to the General Manager, Sales and Service, IBM Data Processing Division, Lexington, Kentucky, asking for help with the new computer department:

> As OBI has just hired an instructor who has over eight years experience in the design and running of computers and data processing installations, it is felt with his help, as well as yours, that approximately 250 students could be exposed to an exciting program in data processing.

On December 23 he wrote:

> Oneida wears a wintry aspect with snow all about, our tree is up and other decorations, we are busy wrapping gifts and preparing the Christmas treat for each boy and girl, plans are underway for

the annual Christmas Dinner, students are practicing the Christmas play, the chorus is practicing its cantata, and the band played so beautifully in their Christmas concert in chapel. Your help makes all of this possible. A very Merry Christmas and warm THANK YOU from ONEIDA.

The Christmas letter was on his desk, ready to be mailed just in time for Christmas. But before he could close out the year he had one more letter to write. It was to tell about five of his kids who needed help. So on December 31 he sat down to write that one last letter. It was to the Rev. Robert Stinson, Pastor, Keysburg Baptist Church, Hopkinsville, Kentucky. He wrote:

> Your letter received today thrills me…I am grateful to know of your concern…thank you very much for $100 designated for scholarships through your church…You have asked about several students and I am sending details concerning several. [Names have been changed.]

> (1) Josh and Isabella…are brother and sister…two out of 15 children…. family lives in a three room house, several miles up Loss' Creek…. family very poor… the children had come without even underwear and carried what they had in a large paper sack. Josh is handsome… over 6 ft…rather shy…won the award for student having made most progress…developing into an outstanding ballplayer. Isabella is a very attractive young lady…in 8th grade…lives in dorm but goes to nearby public school as we have only classes 9-12.

> (1) Sasha and Lonny are another brother and sister…from Jackson County…two of 13 children…unbelievable home situation…some of children mentally retarded. Sasha is very intelligent…already a cheerleader…wouldn't know she is the same girl we first saw… both she and Lonny are very much "diamonds in the rough" Sasha developing into an ambitious, beautiful young lady…has learned so much about how to dress, personal hygiene, etc. Lonny loves to work

on the farm, is a very hard worker but doesn't care much for books…
however says he wants to finish high school…if he does…will be first
male in his family line to do so.

(2) Troy is one of few black students…adopted as baby, then adoptive
parents divorced…. being raised by wonderful old grandmother…
Troy used to running streets…doing about as he pleased…until he
heard of Oneida. Making remarkable progress…every one very fond
of him…he loves Oneida…is 6'3", still growing…quite a ballplayer…
calls coach, "Pops".

(3) Timmy is a sophomore…has a sister here…freshman…used to
walk several miles to meet bus…finally got him to live in dorm…five
children in this very poor family.

(4) Lucinda is one of nine children from Big Creek…father a fine
Baptist minister…graduate of Oneida…brother also on scholarship…
graduating this year…enclosing article on brother who wins award.

Whatever you do or can do, or the people of your church, can do
for our young people will be greatly appreciated and is an investment
not just for time but for eternity as well.

After all, these boys and girls were the reason for which he had done
everything he had done, or would do with all the days of his life, so
long as he was alive, he would be about His Masters Work, right here
at "HIS GALILEE."

Finally he climbed up the hill toward home on New Years Eve. He
had the time to reminisce over the past year and all that God had done,
the deep waters he had come through, the highs and lows, the mountain
peaks and then the valleys deep. He had been ever climbing, holding
onto the Unchanging Hand of the Nazarene.

He had traveled the highways and byways, cities with skyscrapers
and the coastal towns of California, sun-soaked with the ocean's waves
lapping their beaches. He had been to the historic cities of the East, with

spires and gabled ivy-covered mansions. He had flown over majestic mountain ranges, bursting with color, in New England. From the East Coast to the West Coast, from the North to the South, he had been all over the land in his quest for funds. But at the end of each campaign, he was more than ready to return to his Galilee! The village of Oneida was fading into the evening shadows and there was nary a light twinkling in its houses as he rounded the bend to home. He took a moment to stand on the screened-in porch at the front of Burns Mansion, where he could see his beloved school by the light of the December moon hanging low over the hilltops. The moon's rays seemed to shine brightest on that blessed knoll that they called their Mount Moriah.

1974-75
Year 3

*Our primary reason for being in Christian Education is both
ministry and outreach. Some of our work tends more to the one,
some to the other. I would say that Oneida's emphasis is primarily
in "Outreach" as we try to reach those who are not Christians...
and hundreds and hundreds of souls have been reached.*
—Barkley Moore

With thirty new students, 1974 got off to a rousing start. It was cold, but there were no floods that year. Barkley and the staff were ready for the incoming students. The faculty and office staff were busy at their tasks. It almost seemed too good to be true that there was enough money to pay the bills—but there was *just* enough, and the school was expanding all the time. Barkley wrote, "We are having the best year here at the school in many, many years. Financially, operations are still barely in the black."

With more students, more space was needed everywhere. While they had enough room for the staff and faculty at present, they too were cramped in the present housing. Barkley, always on the alert for challenges that lay ahead, tried to stay one step ahead. Some would have called his visions for meeting the needs of the school pure dreams. While the school was safe for the moment, he knew February and March would be the more difficult months financially, as gifts were always down then.

Still, this was the time to trust the Lord and take as much action as he could to ensure the growing needs would be met. He didn't let everyone in on his plans. Brother Sparks could be trusted to keep secret his dreams! He wrote to him early in February:

> I have been sowing seeds since last February toward funds for a new building to replace Melrose Hall…a multi-purpose building including faculty apartments and an industrial arts shop. I have said nothing to anyone because no use having a lot of talk if there are no real prospects. The project would be a little better than $400,000. I have been writing different Foundations, *etc.* I did get in $60,000 this week which I have put into a special capital funds account.

To another friend outside the school he confided that he had been working on a $350,000 gift.

Heavy on his heart, although he had not really said it to anyone, was the need for Oneida to be included to a larger extent in the Kentucky Baptist Convention's funding of its educational facilities. He knew that Kentucky Baptists were evaluating the situation and would be deciding if more funds could be appropriated for Christian education in 1974. Right then the school was receiving just a token amount, or so it seemed to him! Barkley Moore was a Southern Baptist through and through and he considered Oneida to be both Home and Foreign Missions. As such, the school deserved to be funded by Kentucky Baptists to a larger extent. But he also knew this had to be approached with great care and diplomacy. He had deliberately not asked Southern Baptist Churches in Kentucky for any special offering for the school. But he longed to lay his heart bare to his fellow Baptists. He was much in prayer for the Lord to guide him in this.

Making friends was one of the things he did best, next to dreaming big! He already had the secular community applauding him for his accomplishments. Even Sargent Shriver, the first head of the Peace Corps, whom he had never met, fell captive to his dreams for Oneida, and agreed to come for the Commencement in May. Barkley was so passionate about his love for his boys and girls at Oneida that he could persuade almost anyone of almost anything on which he set his heart and mind. Because he brought his friends actively into his plans, they too became passionate. Of course, there were always those skeptics for whom *can't* was the first word and the last word. He had no time for those folks. He would say, "Can't never can and can never loses."

One of his friends said to him that he had missed his calling—he certainly could make anyone "believe white was black and black was white and north was south and south was north". He should have been a lawyer!

Over a year before, he had asked Dr. Franklin Owen, Executive Director of the Kentucky Baptist Convention, to deliver the baccalaureate sermon, and Dr. Owen had, of course, said "Yes". This was going to be the biggest celebration in the history of the school!

He had dreamed of making Oneida a two-year college and had already put the idea before the board of trustees. Soon he was dashing off a letter to the president of Cumberland College, Dr. James Boswell, on the possibility of offering college courses at Oneida, beginning in the fall. He made his plan sound like a golden opportunity for Cumberland. He wrote:

> Several of our staff are perfectly qualified to teach beginning college level courses. Oneida would send Cumberland the tuition fees, pay the teachers out of funds and the remainder of the fees would remain with Cumberland.

So he was off and running, with fresh energy, new dreams—a hope and a prayer in his heart for the coming year—for bigger and better things! Now that the financial crisis was behind him, he was renewed. Working hard sixteen-hour days and taking no days off was his pleasure.

By early March, he was sufficiently confident about one of the building projects that he began telling many supporters of the school that it would go forward. The dream had grown. It would be not one building but two. As always, he was sharing his heart with friends through correspondence.

On March 29, he wrote to a teacher who had only been able to stay for one semester:

It is nearly certain now that we will begin the construction of two new buildings this summer. One will be a faculty apartment house opposite the church where other faculty housing now is. The other building will be across from the Gym where the trailers now are. It will include a new library about one-third larger than our present one, my office and business office, some new classrooms including a language lab, and a CHAPEL on the second floor with large windows overlooking the farm on one side and down the valley on the other side. It is almost ninety percent certain that we will begin a first-year college program this fall in cooperation with Cumberland College and under their accreditation…

This fall we are adding Advanced Biology, Industrial Arts, Vocational Agriculture and Driver's Education…Also, am planning to put our staff on a pension plan this fall.

Enough for now. Keep in touch. Hope to see you at HOMECOMING, Saturday, August first, with your guitar! We did so much appreciate your work here…and wish you could have stayed on and on.

Best wishes. Miss Wilson says "hello".

Sincerely,

Barkley Moore.

He never missed an opportunity to create good will and promote future celebrations. He never failed to invite anyone who had ever been to the school to come back. He thrived on letters from friends of his and friends of the school, and personally corresponded with dozens in any given month. He also wrote thank-you letters to donors; literally thousands went out monthly.

At the rate he was making invitations to come and visit, it would take the rest of his life to show friends just around the campus and feed them meals—and that was just what he meant to do. He a vacation—but so many taking *their* vacations were stopping to see him!

By the middle of April he had $350,000 definitely pledged toward the project. He promptly announced that he had $60,000 in cash. He was ready to begin the formal campaign to get two buildings started by fall.

Another new idea had come to him, and he had already put it into action. He had picked it up from the Peace Corps—the idea of using volunteers. Teenagers from Missouri had worked an entire week and paid him for the privilege of doing so. They had worked nearly a year on various projects to raise the funds to come! Once at Oneida, they had contributed hundreds of dollars worth of paint, painted several buildings, and helped start tearing down an old building in preparation for new construction—and they were Church of Christ people. That summer Oneida would have six Methodist work camps—sixty people in each camp over a period of six weeks. The volunteers would be doing a lot of work in the area—helping old people repair their porches, paint their houses, *etc.*

That very month he was also invited to join the Commission on Religion in Appalachia, Inc. The organization's goals were to promote church "self-help" community economic development in Appalachia, to offer assistance in training, to provide other kinds of support to church-related self-help groups. They invited the school to become a charter member of HEAD, a task force to reorganize itself—principally with church bodies. Through HEAD, Barkley's influence would be felt all over Kentucky!

Graduation was upon the school before he knew it. It went off splendidly. There were forty-four graduating seniors, double the number eighteen months ago. Sunday, May 26, 1974 was the most dramatic celebration in the history of the school. The ceremony was on the lawn between Anderson Hall and the boys' dorm. Everyone marched in to the music of Oneida's band in full academic regalia, never missing a beat. The Associated Press picked up the story, "Veteran of Peace Corps Brings Sargent Shriver to Meet Kentucky Class". It appeared in the Louisville *Courier-Journal* on May 24, 1974. Sargent Shriver had himself seen an article about Barkley released by the Associated Press and had written him. Shriver said, "He wrote back and asked me to come for the seventy-fifth anniversary graduation and here I am. The real reason for my coming here was to find out the secret of his success."

Now it was time to begin in earnest the work of forging closer ties with the Kentucky Baptist Convention. The editor of the *Western*

Recorder, Dr. C.R. Daley, had written a feature editorial in April on the distribution of Christian Education funds. Barkley wrote a letter to each of the members of the Christian Education Committee. He also wrote to Dr. Daley, expressing his appreciation for the editorial and enclosing a copy of a letter he had sent to each member on the committee. It read in part:

> Of course, we are grateful for the support we HAVE received, and have gone out and managed to get the remainder necessary—and we have always worked to get the larger portion of this OUTSIDE Kentucky so as not to "take away" from potential support for the Cooperative Program. For example, in our building program that will begin this summer, we have more than $400,000 in hand or pledged and not one cent of that from Kentucky (but from a variety of sources in other states) for I have made no sort of public effort as yet in Kentucky. But I will probably be forced to do so.

To Dr. Richard E. Walker he wrote:

> We have the three colleges, Clear Creek and Oneida in our Kentucky Baptist Christian Education Family. Each one is doing a vital work I feel…each one goes about the work in a slightly different way and I feel that is all to the good. We compliment and supplement the work of each other in many ways. I see it all in the spirit of *I Corinthians* 12:12: For Christ is like a single body, which has many parts; it is still one body, even though it is made up of different parts.
>
> As you have so aptly summarized it: our primary reason for being in Christian Education is both ministry and outreach. Some of our work tends more to the one, some to the other. I would say that Oneida's emphasis is primarily in "Outreach" as we try to reach those who are not Christians…and hundreds and hundreds of souls have been reached. But of course, ministry is a strong adjunct of that effort.

At meetings with the Education Commission of the Kentucky Baptist Convention, he did not always get what he wanted. He couldn't help but come on strong, and this turned some away. He had to apologize once or twice for taking more time than was allotted to him.

The necessity of raising the remaining funds for the building program now about to begin kept him focused on the immediate needs. The office staff and he got out more than 3,000 letters during June. They were making appeals out of state as well as in Kentucky, trying to win additional friends and supporters. If all went well, he hoped to have the bids on the two new buildings by the end of July.

Summer camps were in full swing, with the heaviest camp schedule the school had ever had. They ran right up to September.

The school had the biggest gardens ever, and there was a major "paint-and-fix-up" program.

Over the summer, Barkley recruited two new teachers. One was a young missionary to Peru, home from the field, with a math major, and she had her own income, so she wouldn't need to be paid. (The last math teacher had been killed in a car wreck four years before and Barkley hadn't been able to find a replacement.) The other was an English teacher, a straight A-B student, who had just finished his degree. To house these additional staff, he had to rent two houses in Oneida.

One of his biggest needs was to find a hostess for his home—if not a wife. Barkley had found someone he hoped would be able to come live in his house and take care of guests. Of course, since he was a bachelor, this person had to be older, He was sure he had found the right person in Betty Williams. He smiled to himself. One of his Iranian friends had inquired whether he was married yet. He had replied, "   No, I'm not married yet but haven't given up. Still run as fast as I used to, and maybe if I get a spare weekend sometime I can get married!"

There had been a few young women who wanted the job, and wanted to be more than hostess—and there would be more. But none would catch him.

The fall semester would be opening soon, with 265 in the high school, about twenty in the seventh and eighth grades. Seventy-five were local; the rest came from at least ten states and five foreign countries. The total was just over double where it had been just eighteen months ago. On the academic side, the school had started a special program for the weak students, and added three advanced courses for the gifted students. The students were especially excited about the new band program. A new arts and crafts program with its own room had been added, and the library had a fresh coat of paint and new carpet.

Bean-stringing and putting up corn was proceeding, the work camps over. A cabin was built for the pageant *Burns of the Mountains*, to be presented at Homecoming. Invitations had gone out in July, and a large crowd was expected. Preparations had been made to celebrate the seventy-fifth anniversary of the first class.

August 31 came quickly. The highlight of the day was the outdoor pageant at 8:00 PM, directed by Linda Hensley. It was presented on the lawn where Melrose Hall once stood. The large crowd sat on blankets spread on the terraced stones, laid over forty-five years before. Ms. Martha Bain was there. She had written the script many years before while a teacher at Oneida. This was its fourth performance.

There was an outdoor supper at 6:30 PM. The following day, Sunday, there was an old fashioned worship service at 11:00 AM in the Oneida Baptist Church, led by the Rev. Lyn Claybrook, Oneida pastor 1948-56, followed by dinner on the ground. Celebrations don't get finer that this one.

Barkley received many wonderful letters commending the school on the splendid revelry at Homecoming. One who didn't get to come was Richard D. Gilliam, an attorney friend in Owensboro, Kentucky, but his heart was blessed by a warm letter from Richard. "Yours is a great institution in a sense the 'lengthening shadow of one man'. But while the sainted Burns started the Institute, it has been and is continually being created by a host of dedicated others whose names tend to get lost in the shuffle." He was most grateful for the praise and in a long letter thanking him for recognizing the present laborers at Oneida he ended by writing:

WHEN WE SHARE OUR NEEDS, OUR HOPES, OUR FEARS AND MAKE AN APPEAL, REMEMBER THE APPEAL IS NOT MADE TO YOU UNLESS AT THAT PARTICULAR TIE IT IS YOUR JOY AND YOUR PLEASURE TO ANSWER IT, THE

BEAUTIFUL PART OF THIS STRANGE WORK IS THAT THE GIFTS THAT COME ARE NOT WITHOUT THE GIVER FOR THEY COME OUT OF THE HEARTS OF OUR FRIENDS, NOT JUST THEIR POCKETS.

The fall semester opened with 265 students and an additional twenty in the dorms going to the elementary school across the river. Barkley felt it was the smoothest opening since he had been there. The ratio of teacher to student was one to fifteen. But by October Barkley had over $25,000 in bills on his desk with no obvious means of paying them. Operating costs came to about $1,100 and he only knew where about $100 was coming from: the Cooperative Program. He also had to find funds for the two new buildings. It is to be noted that he alone carried this terrible burden—the faculty and staff had little knowledge of the situation. He used his correspondence with those outside the school to make the needs known.

He wrote to Dr. Franklin Owen:

We like the way the friends give who DO give. They give as though it is a joy and a privilege, But to carry this work forward is a never-ending strain. The major part of my personal energy is spent in anxiety as to whether or not there will be funds to pay the teacher and staff: feed these growing teenagers three times daily, and otherwise care for and train our our boys and girls. I find myself signing contracts without really knowing if there will be means to meet them. In the past three years, the gifts of slightly over 1200 have made possible our work. But we do so much WANT MORE TO GIVE-how we NEED more to give. We pray that each and every one might become a real part of Oneida. Some could not do much, we know, but perhaps they could get others to help where they cannot help themselves.

We have more mouths to feed, more staff to pay than ever before, prices of every thing jumping, things are financially tight but are holding our own so far...but it is going to be very difficult to make ends meet through the year, I'm sure...spiritually, we see some very real growth…an increasingly active BSU and Al Griffin, our interim pastor, doing a perfectly splendid job. Do keep us in your prayers and, as you go about the state, remember to tell others of our only Baptist high school, His work here at ONEIDA.

A few days later he again wrote to Dr. Owen, "We have several capital needs, and we do urgently need any and all assistance possible." Again describing the needs for more housing for staff and the need for the new chapel/classroom building, he went on for two pages, ending with:

Oneida has always received by far the lowest amount of Cooperative Program funds for operating expenses…its staff has traditionally worked for lower salaries than any other of our Convention Servants. Kentucky Baptist have a very modern multi-million dollar facility…with a quality program…doing a very NEEDED AND VALUABLE work.

Actually, Barkley was beginning to get more help from Kentucky Baptists. The *Western Recorder* was planning a feature article on Oneida, with the new building's blueprints. In connection with that, he had written to the associate editor, James Cox, on December 17, thanking him and inclosing some materials. He described his role as president as one in which he wore many hats.

This morning I have had a few moments to put on my 'Public Relations Hat'. Other roles include, business manager, registrar, development officer, and chief greeter…oh, yes, disciplinarian!

Come spend a day with us when you can, and best wishes for the Christmas season…

Brother Sparks had been away for some time but Barkley always kept him updated. In his summary letter to him in October he wrote:

You have missed the most glorious colors on the mountains that I can ever recall…largest enrollment ever…only lost two from severe homesickness…expelled seven…new dean doing superb job, and keeping place clean...new soccer team undefeated...have added wrestling and boxing...doing better with basketball. Finances pretty tight...behind about $15,000 in bills right now...got about 350 bushels of Irish potatoes, many bushels of sweet potatoes...hope to sign contract for buildings next week...had to pare down cost of buildings...but have a $75,000 pledge...going to try to raise another $75,000 from among alumni...also much more to raise. Tomorrow seventy coming from Porter Memorial, Lexington for weekend retreat...new pastor, Bro. Griffin, doing great job...be really pleased when you get back...

Of the overage from the education funds for the Kentucky Baptist Convention for 1974, Oneida received $35,000, for which Barkley was truly grateful. With this he set up the Oneida print shop once again. How desperately they needed it! By December the school had pledges of $500,000 and $300,000 to go on the building project. To an alumnus who wrote asking about the *Mountaineer* not being sent out, he wrote: "My big failing...among several...since being here is getting the *Mountaineer* out. We are so busy DOING that we don't have much time for telling." Publication of the *Mountaineer* was to resume shortly.

Christmas was upon him and it seemed that in the wink of an eye everyone was gone. It was so quiet when the students were away, he felt a little lonesome. But there was always so very much to do! He and about six of the staff would work through the holidays. He had letters to write.

Our students saw a beautiful snowfall before they left for home...and Oneida nestled by the surrounding mountains is a picture postcard scene with snow. Two of our boys and one girl were baptized at the end of a beautiful Sunday evening Christmas service. The annual Christmas Dinner was very lovely this year, one of the oldest Oneida traditions, the giving of gifts to each boy and girl, and the small children of the faculty singing. Our Christmas week climaxed with a tremendous hour-long Chapel service with our choir and band.

God bless you for remembering us with your good $25.00 gift,
and may 1975 be a year filled with special blessing for you and yours.

But before he could close out the year he had just one more letter to write! It was to apologize to his parents for not being with them that Christmas, and to wish them a happy holiday.

1975-76
Year 4

Our Lord continues to bless in so many ways, and the work here is growing and being strengthened almost daily. There are many difficulties and moments of frustration and discouragement, but we see so many good things happening in young lives. The religious training, teaching values and Christian responsibility, is the most fundamentally important and, we trust, lasting, part of our work.
—Barkley Moore

The staff and students were all back in their places by January 5, the opening day of school. There were more students in the dorms than at the start of the fall semester. By February 25, there were even more—practically unheard of at Oneida. Life was a less stressful for Barkley than in the previous years two and a half years. But it was still hectic!

He wrote to a past teacher at Oneida, Mr. Harold Holderman:

We have bought and paid for: $14,000 for a house directly behind the church...also spent $2,400 for a Universal Weight Set on which 8 boys can work at a time; $2,200 for a Video-Tape Machine that we can use at ballgames, classrooms, etc; $1,000 for large Mosler safe, (they had had a break-in) $7,000 payment for farm tractor; $2,200 for cornpicker; $1,500 for about $25,000 worth of printing and mailing equipment...getting ready to move in that area...paid $11,700, an old building debt, three months before payment was due. Also, through end of January had the operating bills paid. This all seemed too good to be true especially as the bills for the new building were being paid as they came due. However, starting had been delayed because of bad weather. Plans for taking all of the Honor Roll students to St. Louis for a week-long trip near the end of April as a reward for scholarship are made. I'm going to be working more and more in that area…

The building project was finally underway! It would consume almost his every waking moment for the following year. It demanded his attention, if not his presence, constantly. But that meant he was closer to the campus now. In fact he was on campus most of the time, except on weekends, when he invariably had one or more speaking engagements. The days were flying by. On March 10, he wrote, "One day it is spring-like and another day Old Man Winter seems yet with us." Of course, that affected the construction work. But progress was being made, and the funds continued to arrive in $10, $20, $100 checks—and some much larger.

He was invited to join Dr. Franklin Owen, Executive Director of the Kentucky Baptist Convention, Bill D. Whittaker, Chairman of the Christian Education In-Depth Committee, and all the executive committee at a planning meeting to be held on Friday, April 4. They were to meet at the Baptist Building in Nashville, Tennessee. This was of utmost importance, and he would most certainly be there. There was already something scheduled for every weekend until the end of school.

He had already made plans for Homecoming in the fall. The students were to be back on campus two weeks before the event, "so they could take part in the event and so the alumni could see them. We can sort of get settled down and won't have everything to do one weekend", referring to the fact that both opening of school and Homecoming had fallen on Labor Day weekend.

We might have a basketball game or baseball game between the alumni and our students…also the alumni can hear the Band, *etc.* Then we can finish the semester before Christmas vacation, and if anyone doesn't want to come back, they will already be home.

That will get us out of school the first week of May which will give our students the advantage in looking for jobs. The first two weeks after school is over I want to have the rooms repainted in the boys' dorms. Also, I have gotten a lot of extra dressers and want to get three beds in every room…as nearly as possible. For I think we will need them next year, and it is good to have some extra beds when we have guests.

What a different tone! Just the fall before, he was under the crushing burden of fundraising for a project that would cost nearly a million dollars. Now that it was under way, he actually had time to enjoy his students and make plans for the fall and even the next year!

At the end of March came the spring revival. It was led by a missionary home on leave from service in Malaysia. The messages were powerful but low-key. There were no high-pressure emotional appeals— yet there were eighteen professions of faith and twenty-six rededications, and one came by letter.

Easter came, and the beautiful cantata *Celebrate Life*, which the choir had been working on for weeks, was performed in the Oneida Baptist Church. Barkley thought it one of the highest moments in Oneida's history. The program was printed by the new press. He was proud to tell everyone with whom he talked or to whom he wrote, "You will be interested to know that this stationery, envelope, as well as the program are all printed on our own new press!" And then he would ask, "What do you think?" Then he would explain how it would save them money and that they could train boys and girls in the trade.

To a friend giving $20 he wrote:

Our Lord continues to bless in so many ways, and the work here is growing and being strengthened almost daily. There are many difficulties and moments of frustration and discouragement, but we see so many good things happening in young lives. The religious training, teaching values and Christian responsibility, is the most fundamentally important and, we trust, lasting, part of our work.

He was truly proud when he received a letter from Dr. Owen that said, "Dear Barkley, I have another copy of your *Celebrate Life* on my desk which you showed me the last time I saw you. You are to be commended, both in this production and in the nice printing job that you are now capable of at Oneida. May God continue to bless your good work there."

Of course, Dr. Owen would then receive another of Barkley's letters—asking him to help with getting Kentucky Baptists to help out more through the Cooperative Program. He was also pressing C.R. Daley to help. In June he had a letter from C.R. Daley. "Thank you for a word on the fine commencement exercises. It seems that every year things get better and better with you, the school and the church. Your contribution is noteworthy and your influence in the life of the community and also among Kentucky Baptists. I am particularly appreciative of your contributions to the life of the local church. This is a part of the noble heritage and I am glad you recognize it."

In July Barkley just had to share his heart with the friends of Oneida. He was nearly bursting with pride and at the same time was filled with anxiety! Some days he felt like the Psalmist. "…at their wit's end. Then they cry unto the Lord in their trouble, and he bringeth them out…" (*Psalms* 107:27-28) His was a working faith, pray while you work and trust the Lord, but frequently he would open his heart to friends of Oneida and cry out to them for help.

Dear Friend,

On my desk today (there will be more tomorrow) are 417 applications and/or requests for information to attend school at Oneida this fall. The most we've ever been able to accept before has been 265.

Over 60% of these, if accepted will be able to pay NOTHING. They will work. We anticipate $45,000 from our Kentucky Convention for day-to-day bills but the coming year will require more than $600,000 for operating expenses. HOW MANY SHALL WE TURN AWAY?

We have planted 75 acres in corn (for both our freezer and feed for our cattle and hogs to put meat on our table), potatoes, beans, peas, and other vegetables. Fifty of our boys and girls, the largest group we have ever kept in the summer, are working very hard plowing, hoeing, baling hay, stringing beans, cutting up corn, cooking, cleaning, painting. They are WORKING TO HELP THEMSELVES. Will you HELP us help them?

WHEN WE SHARE OUR NEEDS, OUR HOPES, OUR FEARS AND MAKE AN APPEAL, REMEMBER THE APPEAL IS NOT MADE TO YOU UNLESS AT THAT PARTICULAR TIME IT IS YOUR JOY AND YOUR PLEASURE TO ANSWER IT, THE BEAUTIFUL PART OF THIS STRANGE WORK IS THAT THE GIFTS THAT COME ARE NOT WITHOUT THE GIVER FOR THEY COME OUT OF THE HEARTS OF OUR FRIENDS, NOT JUST THEIR POCKETS.

In August Oneida opened its doors for the seventy-sixth year of classes. For the faculty and staff it had really begun three days earlier at Pine Mountain State Park. The faculty conference was a twenty-four-hour retreat for prayer, worship, and fellowship.

The students came just as the faculty and staff returned to campus, and every one was ready to get down to work! They were settled into the full swing of things before Homecoming on Saturday, August 30.

The hills were beginning to change, and soon would be a riot of color. With every letter Barkley would extend the invitation to come: "I want to have the opportunity of being your host. You can do it. How about planning a trip??? I really hope you will."

As always, Barkley was updating Brother Sparks on the school and on his doings. In his September letter, he told him all about Homecoming—how they had dedicated the new faculty apartment building, named it for John Henry Walker, and the new Sylvia Russell Hall, a beautiful chapel. On the old piano in the chapel, he had placed a beautiful vase of red roses in memory of Mrs. Sparks. There was also a vase of roses in the village church—and it was noted in each service.

And to anyone who missed the Homecoming, he had a message!

We missed you! We want to see you NEXT year. Mark your calendar now for September 4, 1976. We had a fine time… weather ideal…campus lovely…food and drink unexcelled…Hymn Service inspiring…soccer game confusing to those who had never seen one…

We are beginning a Dollar a Year Club. It would work like this: Each graduate gives one dollar for each year since graduation…also the same for students who didn't graduate. So, START COUNTING! If you run out of fingers and toes, just send a check for any substantial amount.

In the middle of September he had a letter from Homer Belew, Director of Missions for the Home Mission Board. He was writing a book for WMU promotion of state mission offerings. How eagerly Barkley read, "I would like to include the implication of Oneida for state missions. So, will you send me something of the history of the school, contribution to the cause of the work, any human interest stories that might well be included in the book." As important as this was to him, it was nearly two weeks before he could reply. He wrote, "You would not remember me, but I have vivid memories of you. I was a very small boy when I heard you speak here several times, but I still remember". He always used that sharper-than-a-tack memory to make everyone feel special. And he went on and on about the school, right down to the last detail, along with enclosures, including *The Crucible* and the articles about outstanding teenagers in the *Mountaineer*, which "got to the very heart of what Oneida is all about".

October was a busy time. He had speaking engagements every Sunday. He had joined The Baptist Public Relations Association, and they wrote inviting him to a banquet at the annual workshop session to be held in Louisville, March 28-31, 1977. Of course he would go.

On November 19, he received another important letter from the Kentucky Baptist Convention office of Dr. Franklin Owen. Enclosed was a check for $37,500 to be used for the capital funds distribution voted by the board from surplus funds.

Dr. Owen ended with, "God bless your good work: we're proud of our institutions and I'm so happy to have this small part in this extra for each of our schools, plus the Baptist Student Department."

December had come round and Christmas was upon him. The school had come a long way in the past year. The Christmas letter had been sent to over 20,000. All of his boys and girls were safely home with their families or others who had taken them in for the holidays. Sitting in his nearly finished office in the new Sylvia Russell Hall, he thought about his predecessors. And he thought of a poem that seemed a message sent straight to him this Christmas.

The Bridge Builder

An old man going a lone highway
Came at the evening, cold and gray.
To a chasm vast and wide and steep.
With waters rolling cold and deep.
The old man crossed in the twilight dim;
The sullen stream had no fears for him;
But he turned when safe on the other side
And built a bridge to span the tide.
Old man, said a fellow pilgrim near,
You are wasting your strength with building here.
Your journey will end with the ending day,
You never again will pass this way,
You've crossed the chasm, deep and wide,
Why build you this bridge at eventide?
The builder lifted his old gray head.
"Good friend, in the path I have come," he said,
"There followeth after me today
A youth whose feet must pass this way.
The chasm that was as naught to me
To that fair haired youth may a pitfall be;
He, too, must cross in the twilight dim.
Good friend, I am building this bridge for him."
Will Allen Dromegoole

Yes, he had built some bridges that year, bridges that he hoped and prayed would stand the test of time for his boys and girls. Thirty-five-year-old Barkley Moore had no fears for what lay ahead—although there had been moments that could have turned his deep black hair white all at once!

1976-77
Year 5

Rusty, I want you to know, if you care to come...you are welcome to come to Oneida for a visit after basic and before you go overseas. Even though I had to ask you to leave, you are still welcome here for we have invested a lot of time, thought and energy and prayers in you.
—Barkley Moore

School year number five opened with a blast of freezing rain that turned the Oneida campus into a slippery skating rink for the kids—a disaster for adults like Barkley! But long before school hours every hand was busy shoveling sidewalks, putting salt down. By February Old Man Winter had done his worst, but the school had been open every day. The kids loved sliding down the hill behind Anderson Hall on Saturday afternoons—sometimes on cardboard sleds, but mainly on their own bottoms. Sometimes there would be hot chocolate waiting for them in the dining room. The BSU leaders often planned a "snow" party ending with a devotional time. Adults would volunteer to supervise. The students could always go to the warm gym for make-up games, or swim in the Student Center or just hang out. Of course, this was after they got their weekend jobs done. But snow, ice, rain or hail, they went to school.

Barkley was really proud of this. In every letter that went out, he would mention the "hard winter...much snow and ice and cold". But he would quickly add, "However, unlike the public schools, we are able to go on with our work. We do not dismiss; our young people are here, and they must be kept usefully busy."

The school year was passing so rapidly. Byron Crawford, news reporter at WHAS, Channel 11, Louisville went to Oneida to do a story. It aired in prime time, at 8:54 PM—just before the CBS Friday movie. It was a five-minute film. This was a big thing, and Barkley made the most of it. He alerted hundreds before it ran. Free publicity is the best kind, and this would have cost $4,000 as an ad. (He knew, if no one else did, that his free Peace Corps press releases had cost ACTION tens of thousands.) This free exposure gave him a platform from which to launch his fund raising campaign for Oneida nationally at a time when it was needed most.

It was a fine time to be at Oneida. The new faculty apartments had been finished. Barkley, the staff, and the faculty, especially the faculty, were thrilled with them. Work on the new chapel/classroom building was proceeding beautifully, and the two buildings he had recently bought for more staff housing were almost completely renovated, as were two buildings on the old hospital property. The church was visibly growing as well—more decisions, more giving, higher attendance. The building had been completely carpeted the previous summer, and the church had voted to have air conditioning installed by the time school was out. All the Oneida students attended the church, and Barkley was very active in it himself. They had many challenges, but most of them had to do with growth of the school.

By March, Barkley and the staff had had enough of winter. Everyone was looking toward spring. The whole campus was a beehive of activity. How they hoped and prayed for the new facilities to be ready by September! They were already planning a dedication ceremony for September 4.

April arrived just in time to serve as a backdrop for the joy in the air! After the long winter, the campus was beautiful to behold in its spring glory. The redbud's branches were poking out with tiny purple buds, and the dogwoods just outside the girls' dorm, which had heralded spring for many years, were just about to burst into delicate white crosses. Soft warm breezes were blowing gently through the trees and there was just the faintest hint of fragrance in the air as Barkley hurried across campus to the new chapel/classroom building under construction, to confer with the architect. He wanted to find out the cost of girding up Sparks Gymnasium while the cranes and other heavy equipment were there.

The gym had been built during the Korean War without benefit of architect or contractor. Local people had done the work and no steel was put in those massive walls because steel was very expensive and very difficult to install at that time. He was told the cost would be $24,000. It was a huge expense, but he didn't sleep well nights wondering just when the whole thing might collapse. Great steel girders would be installed. They would run deep into the ground and up the outside walls, and girders would run up the inside at the same points, bolted and welded together, and into the foundation and into the roof supports—in effect, encasing the entire building in bands of steel like a sandwich. The appearance of the building would be improved, and great strength added. Although he didn't have the money right then, he knew it had to be done. Stepping out in faith, he signed a contract to get the work done.

By May 16 construction on the chapel/classroom building was far enough along that Commencement was held in the new Melvin Davidson Chapel, on the second floor of the building. On the night before Commencement, there was an hour-long water ballet performance in the Student Center by the fifteen-girl synchronized swim team, a graceful salute to America's bicentennial. On May 16, in a colorful one-and-a-half-hour ceremony, twenty boys and sixteen girls graduated. Seven graduated with advanced diplomas. The ending of the academic year was thrilling. Barkley rejoiced that he had sent all his boys and girls home with sixteen more of them having made professions of faith in the last six weeks before graduation.

In June he received a letter from Dr. Franklin Owen that truly thrilled his soul. He was being invited to speak at the Kentucky Baptist State Convention on November 9. No such invitation had been given to anyone at Oneida during the school's seventy-six-year history.

The letter from Dr. Owen read:

> Ever since year one the three college presidents have rotated the speaking assignment in behalf of Christian Education generally on the Convention Program. I pointed out last year that we had

an institutional president in you who had been in the convention now a third year and hasn't yet spoken to the Convention and that I thought this should be passed around with the colleges doing more of it. Perhaps, with their larger thrust and greater numbers but that certainly the other institutions shouldn't be left out. I learned, though, that in discussing this, that Merrill Aldridge with all of his years had never been invited and so we invited him first and now we are turning to you for this year…the point is, you are the Christian Education speaker this year…

Barkley, it is real important that you stay within the limits of your time. We think you are great, all of us, but some of the brethren have taken note that you tend to overtime and I am going to get pretty good blame if you don't stay within your time. I realize that it is short but it does get Oneida's President before our Convention, which I have desired to do and which I think his good work greatly deserves. You are a fine speaker and will do a marvelous job. I only have concern about the length, and trust you will forgive my frankness. God bless you.

Barkley was to speak Tuesday, November 9, 1976. He was surely floating on air as he walked over to Miss Wilson's office to share the letter with her.

Summer was nearly over. There had never been another like it at Oneida! So many visitors, so many camps, the first summer school session, college classes at night, the largest gardens and crops ever, moving into the new administration/chapel building, renovation, painting, building new sidewalks, a thousand things. From the number of applications coming in, there was every indication that they would set another enrollment record for the fourth straight year. Barkley was very pleased with the applications, and excited by the prospect of working with these boys and girls. The new students would arrive Sunday, August 15. How fast time had flown!

School opened without a hitch. Every girl and boy was settled into the dorm almost two weeks before Homecoming. Invitations had already gone out and hundreds were expected.

The event was reported by the *Western Recorder*:

> The traditional Homecoming celebration at Oneida (Kentucky) Baptist on Labor Day weekend was highlighted with dedication ceremonies for the new combination chapel and library building. A record crowd was present.
>
> Activities began Saturday morning with registration and a campus tour directed by Oneida President Barkley Moore. Dedication ceremonies in the afternoon included tributes to three former Oneidians: John Henry Walker, Melvin Davidson and Sylvia W. Russell. Walker and Davidson were faculty members and Mrs. Russell was president." Barkley Moore presided over the ceremonies. Music was under the direction of Omer (Blue) Hensley, member of the 1929 class. Other participants were James B. Graham, state superintendent of public instruction; C.R. Daley, Western Recorder editor; Carlyle Hounchell, pastor, Brutus Baptist Church; George R. Bausum, pastor, Oneida Baptist Church; Paul Howerton, Louisville, and Lyn Claybrook, Memphis, former Oneida pastors.
>
> Sections of the building were named for Mrs. Floy DeJarnette, Mrs. Russell and Davidson. President Moore delivered tributes to these and recognized family members. The Homecoming dinner and alumni meeting followed. The celebration continued Sunday with services in the chapel and in Oneida Church. Oneida is a 77-year-old boarding high school founded by James Anderson Burns to bring education and Christianity to a remote and isolated area of the mountains.

In October Barkley wrote to Dr. Owen:

> The Holy Spirit has truly been with us so far this year. Our young people are responding in a manner that has not been seen on our campus since 1951. I was a student here at that time. Sunday before last 42 were baptized...some of these we have been working with and praying for these two, three, in several cases for four years. Four of our young men have surrendered to fulltime

Christian service. One night there were ten decisions…all of them young men.

On October 23, he wrote to one of the trustees:

> The Christian Education Committee is recommending that Oneida's portion for the coming year be approximately $80,000. That beats the $36,000 of five years ago…Though considering inflation, perhaps not much. I've upset the brethren a few times by coming on a little too strong…but at least they know we are down here. I'm to give the "Education Address" at the State Convention this year…the first time an Oneida president has been asked to do this in history.

His message to the Convention got a tremendously favorable response—applause at the end of the address. (He was told that there is almost never applause at the end of sermons or speeches at the convention.) He received many letters afterward. "My appreciation for the great truths that you presented to our convention. I wish every Kentucky Baptist could have been blessed by that tremendous message!" was typical of the comments.

Homecoming was the weekend of Thanksgiving. Wintry weather was coming in, but all the students got away before it arrived. They weren't so fortunate when they headed back! But most returned before the bad weather set in and the roads iced over.

November 27 proved a harrowing day for Barkley. He was to go along with the Boswells and Mrs. Boswell's sister to take one of "his" Iranian boys, Abdi, a Turkoman, back to Cumberland College. They left after the evening church service. Rain was pouring down when they climbed into the van, with Mr. Boswell at the wheel. Barkley wrote to many afterwards, telling them what happened.

> I nearly lost my life last night and feel very grateful to be able to write you once more. Several of my staff and I hit an icy spot and, though going very slowly, helplessly slid over a very steep embankment…fifty feet, perhaps more. We rolled over and over and stopped in the bottom

of a ravine with the van on its end and the headlights in the air. This was about 10:00 PM. With the smell of seeping gasoline, fear of a fire and explosion, we fought to get out. My worst injuries are cut hands because I had to knock the windows out with my fists and we crawled through the windows. One of the women was badly trapped and had two broken legs, another a fracture. We had to get them out and go through a fifty-foot long culver under the highway, wading in water, and then claw our way back up the mountain carrying the woman with the broken legs. All of this in the dark and the constant fear that other cars would hit the same patch of ice (several nearly did) and pile in on top of us. We finally got the women to the hospital, and she needed to be sent on to Lexington, 100 miles from here. By this time, there were so many wrecks on Highway 75, an airplane skidded on the runway at Lexington and four killed, *etc.*, that the highways were closed. They then considered helicopter, but gave that up because of weather, and she is being taken on today. In the meantime, another of the staff had been in an accident but is uninjured, and two of our students returning were in a wreck that totaled their car. Neither they nor parents were too seriously injured. It was all a most harrowing experience, but we feel most strongly that the Lord still must have things for us to do as He has spared us to work a while longer at ONEIDA.

Barkley was back in his office the next morning, ready to be about his Father's business. He had more love than ever for his boys and girls and a new sense of urgency, for one never knew when life would end. When he went to chapel service that morning, he knew the Lord was in the work! He had spared the lives of not only Barkley but Mr. and Mrs. Boswell and Mrs. Boswell's sister as well. He was profoundly thankful.

As he left chapel, a teacher, Miss Debbie Sizemore, came to the platform to tell him of a letter that she had received. He went straight to his desk to write this special young man, who had been on his heart.

I have just come from chapel. Mrs. Sizemore came to the platform after Chapel to tell me of her letter from you…that you have been first in the "mile" runs as well as in marksmanship. I am very, very, proud of you. Yet I am also very concerned. She tells me that your leg has been bothering you. You must be as careful as possible. I, frankly, Rusty consider it a miracle that you got by the Army Physical with that leg. Even more so is it that you are able to run so far, and be "first". That is truly "guts", Rusty, and that is one of your finest qualities…something I've always admired you for. But, also, Rusty, please use common sense and don't do anything so foolish as to perhaps harm yourself for life. But the leg must be pretty strong for you to do what you are doing.

Rusty, I want you to know…if you care to come…you are welcome to come to Oneida for a visit after basic and before you go overseas. Even though I had to ask you to leave, you are still welcome here for we have invested a lot of time, thought and energy and prayers in you.

Mail time was, perhaps, the high point of every Oneida day—the sunny, cloudy, stormy, calm ones! It had always been so. Many were the days Barkley sat down to read the mail so bone weary, worried, worn in spirit and soul, desperately needing a place of sanctuary, a hiding place. It was there at his desk, letters in hand, that the Lord often met him—gave solace to his soul. It was there in those letters—the answers to prayer, the comfort of dear ones praying for him, loving him, and sharing what they had—$5, $10, $1,000 dollar checks. This was his "rock in a weary land", his oasis in the desert. Those letters were the chain of love that linked him to hundreds of friends and gave him strength to continue.

Barkley was always getting letters but this Christmas his heart was especially blessed and strengthened by the gratitude of so many—the love poured out on him.

Oneida was a beautiful snowy winter wonderland the last week before Christmas. On Monday before they left for Christmas, the students went caroling as the swirling, magical white flakes danced in the moonlit night. On Tuesday, the hand bell choir gave a Christmas performance. On Wednesday night, all the students and staff attended the annual Christmas dinner by candlelight. (Each student received a wrapped gift.) On Friday afternoon the year ended with a splendid Christmas concert given by the choir and band.

1977-78
Year 6

We have suffered a sad loss…one that is beyond measurement. Miss Wilson died on September 9th. She literally died from overwork. We have missed her tremendously. She was the greatest human being I have ever personally known, and my dearest friend for many many years. I could not have accomplished what has been done here without her, would not have accepted the presidency had she not agreed to return here with me. She did so at tremendous sacrifice and, ultimately, her life.
—Barkley Moore

January 1977 came in with blizzard conditions over most of Kentucky. Oneida was one of the few schools open in the state for the entire month. Barkley and the teaching staff of twenty-two were carrying on in extremely hazardous conditions, with 320 boys and girls from all over Kentucky, thirteen other states, and twelve foreign countries. Conditions were so bad that he moved nearly all of the community kids into the dorms. Despite snow, ice, and temperatures as low as seventeen degrees below zero, the school was in full operation. Only the stoutest of hearts would not have been in sheer terror considering what might happen if power or water were lost, or if the river flooded, as it often did in January. But snow- and ice-bound, dangers on every hand, he was ever so grateful for the blessings he saw all around him: a band of good souls, his staff eager to teach, love, mold—and his 320 boys and girls, eager to learn, play, pray.

While all Kentuckians hovered close to home in imminent danger from the weather, waiting for the storm to pass, Barkley saw it as a time to rejoice and give thanks. He went to the Lord with thanksgiving and rejoicing in his heart, not fear!

He wrote to his friend Peggy Smith:

> We do not fail to be grateful for: heat, electricity, water, food, comfortable housing, modern classrooms, so many things. We thank God for our friends who make it all possible. We remember in prayer all those in our land and around the world who are not so blessed. We pray for each of them that greatest blessing of all blessings…the knowledge and saving faith in our Lord Jesus Christ.

On their own many of the students were also meeting in the evening for a thirty-minute meditation time.

Maybe it was for just this reason that the Holy Spirit spoke to so many hearts in a revival that sprang up in the church services that winter. Over sixty students made professions of faith, and four dedicated themselves to full time service. They were truly bound together in the physical place called Oneida, but they were also bound together as a mighty army for the Lord. Word of the spontaneous revival traveled fast around the churches in Kentucky. Several of the students were asked to speak at the State Evangelistic Conference to be held at Elizabethtown that spring.

Barkley ended many a letter in January and February with glowing praise for his family at Oneida. As their spiritual father, his heart was overflowing. "Yes, with Him all things are possible." That was a lesson he ever held before the boys and girls at Oneida.

His own gratitude to Oneida's faithful friends poured out in praise for each and every one who gave a gift, whether it was $1, $10, or the $3,000 he had received on February 3, 1977.

One of his first letters of the year was to Brother Sparks. The letter began, "Happy Birthday". He then told Brother Sparks of plans for another big party on his eighty-fifth birthday. As always, he then jumped right to the school's news.

Today we have 320 students and this is our first week of a new semester…We have graded the bottom beside the campus next to Goose Creek. This spring will complete a new regulation size soccer field with portable goals. The other side of the field will be a softball field for girls…and we plan to add a regulation size track.

Oneida's runners have never had the benefit of a paved track. Since the finishing of the two buildings, started just over a year before, all the bills are paid to the contractors, except for $15,000 I am holding until they finish the bell tower and the cross on the chapel. Not only that, we have paid for all the renovations! We have one loan taken from the endowment fund and it is being paid back monthly…The school's operating budget has increased over $500,000 the past five years to a total of $739,000 the last year.

It is a constant effort, of course, to keep up with the daily bills, but the Lord has blessed us and we have been in the 'black' each year while adding one million dollars of new buildings and equipment.

Brother Sparks had inquired about the *Mountaineer* in his December letter. Barkley was glad to be able to say that, with the new printing press, the paper would be more regular. Brother Sparks was the one person who understood why so few *Mountaineer*s had been published.

Barkley said being in charge at Oneida was like "riding a tiger", there were so many things happening at once. Oneida's alumni could be very much like a herd of tigers themselves, roaring when they missed their *Mountaineer*! The *Mountaineer*, begun by Paul Hounchell and Roy Helton in the early 1940s, was and is the school newspaper. Normally it would go out monthly or bimonthly. However, Barkley had not had the time to publish it regularly since becoming President, as he and the office staff were the last ones to receive extra help. The *Oneida Mountaineer* was a little sheet with a mission—it offered hope and inspired imagination! From its earliest days the paper presented the burdens and aspirations of the boys and girls of Oneida to a more fortunate society. The *Oneida Mountaineer* was the most welcome publication to arrive in the mail for the alumni of Oneida Institute, and the many friends of the school who also received it. From all the complaints, one could imagine a mighty jungle of tigers all over the land ready for a great hunt—his head being the prize!

How could Barkley tell them that for the past five years, he had been just ahead of a pack of wild wolves at the door to their beloved school? How could he tell them what it had cost him to get the alumni mailing list in a condition to use—the endless hours in the office in the middle of the night, meticulously laboring over each name, dropping over 600 "dead" names, and hundreds of others with wrong addresses to end up with just 7,000 names? How could he really tell them what it was like to travel the land speaking, in a fight-or-die effort to get more names on a new list—mostly people who had never heard of Oneida? What he could tell them and Brother Sparks this day was that there were over 30,000 names with correct addresses on that list, and that there was a printing press now printing 30,000 *Mountaineer*s that each and every one would be receiving.

Another ministry for which the Lord had prepared Barkley was consoling many of the aging friends and donors of the school as they lost their life partners or became infirm themselves. He loved and appreciated every friend of Oneida and had such reverence for those who had gone before him: leaders, teachers, ministers, students who had been at the Institute, fathers, mothers who had stood in the gap for Oneida's children. They were the same as family to him. They could have been his own grandparents, his own teachers. As far as he was concerned, they were due respect, dignity, and a place of honor. They could never be relegated to out-of-the-way positions. He took the Bible very seriously as regarding the care of the elderly in Oneida's family. It was a sacred duty to love them and lift them up in honor. He mourned with them when they mourned.

This endeared him to thousands over his lifetime and beyond. He always remembered the details of their lives in relation to Oneida. In February he wrote to one such family who had lost their mother:

> Yes, your father and mother were great and generous friends of
> Oneida and these boys and girls. In 1975, your mother established a

$5,000 Scholarship Fund in memory of your father and herself. In 1972 she sent us $1,000 when we were seeking to raise $60,000 in order to qualify for a $40,000 matching gift. Many other times they generously remembered the Lord's work here.

I believe it was Thanksgiving, 1963 that they visited Oneida just before Thanksgiving. They were on their way to visit your uncle, I believe, who lived in Louisville. The turkeys were being prepared, the girls pilgrim hats and all, and your parents seemed to enjoy it all very much.

We appreciate so very much your mother remembering us even in death. Her provision for our work in her will is most generous.

I know you must be lonely but I am sure you have many warm memories to sustain you for, apparently, your parents lived their lives usefully, concerned for the well being of others, and reflecting the love of God in their hearts and lives…certainly this always came through in your mother's letters and gifts.

Would you consider our Oneida family as being your own??? Certainly, in our mind and heart, you are a part of our Oneida family. I do hope that you might come and visit with us sometime as did your parents…and that you might have the same warm feeling…if we can assist you in anyway at anytime, let us know. You will be remembered daily in our prayers at ONEIDA.

When the first signs of spring appeared, crocuses and daffodils began poking their heads up here and there, and birds began arriving and nesting in the towering beeches, oaks, magnolias. From the many white dogwoods and redbuds came a riot of birdsong as robins, sparrows, indigo buntings, and chickadees sang their choruses, perched on low hanging limbs. On the banks of the Bullskin and Redbird Creeks and the Kentucky River the sycamores waited patiently to unfurl their leaves. Bullfrogs along the water's edge croaked long and loud in the warm evenings. In front of Anderson Hall, the ancient star magnolia opened its lovely flower heads into fragrant masses of first pink, then white petals that drifted through the air with any warm breeze on its way north. All of the staff and kids at Oneida rejoiced in the glory of that spring as they traversed the walks to class and spread out blankets under the trees during free time on Saturdays and Sundays.

It was just a little bit of Heaven on Earth for a few weeks. The spontaneous revival that had begun in January, led by students to students, continued in the dorms and in chapel. By April 24, there had been eighty professions of faith.

That spring the seniors took their annual trip to Washington, D.C. And there were "first" times for several types of outings for the students. All of the geography students went to Mammoth Cave, the seventh grade to the state capitol, and the art students to the Cincinnati Museum. The honor roll students went on various trips, including one to the restored Opera House at Lexington to see a ballet.

In the Greyhound bus, purchased that spring, the twenty-six-member choir and their chaperons went with Barkley to many services when he spoke. On May 4 they left on a 2,000-mile twelve-day sixteen-concert tour in Tennessee and Kentucky. This was a year of "firsts"—the choir tour was only one of them. They presented either the cantata *Alleluia* or *The Fabric of Freedom* in many churches and Christian schools in Kentucky and Tennessee. They also sang at the wedding near Nashville of two students who had just graduated. Mixed in with the singing and work were recreation and educational side trips to see the Parthenon in Nashville, the Country Music Hall of Fame, Andrew Jackson's home, Opryland, the Baptist Sunday School Board Headquarters, Cumberland Falls, *etc.* Many churches had been gracious hosts along the way. Oneida's boys and girls had been truly blessed, and Barkley hoped they had been a blessing.

Two days after they left, the bell tower and cross were put into place on top of Sylvia W. Russell Hall. It had been nearly a year since the building was finished—while the school's original bell, made in 1869, was being restored. The bell had rung out from atop the second school building, Marvin Hall, built in 1902, until early in the morning of September 29, 1966, when the building burned. It had been salvaged and put in storage all those years ago.

When the Greyhound pulled onto campus, the bell tower and the cross were gleaming in the crystal-clear night sky, lit by a million stars and by spotlights playing on it from below. Barkley and the twenty-six boys and girls disembarked, amazed. They stood in silence, as if they were on holy ground, awe-stricken with the beauty of it!

Barkley was refreshed and ready to plow into the summer activities. Ahead lay a very busy summer of farming, camps, summer school maintenance work and building. Before summer was out, he intended to have added three more faculty apartments and to have started the construction of an industrial arts building. In his many letters, he always ended with, "It is exciting to work for the Lord and with these boys and girls who come our way to be ministered unto."

On May 17 he took one of his boys to dinner. He told about it in a letter dated May 18 to a special donor:

> It was Steve's 18th birthday. He was brought here four years ago by his mother. I've never seen that woman since. We've never had a phone call, nor a letter, nor a dollar from her. Steve was her only child by a first marriage and apparently, has been more ignored than anything. He has about an 89 IQ and is not going to be able to finish normal high school work. But he is such a fine boy…and a tremendously hard and faithful worker. He and one other boy keep the many acres of our campus mowed and looking so beautiful. He has asked me if he can quit school and just work here for Oneida…and let this be his home. That seems the best for him for he is just wasting time in class.
>
> Yesterday was his 18th birthday. To my knowledge he received no kind of greeting from his family or anyone. He worked as usual all day. But last night, at suppertime, I announced to him that he was going out to dinner. He was quite surprised and pleased. We had to drive 40 miles to find a restaurant that serves T-bone steak…but that is what he had. The cost of it came out of your 'Student Aid' fund. I don't know when I've done anything that gave me more pleasure or for one more deserving.
>
> I thought you'd be interested in knowing.

Out of his personal income he made a $1,000 loan to another Oneida boy who was on his own for the summer months. He received a beautiful letter. "Dearest Barkley Moore" it began, thanking Barkley for the generous loan, and assuring him he would work for the school the next year. In his reply, Barkley said:

> I too believe that Oneida is the nearest thing to happiness one can find. Today has been a great day…and your letter added so much.

On July 19 Barkley wrote to another student who had just graduated:

> We had a simply wonderful year. I think it must have been the greatest of our history. Do keep in touch with us, come to see us when you can for you will always be welcome, and in our memory you will always be a part of ONEIDA.

Barkley's letter to Brother Sparks on June 10 was full of updates on projects all over campus, and all the news of the camps going on right then and more to come.

> …twenty-four here for summer with Youth Conservation Corps, 67 Methodists arriving from three different states for week long work camp…similar groups coming for next 7 weeks…and 100 girls arriving the next day…Mountain Mission Conference in July with Wendell Belew leading the Bible study…We have the drawings for the new Industrial Arts-Maintenance Bldg. Write when you can and we are going to be looking forward for you for Preacher's Camp… spoken at Walnut Street Baptist Church in Louisville Sunday…one of the brethren wrote a check for $1,000…several others slipped me smaller ones…a good evening!

In just three short months Oneida and Barkley would suffer a tremendous blow. On a beautiful September day that had been glorious in every way, his dear Miss Wilson would suffer a massive heart attack. The chimes on top of the chapel played a beautiful melody at 7:00 PM. Miss Wilson, Barkley, and several others were back at work after a dinner break. In her office next to his, Miss Wilson pecked away at her typewriter. At 8:00 PM the chimes rang out again, resounding over the hills. In his office Barkley was busy typing letters. At 9:00 PM Barkley heard her fall. Rushing to her office, he found her gasping for breath. In just minutes an ambulance arrived, and, with Barkley following in a car, it headed for the University of Kentucky Hospital in Lexington. Near dawn, Barkley returned to the campus, planning to return as quickly as he could.

I was sitting by Miss Wilson's hospital bed. After a brief call from Barkley, I had driven through the night from Rockford, Illinois to be by the dearest friend I had ever known. At daybreak Miss Wilson, very weak, but seemingly her old self, was alert and inquiring about one of her namesakes, my daughter Mary. Without a trace of fear or concern for herself, she had one last conversation with me. I left for a short time to have breakfast with a former trustee of Oneida, Mrs. Encil Deen, now 107 years old, another of Oneida's treasures—one who took me in as her daughter and saw to it that I could go to college. While Mrs. Deen and I were eating, the phone rang. I should return immediately to the hospital.

The golden bells of Heaven had rung for dear Miss Wilson. She had been called home by Him who carries each of His children through life, He who had paid for her eternal life with His own blood. He, the sweetest Dove of Heaven, had called her name! The hush of angel wings softly filled the room with a heavenly peace, with a beauty that lingered on her still and silent form. An aura of peace too precious for words hung in the air as the rays of morning sunlight filtered through the blinds and caught the softness of her gray hair. The essence of a saint called home left a fragrance that perfumed my soul as I sat holding her hand. It was out of that sacred time alone with her that I found the strength and hope to carry on. How sweet would be the sound of the chimes I heard on coming into Oneida two days later!

Barkley sat alone in his office. The loss was almost more than he could bear. He had experienced many deaths: those of his own little brother George, dear friends, and many adults and children in Iran. He knew pain and suffering. But he also knew that, as the writer of Ecclesiastes had said over three thousand years ago, "There is a time to die."

Barkley also knew grief and now it had struck a blow in the deepest recesses of his soul. But in his heart he knew that he knew, a joy still deeper.

Oh, the love that drew salvation's plan!
Oh, the grace that brought it down to man!
Oh, the mighty gulf that God did span at Calvary!

That love made it possible for him to take the next step. That love stretched from his thoughts all the way to eternity through the eyes of faith. One day he and Miss Wilson would meet again on Heaven's shores. Now, he had so many calls to make, so many to tell of her death, and, on campus, so many to comfort! It was with superhuman grace that he began:

We have suffered a sad loss…one that is beyond measurement. But now her labors are ended and she is with our Heavenly Father. "Miss Wilson died on September 9th. She had worked seventeen hours that last day…arriving at the office at 4:00 AM which was her custom for many years. She literally died from overwork. We have missed her tremendously. She was the greatest human being I have ever personally known, and my dearest friend for many, many years. I could not have accomplished what has been done here without her, would not have accepted the presidency had she not agreed to return here with me. She did so at tremendous sacrifice and, ultimately, her life. Her body was brought to the Chapel at 6:00 PM the first to lie in state in the new Chapel. Several times during the next 22 hours, there were lines of over 100 waiting to pass her body. At 9:00 PM, there was an hour-long hymn Service which was, I believe, the most beautiful service I ever had part in…a packed Chapel which sat for many minutes in total silence. After the service concluded, no one moving, everyone present conscious they were in the presence of a true saint of God. She had no close family but she had taught for fifty years…very strict and much loved by so many. So many of them had come to say goodbye…Cliff Hagan, the all-American basketball star and St. Louis Hawks professional, now Athletic Director of UK, sat nearest her casket with his family. He gave a moving tribute and then wept…he, too, had worked with her, and so many…Dr. Conley Powell, the atomic scientist, was here…The Sermon on the Mount was read in its entirety.

Blessed are the meek, for they shall inherit the earth. Blessed are they which do hunger and thirst after righteousness, for they shall be filled. Blessed are the merciful, for they shall obtain mercy. Blessed are the pure in heart, for they shall see God. (Matthew 5: 3-8)

Barkley had come to a new level of understanding of the promised blessings—of his mission at Oneida. Oh, how he longed for every boy and girl to know his Savior before it was too late, before the evil tide of sin ran its course, before it was too late to change the course of their lives! He would go on without Miss Wilson, but he would not be alone. The Savior would show him the way to the hearts of these young people—how to win them to Himself. He would more diligently teach them about the right time to do everything, so they would learn in their youth to care that the Lord of the Universe had paid the price for their redemption. He longed even more to see each give his heart to Him. He did not want one of them to spend one hour in vain. He had a message on his heart when he climbed the steps to the chapel.

Years I spent in vanity and pride,
Caring not my Lord was crucified,
Knowing not it was for me He died on Calvary?
Mercy there was great, and grace was free;
Pardon there was multiplied to me;
There my burdened soul found liberty at Calvary.
By God's Word at last my I learned;
Then I trembled at the law I'd spurned,
Till my guilty soul imploring turned to Calvary?
Now I've giv'n to Jesus ev'rything,
Now I gladly own Him as my King,
Now my raptured soul can only sing of Calvary.
William R. Newell, 1895

Brother Sparks was unable to attend the service, but Barkley wrote him with all the details. He also spoke of the second funeral he attended in Owensboro with her family and so many friends who had known her from former Oneida days—Don and Peggy Coleman, Francis Patrick Black, Martha Bain and her husband. Then he told him what he was going to do to honor her and keep her memory always before him.

At the entrance to the Chapel, we are cementing river rock and in the center will have the symbol of the fish in tan mosaic work. Inside the fish in black mosaic will be the Greek symbols for "Jesus Christ, Son of God, Savior". A plaque at the head of the stairs on the outside of the Chapel will read:

MARY NANCY WILSON
1908-1977
Devoted Servant of Christ
50 Years an Educator
In Life She Ever Refused Praise,
In Death She Is Too Great For It.

On November 21, he had more sad news for Brother Sparks. One of Brother Sparks' and Miss Wilson's former students, Harlan Woods Jr., and his wife, he thirty-two years old, she twenty-nine, had been killed instantly in a car wreck, and their little daughter Traci, four years old, was being kept alive only by a machine. Harlan had been Barkley's first principal. They had been at Oneida just three weeks before for the funeral of Miss Wilson. This too was a great loss to Barkley and very sad. So many things had happened that fall—most of them good things, but this was a deluge of suffering that seemed unbearable. He again wrote to Brother Sparks:

We buried our former Principal Woods and wife this past week… killed instantly in a car accident and their one daughter, born here at Oneida, near death. I had charge of most of the arrangements and spoke at three different services in their honor. He was only 32 and she 29. He was one of the most remarkable students Oneida ever had…came here ranking 64th out of 64 in his entering class and graduated valedictorian, from a family of nine that paid $5 per month. He got his Masters with a perfect academic standing. He was my principal when I came here as President…so in the past three months have lost the three people closest to me in that difficult time five years ago. All three of them have lain in state in our new Chapel, and it doesn't seem possible…but it has happened. Their loss five years ago might have very nearly closed the School…but today the work is on a far stronger footing and we go forward. Having so narrowly escaped death myself just one year ago in a car accident, I wonder sometimes how long it will be until, I, too, will lie in the chapel. But God has blessed us thus far with health and strength, but the burden grows heavier and I am very tired at times.

These deaths had dealt a severe blow to Barkley. He continued with the running of the Institute, but for a few months he felt terribly low. On December 9, he wearily wrote to another who had been very faithful in supporting the school:

Thank you for your good letter and for the $75 contribution… both much appreciated. At the rate we are going, it will take one million dollars to operate Oneida this fiscal year (as compared to $190,000 six years ago), and that is a tremendous undertaking. It means working sixteen and seventeen hours seven days a week, literally and still being far behind and many things going undone… and most of the staff putting in fourteen hour days.

When the kids all left for the Thanksgiving break, Barkley was alone at the office for nearly the first time since he had come those five long years ago. Miss Wilson should have been working in the office next to him—how he missed her! He set about cleaning out his files and all the miscellaneous materials scattered on his desk. Occasionally he would find a note of hers clipped to a file.

Pres and Ruby Baker had invited him to Thanksgiving dinner

with their family. They were lifelong friends, and Pres was a trustee of the school. What a blessing it was to him that day to anticipate their company! Ruby was the best cook in Clay County. She made the most wonderful biscuits, and her rolls melted in your mouth. He could taste the pumpkin and chess pie before he got in the car. The drive was as picturesque as a Currier and Ives Thanksgiving picture. The white clapboard house and the farm lay in a beautiful valley, with Little Bullskin Creek flowing peacefully beside the road. Numerous cattle grazed in the fields enclosed by a white farm fence. In the distance he could see the well-kept weathered gray barn.

There was smoke curling from the chimney. The glowing embers in the fireplace welcomed him into the front room when he arrived. On the long sideboard, Ruby had set a feast worthy of her reputation. There was cured ham, fresh turkey right off the farm, dressing, cranberry sauce, mashed potatoes, green beans, sweet potatoes, apple stack cake, pumpkin pie, chess pie, and fried apple pies.

Barkley stayed so late into the night, reading by the fire after others had gone to bed, that Ruby made a bed for him in one of the guest rooms. Early the next morning there was a wonderful breakfast on the table—biscuits, eggs, bacon, home-made strawberry jam! He ate in a hurry, eager to get back to the school. He knew more than ever that "Each day is God's gift; it's all you get in exchange for the hard work of staying alive. Make the most of each one." (*Ecclesiastes* 9:7-10.)

It was back to work as soon as he arrived on campus. It was cold and snowy all that week. His was quite a job, trying to provide water, heat, food—supervise and discipline all those kids and keep enough money coming in to pay the tremendous bills. But he was glad for it!

Barkley wrote to a family friend:

> It will cost one million dollars to run the school this year...think of that! It frightens me to death at times, but so far we are paying the bills but we are always on razor-edge. Of course, I keep adding to the program and the facilities. If I just sat still, it wouldn't be so hard to pay the bills...there wouldn't be so many to pay...but when

you stop strengthening you start dying. I want us to do a better job all the time.

Reflecting on it all, he was heartened. There would be another day, another year, and he would make it, with God's help and the good friends of Oneida. The rhythms of the seasons, the traditions, were like a warm blanket wrapped around him that night. There would be a time to mourn and then there would be a time to rejoice!

It was time to get back to work. He finished reorganizing his desk and the boxes stacked around it. After he finished, he had an organized stack of letters to be answered, and the Christmas letter needed to go out.

The bitter cold air cleared his thoughts as he made his way up the hill that night through snowflakes that continued to fall off and on all week. Several nights the first week of December he didn't get to bed until after 4:00 AM and then he was back up at 8:00 AM. But by the end of the week the Christmas letter was finished and ready to go out to the more than 35,000 on the mailing list.

Christmas was celebrated in the usual manner—Christmas trees in the chapel, the dining room, and each dorm lounge—a big candlelight dinner—Christmas carols—gifts for each student. But this time it was a gift of books. Candy Meyer of Scottsburg, Indiana had given thousands of books to Oneida. For Christmas, every student got to go to the library and choose up to seven books. The library staff had divided them into categories and stacked them on tables.

And then the students were off to home, with a light snow falling as they left. Barkley sat at his desk alone for a brief moment. He began a thank-you letter to a donor:

> We haven't had so much excitement in years and we've seen kids reading, we have never seen reading before. We were really surprised at their response. Just to have seen these with your own eyes would have made the ENTIRE PROJECT worth while.

Christmas giving was good, with well over two hundred people donating for the first time. Barkley's prayer was that it would continue so in 1979. He and his office staff would work through the two-week break, trying to catch up with the mail—but they didn't, as the new year rolled around. He wrote, "We Never Are".

Why would a thirty-seven-year-old who had not had a day away from the burdens of running this place for six years be willing to give up every waking moment to the cause of Oneida Institute? It was because the mission of giving himself away on behalf of these boys and girls was being repaid with blessings far greater, in the joy he felt in his heart when he looked into the faces of his boys and girls filled with such promise! And he knew that "Or ever the silver cord be loosed, or the golden bowl be broken, or the pitcher be broken at the fountain, or the wheel broken at the cistern. Then shall the dust return to the earth as it was; and the spirit shall return unto God who gave it." (*Ecclesiastes* 12:6-7)

The other thing Barkley fully understood was the gift that he had been given by his Maker. *"Not even God a greater gift could give. Nor Heaven itself a greater boon impart. When Jesus came, and died that he might live, God gave without reserve His very heart."* (Larry Windom, *Glorying In the Cross — Why Jesus Came Into the World*)

He would never be able to out give God!

1978-79

Year 7

About six weeks ago we received $5 in the morning mail.
That was it. I had that day's bills and about $30,000 other
unpaid ones and felt like all the world had forgotten us. That
afternoon one of my teachers came to me with a letter from her
sister...and a check for $2,000 enclosed. I nearly cried.
—Barkley Moore

While the energetic old Barkley had not died, not by a long shot, the new Barkley was ever more gentle to the suffering souls he often met through his ministry at Oneida. His faith in God had been severely tested, and out of that testing, his love and empathy were deepened. With the grace that he had been given, with the love that he had been shown, his heart was filled with a new tenderness. So when he heard of Miss Bessie Bigler's loss of her sister, he personally wrote her a long letter. The following is a short excerpt from it:

I know that these are difficult days for you...missing the companionship of your dear sister having lived together for so many years. But God as He walks about His garden occasionally picks a rose for Himself...his due as Creator and giver of all things. I'm sure your sister would not come back if she could nor would you want her back. But of course it is natural to miss her and wish for that love, companionship and friendship that you shared as sisters, both natural as well as spiritual.

He then shared his own loss, so on his heart, as he continued with the day-to-day duties of the school: "I do miss them, but they will live eternally."

In February the weather repeated its onslaught, as in the year before. Four inches of snow fell on February 2, and during the following week forty students and seven teachers came down with the flu. The school made it through the month somehow. Schools were closed all over Kentucky for almost the whole month; they accumulated a total of six weeks of makeup days. But not Oneida! The activities of school went on as if there was no snow.

Barkley had moved into Miss Wilson's efficiency apartment in the boys' dorm. There he felt a sense of her presence as he sat at her father's big roll top desk. But he never forgot the sacrifice she had made to come back to Oneida with him, a sacrifice that he knew had cost her life.

Barkley continued his letters to Brother Sparks. He sought his counsel even more now that he didn't have Miss Wilson. On February 2, he typed a three-page single-spaced letter giving him all the news. If Brother Sparks really questioned the wisdom of any plan, he would send back a handwritten letter. (While there was sorrow and suffering, there was never a word of complaint to Brother Sparks about his added burdens.) He was willing to heed Timothy's admonition, "Thou therefore endure hardness, as a good soldier of Jesus Christ." To remember, "If we believe not, yet he abideth faithful: he cannot deny himself." (*II Timothy* 2:3,13)

There would be no return letter this time! On March 27, Brother Sparks, at the age of eighty- five, died of a heart attack while visiting in Springfield. He too would lie in state in the chapel at Oneida. This time the chimes that rang were surely ringing for an old saint gone home.

When They Ring the Golden Bells
There's a land beyond the river
That they call the sweet forever
And we only reach that shore by faith's decree
One by one we'll gain the portals
There to dwell with the immortals
When they ring the golden bells for you and me

Don't you hear the bells now ringing
Don't you hear the angels singing
'Tis the glory hallelujah Jubilee
In that far off sweet forever,
Just beyond the shining river
When they ring the golden bells for you and me

We shall know no sin or sorrow
In that heaven of tomorrow
When our hearts shall sail beyond the silvery sea
We shall only know the blessing
Of our Father's sweet caressing
When they ring the golden bells for you and me

When our days shall know their number
When in death we sweetly slumber
When the King commands the spirit to be free
Nevermore with anguish laden
We shall reach that lovely Eden
When they ring the golden bells for you and me
Daniel de Marbelle, 1887

On the first day of April, the funeral of Brother Sparks was held. On April 12, the *Western Recorder* ran a full-page story on the death of Brother Sparks, Miss Wilson, and Harlan Woods and his wife. It was written by the Editor, C.R. Daley, who had often preached and fished with Brother Sparks. The *Mountaineer* also had articles about all three of the beloved members of Oneida's family.

The school was well into the second semester when Barkley returned from Brother Sparks' funeral. While Barkley had been tried to the very depths of his soul, it was time to move ahead. He was so proud of the way the staff and students had performed while he had been occupied with the responsibilities attending the deaths of Oneida family members. Those old mountains never looked more beautiful. The dogwoods and redbuds were just opening into their delicate whites and purples. Easter was upon them! What a glorious re-birth their new spring coats announced! God preached a message that spring in words that couldn't be uttered by mortals, a message that echoed from mountain peaks to valleys below. If these children of man would look to him, they too could see beyond to the lovely Eden that awaited them. It was a time for hope. Barkley's hopes for the year 1978 went beyond mere buildings. He was building into the lives of these young people a hope that would see them through their lives, whatever lay ahead.

There was a rich harvest of souls in a week-long revival at Oneida that spring. Reverend Calvin Fields, a former pastor of Oneida, led the services. There were thirty-five decisions made. Brother Fields had preached not only in the evenings, but also every day in chapel. Barkley was present at every chapel service and at every revival service in the evening. He could never worship the Lord too often. He was ever learning from the Godly men who came to the campus, as he hoped and prayed the students were doing also. His own sermons when he traveled were straight out of the Bible, given with a didactic reading of Scripture—and always about serving the Lord at Oneida. To him, Oneida was the State Mission Field, the Home Mission Field, the Foreign Mission Field of Kentucky Baptists.

He would make plans and they would be carried out by many others willing to give and to labor in the work of God at Oneida. His heart was renewed. Now he looked to the needs of the school. An industrial arts-maintenance building, and another apartment building, with at least four apartments. Purchasing the historic Britton house in Oneida was on the list as well. The staff housing was completely filled up, and he couldn't add any more staff without more housing. The school was producing a twenty-eight-minute 16-mm color film of Oneida, to be finished in the spring. In addition to planning additions to the physical plant, he began thinking about the needs of the farm, and about additions to faculty the staff. He was always looking for the best teacher, the best farmer, the best maintenance man. If he saw the qualities he needed in someone, he would make it almost impossible for that person to turn him down.

He had writing to do for the *Mountaineer*. He wrote articles on the progress of students, including some who were no longer at Oneida. Take Jen-Hsun Huang and his brother Jeff:

> Jen-Hsun Huang, who came to Oneida three years ago from Taiwan, was mentioned in the January 30th issue of the national magazine, *Sports Illustrated*. Jen-Hsun was called "perhaps the most promising junior ever to play table tennis in the Northwest." This fine young man now lives in Portland, Oregon, where his parents have emigrated.
>
> Last year Jen-Hsun and his older brother, Jeff, left Oneida to join their recently arrived parents…
>
> The *Sports Illustrated* article tells that Jen-Hsun "earns his money to travel to tournaments, to take part in clinics and to play table tennis by scrubbing floor…He is a straight-A student and very hungry to become table- tennis champion…Watch out for him."
>
> This describes the same Jen-Hsun, we had the privilege to work with at Oneida…straight A's, scrubbing floors, table tennis and all! *Mountaineer*, Spring, 1978

Barkley was proud of both of these boys, and considered them "his" boys. He would continue to cheer them on and to be proud to have served them when they needed a home in America. It was for such young men as these that he had struggled to provide all the opportunities for the best education to be had at the time—such as the first computer lab in a Kentucky high school, open to all students even on the weekends and evenings, with trained staff on hand!

He would really be proud, were he alive today, to see the results. Jen-Hsun Huang has gone on to build a *Fortune 500* company, Nvidia, the world's leading visual computing company.

It was plowing time at Oneida when Barkley returned from speaking in western Kentucky, where he gave fifteen speeches in seven days. The students were busy with work, classes, and athletics. Baseball, track, table tennis, fencing, and tennis teams were all busy with their games and meets. The tennis teams had to go all the way to Manchester, seventeen miles away, to practice.

After the harsh winter, Barkley wrote to a friend:

> It was so good to see the green grass, budding trees, the redbud and the dogwood! It was a blessing of God to see and be a part of this renewal of life…the renewal of Nature as well as the Spiritual renewal in many lives at ONEIDA.

The days flew by. It was June before he had time to catch his breath. Commencement weekend was June 3 and 4. He wrote to every donor with a glowing report and a warm "Thank you".

> Commencement weekend was so very beautiful. Many hundreds of friends and guests shared one or more of the events with us. On Saturday evening, a fine Dinner honoring Mr. Joe Tigue for his 35 years of service on our Board started the activities. Then our seniors did a superb job presenting *Our Town*, by Thornton Wilder. The evening came to a close with the showing of a professionally done film called *Oneida—for Time and Eternity*. It was 28 minutes long, in color and with music and narration. On Sunday Rev. Bill Messer, pastor of the Sand Springs Baptist Church, Lawrenceburg, preached a memorable sermon to the graduating class in the Oneida Baptist Church. Fifty-four graduates were given their diplomas in a beautiful and moving service. The Class of 1928, eleven strong, marched in academic procession and were recognized on the occasion of the 50th anniversary of their graduation.

Work began on a new 6,000-square-foot apartment building. Camps were in full swing. There would be over 200 campers at the Institute weekly right up to the fall term.

By July the Institute was facing a deficit for the first time in six years. The operating budget was up to $1,100,000 compared to $228,000 just six years before. Inflation was causing serious problems. He sent out a letter to 35,000 asking for help.

He really meant it when he asked "Which child shall we turn away? How could we refuse a child because he was unable to pay?

"SHOULD WE BE JUST ANOTHER PREP SCHOOL FOR THE WELL TO DO? NO! THAT MUST NOT BE!"

He always loved to have Dr. Franklin Owen speak at Oneida. This year Dr. Owen would be the leader of the Mountain Missions Conference Bible Study. Barkley had a letter from him; he was coming in a motor home that he had bought but hadn't had a chance to use much. By then Barkley had established a motor home campsite, and he was glad to tell Dr. Owen that it was fully ready.

In July he got a letter from Tim Lee Carter, a member of the Kentucky delegation to the House of Representatives. He had met Monoutchehr (last name omitted for security reasons), Barkley's Iranian friend, with whom he had roomed at Oneida as a high-school boy; Monoutchehr's father had been Iran's Ambassador to the U.S. They had had lunch and, said Rep. Carter, "He told me, you have helped provide an education for fifty young people from that country…Let me commend you on this endeavor. I look forward to visiting you at your Institute on my next visit to that area."

Almost no one at Oneida, except Miss Wilson, knew that he had brought so many Iranian boys and girls to the states. But he had, and had paid their way out of his own meager salary at Oneida; when he ran out of funds, he had borrowed whatever it took. He had gotten scholarships for a number of them at various colleges, including Cumberland, Campbellsville, and Alice Lloyd. Since many of them were in high school when they arrived, Barkley gave them scholarships at Oneida, and he assumed responsibility for them until they were able to make it on their own. One whom he was helping, a most hard-working and deserving boy, had died of typhoid fever, just weeks before Barkley could have gotten him out of the country. For each student, there were long forms to be filled out, diplomatic procedures, and finally a long waiting period while he got his passport.

Help for the school came from many sources. Barkley's work with the Christian Appalachian Project paid off with a $1,000 scholarship. He had found real friends in Dr. C.R. Daley and Dr. Franklin Owen. Dr. Daley's brilliant editorials in the *Western Recorder* were to Barkley as iron sharpening iron, and Dr. Owen was a father figure to him.

They would both mentor him through the years ahead. He was ever appreciative of their help, and he felt free to call on either when the need arose. He frequently sent them long letters, usually just updating them on something with which they were involved, as he had done with Brother Sparks. But the letters were not quite as long; he knew they were both extremely busy in their roles as leaders of Kentucky Baptists.

When Barkley was sure that the industrial arts building and the new apartment building would be ready by Homecoming on October 8, he wrote to Dr. Owen, asking him to speak. He gave him an updated schedule for the rest of the summer, and told him that by the end of summer the school would have had over 1600-1700 campers. He shared a sad story that had been in the *Mountaineer* about a boy whom he had had to let go:

> Sometimes those you have worked the hardest and most patiently with and ultimately have to let go are the least appreciative…and their parents! I took a real upbraiding this morning from a mother in such a situation! It is really discouraging at times and I don't have Preacher Sparks, Miss Wilson and several others who meant so much in similar situations in times past.

But he still had his Oneida family and drew on their fellowship and strength. That fall he would take the faculty and their families to Cade's Cove in the Smokey Mountains for a retreat before the fall session began. There they worshipped in a 150-year-old Baptist church, attracting the attention of many tourists passing by, some of whom stopped to worship with them. Afterward, Oneida's group all boarded the Greyhound and explored the Cove, with the bus stopping at points of interest. Later in the afternoon they enjoyed a picnic supper in a valley, with the towering mountains in the distance. From there they went to Pigeon Forge and saw the Passion Play. Late in the night they arrived at their sister Baptist high school, Chilhowe Academy in Knoxville, Tennessee. On Sunday morning they worshipped together one last time and had a wonderful time of fellowship. Standing in a circle, holding hands, they sang *Blest Be The Tie That Binds*. It was time to get back to the students now arriving on campus.

For some time Barkley had wanted to find a person to help beautify the campus gardens. In a conversation with Mrs. Wasson of the Oneida staff, he mentioned the need. She said she knew someone who would be perfect—her grandfather, a dear little man named David Cooper, who was in his eighties. It didn't take Barkley overnight to decide that he wanted to talk to this man; it was just that it was too late that night. When he couldn't get him on the phone the next morning, he wrote to him:

> For some time I have been conscious of the need of, and have been praying for, a retired man who knows how to work and how to make flower beds, *etc.*…a man with a "green thumb"…I feel this so keenly and you sound like just what I've been looking for.
>
> We have several acres in our campus, and thousands of people visit here each year. There is so much that could be done with just a little work, but I never have enough staff to do all that needs doing. It is beautiful here, and could be so much more so with someone who could give his full time and attention to our grounds.
>
> I HOPE YOU WILL THINK ABOUT THIS, PRAY ABOUT THIS—and come visit and see FIRSTHAND the OPORTUNITY FOR SERVICE.
>
> How about it?

Mr. Cooper did come. It was a wonderful thing for Barkley, as dear Mr. Cooper did know flowers. He had spent years at Calumet Horse Farm, one of the oldest horse farms in Kentucky—aristocratic, beautiful, stately. Once Barkley got him to Oneida, he worked from daybreak until dusk every day except Sunday, on his hands and knees planting, planting, planting! This was the beginning of the many beautiful perennial gardens that grace Oneida's campus today.

In November the C.R. Clark Press for the Publication of Historic Documents wrote to Barkley. They were working on the Claude Matlack Collection of historic photographs taken in and around Clay County in the early 1900's. Would Barkley help them with identifying the people in these pictures? The book they would be printing would be similar to the *Foxfire* project at Berea. They had an incredible collection of photographs depicting logging, rafting, hillside farming, transportation, roads, cabins, mining, and, of course, the Institute. Members of the Press wanted to meet with him again. (They had paid him a brief visit earlier, but hadn't shown him the pictures.)

Barkley was ecstatic! His beloved Oneida would come to life in pictures from the turn of the century that had been stored away in boxes all this time. Of course he would work with them. Would they be able to come during either the Thanksgiving break, November 21-25, or Christmas break, December 23-January 6? There was an old man, ninety-six, who was principal of the school when those pictures were taken; his name is now unknown. He lived seven miles from Oneida. Though he had suffered a stroke, his memory was as keen as could be and he could recite fascinating stories with detailed conversations of seventy years ago. A day spent with him would be like digging in a goldmine.

Barkley pressed them to have it done by 1979 Homecoming, when the school would be celebrating its eightieth anniversary. "We have 34,000 on our mailing list. Out of that number I am sure thousands would be interested."

Thanksgiving found him giving thanks, but he had thanksgiving in his heart every day at Oneida for all the wonderful things the Lord did with His people who loved Oneida and gave as if giving to the Lord, with generous hearts and generous spirits.

By December, the new apartment building had a beautiful stand of grass around it. All over campus the beauty of new growth reflected the life that goes on for a Christian, leaning hard on the Lord, even in the darkest of times.

He had looked into the eyes of young men and women who knew nothing of this kind of love and caring. The Christmas letter reflected the needs of those who didn't know the Lord—who didn't know such a wonderful life—or even dreamed of its existence. Every day brought letters from former students who had been blessed.

Dear Friend:

I failed to do what I promised you even though you could have kicked me out at any time. I was a very mixed up kid then. At the time I hated your school because I had to go there.

I'm at University now and I am doing great because you gave me a chance I did not deserve. I will always remember how you helped me. I am sorry I disappointed you. I learned a lot about life from you and your school.

In the same mail was this letter from a boy recently expelled:

I'm very sorry about what I've done in the school. I'm giving my word that it will not happen again. I hope you will give me "one" more chance. It would be a favor to me and a big surprise for you how much I will stand up to my word. I'm not just saying this to get back and cause more trouble. I really mean it.

It was just about Christmas. Barkley had to decide.

SHOULD WE TAKE HIM BACK?

Jesus, whose birth anniversary we soon celebrate, told his disciples that "Inasmuch as ye have done it unto one of the least of these, My brethren, ye have done it unto Me."(*Matthew* 25:40)

While remembering others, won't you give Jesus a birthday gift by helping His "little ones" in Oneida School this Christmas season? And during the coming year, our 80th year of extending the helping hand and providing a quality school as well as a home for hundreds of boys and girls "away from home"?

Have a good Christmas and may its glow extend all the way to ONEIDA.

He believed that the Lord always gave second chances to His children. Yes, he could return—and so could dozens more who had lost their way, if they asked for a second chance.

Barkley had one more letter to write before Christmas. It was to Dr. Owen, giving him a final update on all the doings at Oneida during 1978. "Grace had brought them safe thus far and Grace would lead them home."

1979-80
Year 8

Henry never knew a father. He hadn't seen his mother for many years. He is a follower…doing whatever the crowd is doing in his craving to be accepted, to "belong". He has so much potential, but like all teenagers needs the security of people who care enough about him to lay down some dos and don'ts. Oneida so cares.
—Barkley Moore

School opened for the spring semester on January 7, 1979. There was an ice storm to the west and north of Oneida and it was headed toward the school. It would be days before all of the students would be able to make it to campus. Barkley was working in rounds of different activities, helping the students register and get to their rooms, talking to parents, leading tours around the campus, and in odd moments trying to get through the mail and answer the phone which rang incessantly.

"Carrying on" was not easy that first month. Walks all over campus had to be cleared, supplies had to be gotten in, the cattle and hogs had to be fed. (Four new calves were born during the month.) There was a flu outbreak, with seven teachers out. That meant others had to fill the gap, so teachers had to give up their "preparation periods" each day. Barkley wrote, "Courage has many faces and I have seen it exhibited by my staff various times in these difficult circumstances."

When all the students finally got back, there were over 340, with thirty new ones. Everyone was glad when the weather finally broke;

snow was one thing but ice really crippled every activity. But they had weathered the storm.

There were three new teachers, all of whom Barkley was happy to have, all prepared to do a great job academically. There were Harold Holderman's daughter; Mr. Rick Coffey; and his own Iranian "kid" whom he had put through college. Several already on staff had stepped into new positions. There were new babies as well; the Grittons had a son, and soon there would be others born in several young staff families. (You would have thought Barkley was a grandparent, he was so proud of them!) His was a growing family, and the more the better. They had added a day care center in the church basement for children ages three to five. Everyone was doing a fine job, according to him, and he ought to know! So, he set about spreading the good news to anyone who would listen or read about it.

The village streets of Oneida and the roads on campus had all been blacktopped, and he was proud of that too. He had a new farm manager, Mr. Zane Fraker, and his wife, and he was relieved and proud of that. He had a classmate of Miss Wilson's in Anderson Hall. She also worked in the office, and he was comforted by that.

Many of the hundreds of people to whom he wrote in the next few weeks received a letter that said in part:

> The following are highlights of the month of March: Our Seniors in Washington, D.C. and other students on 'spring break' for 9 days...more seniors this year than ever before, two buses necessary for the trip. A break from normal routine, the Washington trip is never a break in terms of rest for the staff members who drive and chaperone, but all feel this 30 year tradition is one to maintain for it is always an unique and educational experience for all involved. Spring arrives (our principal has already spotted some daffodils) and everyone ready for it after another hard winter. Many visitors are coming this month...WMU groups from different parts of the state, several youth retreats, and more than 100 Royal Ambassadors here from Elkhorn Association for their third annual weekend Basketball Tournament. Also, by the end of this month I will have spoken before

at least fourteen different groups in various parts of the state. I enjoy presenting the cause of Oneida, but it takes much time, energy, and traveling. There is always a mountain of work and decisions to be made upon one's return to the campus. Our third quarter ends, fourth begins.

Six of our boys took part in a two-day "Trivia Tournament" sponsored by Berea College several weeks ago. Competing against ten college teams, Oneida won the championship in a Quiz-type competition and one of our freshman boys was voted most outstanding in the "Tournament". The boys were very proud and we were quite proud of them…high school kids defeating scores of college students in a competition on general knowledge! Also, we were very proud of our Junior Class production of *Charley's Aunt*. The students put in two months of daily practice and a beautiful performance when the big night came. The audience, larger than last year's, laughed uproariously throughout most of the performance as each one so skillfully played their role in this hilarious comedy. The basketball team ended the season with 20 wins, 13 losses and now it is baseball, tennis, and track season…with fencing (Oneida competing in a National competition this month) and table tennis continuing. Our daily worship experience, all teacher and students attending, is a highlight of each day and several recent services have been real mountain-top experiences. Pray that we may have a revival this spring such as last fall.

Letters, 1979

Only to his mentors and friends would he confide just how tired and weary he was. In this letter he asked for prayer:

…that our endowment might be substantially increased and that we might be able to meet the day-to-day bills: believe me that is a burden never away from my thoughts. I get very discouraged and then feel guilty at my lack of faith. About six weeks ago we received $5 in the morning mail. That was it. Much appreciated but the bills that day ran over $2,700. I had that day's bills and about $30,000 other unpaid ones...and felt like all the world had forgotten us. That afternoon one of my teachers came to me with a letter from her sister...and a check for $2,000 enclosed. I nearly cried.

He ended that letter with, "I'm leaving within the hour on a nine day speaking tour."

On March 28, the headlines in many a U.S. newspaper would be "Turkoman battle police in Iran." This was in the same very little town he had served not so long ago, when in the Peace Corps. It grieved him to think of his boys left behind. It was hard to imagine fighting and killing in the streets of Gonbad, with perhaps his boys in a battle for their lives. All he could do was pray for them and pray that, by some miracle, a reasonably democratic system might emerge. His Iranian family preyed on his mind more than anyone could possibly have imagined.

In April a very fine article about Oneida appeared in the *Western Recorder*. Barkley was delighted; such articles helped win new friends for the work by making more people aware of how the Institute worked with individuals, and of the scope of the work.

In May Barkley invited Frances and Andy Clark, who lived in Nashville, Tennessee, to come for a visit. They were friends of his and had been friends of Miss Wilson. He had last seen Frances at Miss Wilson's funeral. About that he said:

> She will soon have been gone two years yet, in so many ways, she still seems to be here. I think of her so many times each day and often find notes and letters she wrote in varying files that I had never seen before...and for a moment, she's back in her office pecking away! I know she is interceding for me and for this work every day.

It would be a long time before he could fully let her go!

On May 29, an article about Barkley, *A Work of Faith*, by R.G. Dunlop, appeared in the *Louisville Courier-Journal*. Of course if it was about him, it was also about the school. The heading of the article read *School Gets Young People Ready for Life*.

Barkley had been interviewed on campus. Just as the reporter had shown up, Barkley was in the act of administering a paddling to one of the boys who had just confessed to smoking marijuana. "The handsome boy. dressed in a yellow t-shirt, blue tennis shoes, and jeans, had an impish look on his face as he walked out of the office straight into the reporter's gaze." There was nothing for Barkley to do but to explain the situation to the reporter. "The school permits paddling in small doses," he said—so he had doled out a couple of whacks. But he had also let the boy know that he had done the right thing by unburdening his conscience.

"The boy thought so, too."

"I think I'll make it," he said. "I'm doin' all right here—because you gotta."

Barkley was quick to point out that "Oneida has never kidnapped a student. Those who come must play by the rules, and those who don't leave."

The story was really quite humorous and went on to give a really good pitch for Oneida and Barkley. But as many a parent will tell you, just when you want your kids to be on their best behavior, they go and embarrass you at the most inopportune moment.

He must have felt a little nonplussed. However, the show went on, with the "Tour" being the next part of the interview. Of course, as they walked, or should one say jogged, around the campus, Barkley was giving him the normal tour and that meant—let's let the reporter tell it because he got all of the following information from the "Tour". As they walked, Barkley began:

> We're not a school for angels...we go not only for the 99 sheep in the fold, but also for the one outside...nobody ever comes here by accident...have about 340 in the fold...attending grades seven through 12...majority of students graduate, and more than half go on to college or some other form of further training...some applicants are denied admission because all the beds are full or Oneida isn't the place for them...but no one is turned away for lack of money...majority of Oneida students in fact pay nothing, and none pays more than $150

a month-half the actual cost. Arrivals come at all times, including the mid-semester and midnight...I'm usually the first one they meet... our students get up at 6:30 AM, attend chapel in the morning, go to classes during the day, work in the afternoon or evening, have study time at night and lights out at 10:30 PM, each Oneida teacher has about 15 students and faculty live on campus...boys' hair below the collar is taboo, as are liquor and drugs...not even an aspirin or cough drop is allowed without staff permission...more students are expelled for lying than for all other transgression combined...Oneida neither advertises for students nor solicits contribution, so the applications and money received are the result of a word-of-mouth network... have 10 students from Iran...others from Ethiopia, China, Mexico, Japan, Thailand, Guatemala, El Salvador, and Cambodia...even have a Ghanian prince in student body, but Oneida doesn't stand much on ceremony. Work is an integral part of life at our school, and the prince is just as likely as a kid from Corbin, Paducah, or Louisville to be found swabbing dormitory floors or picking corn on the farm. We're getting our people ready to live, and work's a part of life... Oneida differs from most other schools, public or private, in a variety of ways...no janitors...students fill that role...no budget either, despite fact that running the school for a year is an $800,000 proposition... began this year not knowing where more than half is coming from...a recent day's mail...brought about $700 in contributions, many from people who had never seen the school or Eastern Kentucky.
Louisville Courier-Journal, A Work of Faith, Roger Dunlop, May 29, 1980

As they walked around campus, he talked as they went—stopping at each building, giving out its name, telling a little about the person for whom the building was named—that person's history in relation to the school. He led the reporter on a tour through Sylvia Russell Hall—the Floyd DeJarnette Library— the Melvin Davidson Chapel.

In about forty-five minutes, the reporter's head was spinning with facts. If they met a student or faculty member, he got that person's history also. Barkley also had some words of praise for each person they met. The article brought lots of inquiries and letters and many new friends to the school. For every inquiry, a letter went out immediately, with brochures and a personal letter from Barkley. He alone knew just how much he depended on the Lord to give him enough faith to keep on keeping on! Right then the school was operating with a $6,000 monthly deficit.

In June Barkley sent out another appeal to the friends of the school. It started with the story of two young people at the school right then.

Henry never knew a father. He hasn't seen his mother for many years. He is a follower...doing whatever the crowd is doing in his craving to be accepted, to "belong". He has so much potential, but like all teenagers needs the security of people who care enough about him to lay down some do's and don'ts. Oneida so cares.

Etta is one of thirteen children and has grown up in poverty. That cycle can only be broken by removal from that environment and getting a vision of something better. She, like Henry, needs much love and security.

Jimmy's mother died when he was nine. The father remarried and Jimmy's young step-mother did not want to be bothered with Jimmy. The resulting domestic turmoil left Jimmy without a home until he found Oneida.

Yes, we have these children and many, many others. Unlike the situations described above, the majority of our boys and girls come from more normal home lives—many from very solid, loving Christian homes. But they have a "need" also—they come seeking the quality academic preparation and the atmosphere of concern and individual attention that Oneida provides, which often can't be found in their home school.

Henry, Jimmy, Etta...and so many others...need friends like YOU who CARE enough to DO something...who care enough to share. Will you be such a friend? Today? Monthly?

In June a group of men came from the Ephesus Baptist Church in Winchester, Kentucky. They had come in response to Barkley's appeals for help. They took it literally—and there they were. They helped repair the corn crib, worked on the water plant addition, both roof and wiring, and painted the school's name on the buses and on signs about the campus.

This opened Barkley's eyes to new ways to get things done with volunteer labor. He had come a long way from those first years when he had modeled "Volunteerism" after his Peace Corps' experience. He was truly grateful. He wrote to each of the men:

> Not only are the things you did for us a great help to us, but the influence of your effort here is going to be immeasurable. I had never thought much about the potential of this type of volunteer work, how much it could help us, how much money we could save, how we could get so many things done that often must wait, if we had more groups like yours to come here to work as you men worked. I am going to write an article about the project and print it in the next issue of our little paper, the *Oneida Mountaineer.* That paper goes out to 34,000 people all over the United States. I am going to use the picture made by the Courier-Journal photographer of Mr. Crowe working on the bus. I am sure this article will be an inspiration to many and that many others will soon want to do what you have done. Thank you, Ephesus Church, for leading the way in this. This is missions at its best…putting into daily practice God's love, to SHARE with others, to help 'even the least of these' as Christ commanded. There are so many young people here that we are serving, that we are teaching God's love by example, and yours is a wonderful example. When our young people see men like yours coming here to work for nothing, it must have a valuable effect in the molding of their own characters.

The inspiration for using church members for short term help soon grew all over Kentucky and beyond. Who knows, it may have even been the start of the program of almost every Southern Baptist church in America—for today it is as commonplace as taking the offering. For Oneida it would bring literally thousands of trained laymen to help who would give small portions of themselves to help Oneida. That would be their offering.

The school was being promoted by more Kentucky Baptists and help was coming in from many churches as Barkley traveled and wrote. The choir was away on many weekends as well. Most of the time they were with Barkley but many churches just had the choir, especially if Barkley was already booked. By then Oneida was the fastest growing boarding high school in the nation. In an article written by C.R. Daley, editor of the *Western Recorder*, on April 18, 1979, and reprinted in the *Mountaineer*, which went out to 34,000, many hearts were touched to help him with his great mission at Oneida.

Keys to Oneida's Unusual Growth

At least three reasons occur to this writer for Oneida's success. Each one seems directly related to the others.

The first and most visible barometer is an Oneida graduate who returned to his alma mater after six years in the Peace Corps and became the school's president in 1972. Barkley Moore, still single at the age of 37, obviously eats, sleeps and breathes Oneida 24 hours every day, seven days a week, 52 weeks a year.

More often than not he puts in a 17- or 18-hour day, a tremendous example of commitment to his 52-member faculty and staff. Moore's busiest day of the week is Sunday when the campus is often over-crowded with visitors. He conducts an average of five to seven tours on any given day of the week.

A University of Kentucky graduate, Moore comes on strong whether he's leading one of the "Tour"s for which he has become famous or speaking in behalf of Oneida at a church somewhere across Kentucky. His locks of black hair, ruddy complexion and robust manner offset his overweight, suggesting a man whose youthfulness has helped him in his ambitions drive to see the institution so dear to his heart succeed. An astute observer once likened Barkley Moore to a "steam engine in britches". It couldn't have been better put.

When the executive board of the Kentucky Baptist Convention meets in semiannual session, veterans on the board knowingly smile as the time approaches for Moore to report on Oneida's progress.

They realize they are in for an address instead of a mere report because Moore's exuberance for the institute can't be contained.
Western Recorder, April 18, 1979

The May/June *Mountaineer* reported that the now tangible help in terms of real dollars was $125,000 of Oneida's $800,000 budget, the funds coming through the Cooperative Program. He couldn't have been happier, unless, of course, they gave a lot more!

You would never have known at Oneida how successful Barkley was in the world outside the school. On campus he was always running as fast as he could go, wearing one of three or four suits his mother tried to keep clean for him when she came on the weekends from Lexington. He put on whatever was in his closet paying little attention to such details. But there were no expensive linen or silk suits. He wouldn't have worn them if someone had given them to him. In fact he once returned a tie to the giver because it was too nice—this person "should give it to someone who needed it". In those size-twelve shoes of his, he made a big imprint, but it was his big heart that left the largest imprint. He had begun to tiptoe his way into so many hearts, the funds would come!

1980-81

Year 9

*Oneida is big enough to have a strong program, yet
small enough that each boy and girl can have a part, be
a SOMEBODY and all can know one another.*
—Barkley Moore

A new year, a new decade—it is a time to look where we have been and to consider where we are going. This is the beginning of Oneida's ninth decade of service in the training of boys and girls for Christian living. Overall, there is a far greater need today for Oneida's work than when our work first began.

(1) When Oneida was founded in 1899, every public school in America was a Christian school where the Bible was taught, chapel was regularly held, and prayer was a daily part of the day. That is not true today. So there is an even more compelling need for private Christian schools, not supported by the tax dollar, where the foregoing can all still be a part of the education process. Because of YOUR help and of others like you, we can have daily worship, prayer, and teach the Bible as a part of our curriculum at Oneida.

(2) When Oneida's work began, nearly every high school in America was a small school with several hundred students at the most. But, today, the grate majority of our public schools have a thousand or more student….many two or three thousand. But there is still a need for smaller schools where there can be more of a sense of community, discipline, where students can be given more personal,

more individual attention. Oneida remains such a school. We are such a school because of friends like you who make it possible.

(3) Divorce was nearly unheard of when Oneida first opened its doors. However, today nearly one out of every two marriages end in divorce court. One or the other is given custody and that parent nearly always is forced to work outside the home trying to be both father and mother, housekeeper, cook, etc. Oneida has always been a HOME (away from home) as well as a school. All the teaching and administrative staff live on campus, and our young people have 24-hour a day Christian supervision...a wonderful program of study, athletics, work and worship, always something useful to do and someone to do it with under adult supervision. Oneida is big enough to have a strong program, yet small enough that each boy and girl can have a part, be a SOMEBODY and all can know one another. Yes, YOU and others like you CARE and make this possible.
Letters, 1980

As always, Barkley was planning for the needs of the coming year. As he looked back to the previous year he could see some real improvement in the financial situation. About $400,000 in buildings and equipment had been added in the last fiscal year, without borrowing, taking from the endowment, or having a special fund drive. The school year had opened with $100,000 in unpaid bills and no money. Before the month was over, $55,000 of that had been paid, even with 13.2 % inflation. There were thirty more students than the year before. Five had been added to the staff. Looking forward, he saw many ways to cut back on operating expenses and reduce payroll. Volunteer help looked very promising!

Even so, there were many projects that needed to be done in order for the operation of the school to proceed more smoothly. There was always maintenance work that had to be done. He planned to put a new roof on one house; build a new storage shed; partition off another classroom in the student center; paint the new firehouse, water plant, and water lab building; rewire Anderson Hall; and add another house for faculty housing.

There was at least one new project. He planned to build a small stone prayer and meditation chapel near the girl's dorm. With all of these projects he hoped to use volunteer help. He had already gotten commitments from many churches to send men to help. The article he had run in the *Mountaineer* had reaped rich results!

Being Barkley, he put his thoughts into action! No time was wasted daydreaming. He thought, he sprang into action! He finished the details in his mind as he walked to see the farm manager, Mr. Zane Fraker. He had so much confidence in his ability to get things done.

One of the secrets of Barkley's success with all the projects under way was delegation. He put full confidence in anyone to whom he had entrusted a task. That is not to say he wasn't involved—he would stop and praise the men as he made his way across campus so many times during the day. He never forgot to say thank you to his laborers. In fact, if he was leading a tour, he would stop to brag about the work they were doing. That sense of his involvement in every project stimulated those one hundred souls now under his leadership to be confident, industrious, and persistent in whatever the task was. He was each and everyone's cheerleader!

He believed and counted on God even as the bills piled up or circumstances gave no evidence that God was acting. His faith gave him the fortitude to act, before the funds arrived, while it was still winter, while the snow lay on the ground.

In the same spirit he counted on others before they volunteered, before they gave. In the same spirit he never failed to thank and praise every person who sent any gift whether it was used clothing, a few dollars or thousands. He made them feel a part of the work—he shared the school's needs with everyone outside the school as though they were indispensable to the Lord's work.

When laborers started coming to the school to help, he doubled up on the praise and thanks. That, in a real, tangible way, was an immense help and he let them know it. Work, real work, was Godly to Barkley and all those who arrived to work were on mission for God. He could never praise or thank them enough.

When the needs were overwhelming he would turn to Dr. Franklin

Owen, churches and friends outside the school. He would write to them, unburden his heart, and appeal to them for help. It was totally without guilt or shame that he brought Oneida's needs before them.

On March 29, he wrote to Dr. Owen, thanking him for all that he had done for the school in raising the funding for Oneida.

I am sure you have done the best that can be done. I am fighting the financial battle daily, as I assume most are having to do. We have cut back some on operating expenses and I'm hoping to reduce our payroll next year by $20,000…will accomplish this by use of additional volunteers. Prospects look bright to have at least four additional staff next year with Masters degrees, each with years of experience, and each financially able to be VOLUNTEERS. Also, I will have at least two young people…one who has completed his third year of college and will come for a year of volunteer service…and one who will serve a year before going to college…to help us in our "special help" program. For some months I have had a dietitian (she owns a Day Care Center in Shepherdsville and is paying someone to run it while she works here for nothing. Mrs. Betty Hasty…she is in the kitchen by 4:30 AM each day! She has cut our food cost back by $3,000 monthly while providing better meals. Our new maintenance building is making for a more efficient operation in that department and consequent savings.

While trying to save in operations, we are still improving our plant. We have gotten 69 year old Anderson Hall rewired this month…the work donated by four electricians from Ohio. They are coming back in April to rewire 26-year old Gym putting in mercury vapor lights which will give us much better lighting at less cost than the present system. They are also donating their labor for that. Plans for the summer include: construction of a 74-ft long shed addition to one of our barns by a church group from northern Kentucky for use in storing equipment like our tractors, etc; a new roof to be put on one of our faculty houses by a church group from Winchester; painting of our water plant and new fire house by another church group; partitioning in our Student Center to provide two additional classroom and some work in basement to provide another faculty apartment; hopefully new sidewalks for most of the campus; and construction of a stone prayer and meditation room for our girls near the girls' dorm.

His letter to Mr. Hiram Campbell expressed his gratefulness to just one of the volunteers. He wrote hundreds.

Dear Mr. Campbell,

Words are inadequate to express our genuine appreciation of your hard work, and for the fine job you did on the Anderson Hall, as well as the work on the farm and the other work. It was such a needed job and I am resting much easier. I had feared an electrical fire for years.

As I told you, our boys and girls are what it is all about. Your knowledge of what the school is meaning in their lives highlights the importance of what you have done, are doing, for us at ONEIDA.

Always it was about the boys and girls, but it was also about the extended family that belonged to Oneida—those who had served the school, who were serving the school, or who had attended the school.

He took every one of them on his shoulders. If they were old, he revered them in word and deed. When they died, he wrote comforting letters and made calls to the family. If they were due honor, he was the first to honor them, in as many ways as he could he connected every one to each other, in ways that made for a strong cord. He firmly believed that a cord of three made a stronger rope.

He had a way of giving kids who didn't have family roots—roots at Oneida—that would last for life. He was fond of saying, "You don't have to be anyone to come to Oneida, but you will be somebody when you leave."

When Dr. Paul Hounchell, a former president of Oneida died, Barkley wrote his daughter a long letter, about her roots to Oneida.

Your father was the last surviving member of our FIRST graduating class. He later served the school as Dean, teacher and Coach for seven years and founded our little paper, THE ONEIDA MOUNTAINEER, in 1915 and was its first editor. He played a very significant role in those early days. That is recognized with the name HOUNCHEL on one of our newer buildings...honoring him and Dr. Saul.

He always loved Oneida. His 'roots' were here on Beech Creek and here. We have a picture of your father and the remarkable 1912 baseball team that he coached...a book will be published later this year called DAWN COMES TO THE MOUNTAINS that will include several pictures of your father.

This morning your father was remembered at some length in our daily Chapel worship, all teachers and students attending.

A Time to Reap

On April 4, he was to have a door opened to him that would give him an opportunity to make others aware of Oneida's needs and take some of the financial load off his shoulders. One that up to this time simply hadn't existed. The Lord was surely in this and it was an answer to his prayers—but he didn't know it yet. It came in a letter from James H. Cox, Associate Editor of the *Western Recorder*.

I want to inform you of an advertising package Western Recorder has put together of offer a permanent, weekly voice for KBC institutions going into 60,000 Baptist households across Kentucky every week. We believe it may be a significant break-through for the communications programs of several agencies. It was prepared at the request of one agency, but we believe it should be offered to the presidents and administrators of all others as well.

Basically, it involves a year-long commitment on the part of an institution to a significant amount of advertising space at a greatly reduced rate...

What could this mean to you? You might like having an editorial type column going into our Baptist homes weekly...Imagine the points you could get across and friends you could cultivate through weekly contact with so many Baptist readers.

The Lord works in mysterious ways his wonders to perform. This was one of those times; even the leaders at the *Western Recorder* didn't know what they had done for the future work of Oneida and the other small institutions, like Clear Creek and Glendale.

Every one of these 60,000 households represents an average of two to three readers. Can we help you get the things you want to say before them permanently?

Barkley quickly added it up—his mailing list of 34,000, plus 60,000 times three—214,000 hearts to touch for Oneida!

The cry of Barkley's heart was for just such an opportunity—had been those long hard years. It took his God to devise a way! Now he could share with his beloved Baptist friends his heart's desire, and occasionally his heart's cry.

On May 8 he received and signed the contract with the *Western Recorder*. The *Oneida Journal* was launched!

As soon as the first *Oneida Journal* appeared, it gained friends for the school. Letters poured in! Many with generous gifts.

In September he had a note from C. R. Daley, Editor of the *Recorder*:

> I feel that the column appearing in the *Western Recorder* this week, *How Green Was His Valley*, is the best one yet. If this isn't some of the best public relations money can buy, I'll eat my hat!
>
> I would be curious to know if you get responses to this particular column. It is a heart touching story that should motivate several people to give and give generously. I trust all of this is doing the job you want.
>
> Thanks for sharing this kind of story with all of us. It blesses our hearts, too.

How Green Was His Valley

A letter and a $350 gift to help support a scholarship for one of our girls came recently from Mrs. Matha Nolan of Lehigh Acres, Fla. She wrote in part: "Had it not been for Oneida, I would never have met Pearl Nolan, a wonderful product of your school and my late and beloved husband. He told me many times how the school was responsible for his education, and even for his life. He said he felt sure he would never have made it if he hadn't gotten the chance to go to Oneida.

The many letters from our friends show you were justified in giving that little redheaded freckle faced boy a chance. He was considered a valuable and good citizen. He always stood for the right as he saw it which was many times in his 70 years of life."

Paul Nolan graduated from Oneida in 1922, and his first job after leaving Oneida was as a printer's "devil". His entire life was in journalism. For most of his life he was a publisher of one or more newspapers. Several of Kentucky's most outstanding journalists began their careers under his tutelage.

Pearl, himself, began his newspaper career in Oneida's print shop helping to print our little monthly paper, the Mountaineer. Mrs. Nolan's letter caused us to look back in our files and find a letter from Mr. Nolan, written in 1942 as he sent a gift for a scholarship. It reads in part:

"I am reminded of the many pleasures and hardships at Oneida during the first World War. I remember our oatmeal without sugar at the dormitory. I remember how we sawed wood and dug coal to keep warm, and how we worked on the farm in the spring and summer, raising all kinds of crops and fruits and vegetables to take care of our winter needs.

"I wonder how many think as pleasantly now as I do of all of this...plowing and hoeing, driving the wagon, mowing and pitching hay, milking nine cows, janitoring and dozens of other things. More pleasantly than anything else I remember working on the *Mountaineer* by lamplight, sometimes until early in the morning, especially of kicking off a 40,000 run of a single issue, one page at a time on the old foot press. No wonder I could boast of my muscles, my ability to run and jump.

"How well I remember my first coming to Oneida, how I was singled out and taken to be fitted with second-hand clothes; how I had pellagra and the others were afraid to stay near me. I remember the time when I became discouraged and dissatisfied and on the way home meeting Prof. T. L. Britton and how he reached down from his horse and picked me up from the creek, saying, 'You are going back to school.'

"I also remember the lessons, and can still repeat many of the hundreds of poems and songs we memorized. We learned from books and from the lives of our teachers and from our own experience and struggle. I remember it all, the easy and the hard, and now everything is a pleasant memory about Oneida.

"I remember agreeably the speech Mrs. Russell, then president of the school, made about me, of how I had worked and paid all my way. But I have always felt that I still owe everything to Oneida and the good people who helped me. I am proud of being a product of Oneida, and that we live in a country where even the humblest and poorest has an opportunity to advance and make good.

"I realize that nothing is valuable unless it is worked for. The high ideals and principles instilled at Oneida have always stayed with me and have gone into my work wherever I have been."

These lines from Pearl written nearly 40 years ago suggest, "how green was his valley" at Oneida. His widow continues to invest in young lives here today knowing the dividends that came from such investments. A great-nephew of Pearl Nolan is one of our eighth-graders this year.

Western Recorder, September 1, 1980

Barkley was touched. He had many more wonderful stories to tell. The year 1980 saw progress all over campus, even more than Barkley had planned. In his correspondence with many hundreds he shared the good news. In words dancing across the page, as his typewriter spit them out, he told of the year past:

So much is happening here, I don't know where to begin. We've had a most busy summer: Gym totally rewired…stone prayer chapel built…new roof for girls' dorm…dining hall renovated…you would scarcely believe it…solid ceilings in boys' dorm…all rooms painted in lighter, brighter colors...total Anderson Hall Renovation under way...going to be something to see when it is finished...old one room school rebuilt on campus...center portion of Student Center being used as study hall, so net gain of three classrooms...varsity dorm air-conditioned...beds painted...shop building well organized... barber-beauty shop in full operation; apartment for single staff on second floor Brittan house...firehouse completed, painted...Old-fashioned supper to pay off new fire truck...7,500 flowers in bloom... more work on Allen Trail behind Chapel...Miss Wilson's memorial plaque in place...memorial column made of old Marvin Hall brick near old Melrose Hall...much new shrubbery planted. It has been a very busy time.

We lost two teachers and added six...smoothest and best opening since I've been here as President. Oh, yes, we have put new ceiling in church sanctuary; new guttering; and getting ready to paint there. *Letters,* 1981

And then there was a letter to former teachers Laura Neil Mobley and Bill Branan, in response to a beautiful Christmas card that she had designed and painted herself, just for him. There was news he wouldn't mention in full ever again.

I love your card. I am tired. Sometimes discouraged, though an activist and optimist at heart, I don't allow myself to get "down" too often. But I was unexpectedly hospitalized for several days while on a speaking trip to Owensboro a year ago (kidney stone attack...had no idea I had such a problem.), and then was rushed to Lexington hospital in June and was hospitalized for about a week... they thought initially I was having a heart attack. But it turns out I've got some lung damage caused by they don't know what... perhaps something I picked up in the many years in Iran: they said it was as though I had worked in a coal mine for forty years, etc. I was so tired this fall that I felt I couldn't make it through another year: I sensed that I was getting about where Miss Wilson was just before her death.

I got this inspiration to get the work load off myself…onto another. I would make Mrs. Erma Smith the Dean of Students… the position Mai Mai Sparks had held years ago. Mrs. Smith has five and one half years of incomparable 'experience' already in the dorm. The five house parents would report to her as well as the principal. She would have authority to expel students when necessary. And she would make the work assignments, a huge undertaking every week. I have very little to do with all that now…sometimes am not involved even ten minutes a day. I used to spend as many as ten or eleven hours daily with all that nitty-gritty, exhausted emotionally and physically and harassed with all the other things I needed to be doing and couldn't get to.

She relieved me of all that burden, so I'm beginning to get a "second wind" back and putting my attention more fully on other things that have always needed doing. (This very likely saved my life.)

He labored on, knowing his Time was in God's Hands. He would make it count FOR TIME AND ETERNITY.

As in every Christmas past he anticipated the festivities that led up to Christmas Eve—and this year the joy he felt in every moment was deepened—from the special Christmas emphasis—chapel every day to the special dorm activities—to the Sanctuary choir performance—to the Oneida Choir Christmas "Special"—to that final night with the faculty at his home.

And as it had been now for several years, Old Man Winter brought them a snow early in December. Theirs had been a wintry wonderland with kids frolicking in the snow, having many a snow ball fight, mussing the clean snow with trails all over the campus. They had all left now and he felt quite alone, but he really wasn't. There were four of his boys at his home on the hill waiting for him. Thirty-nine-year-old President Barkley Moore gathered his rumpled coat from the old leather sofa in his office, locked the door and headed into the cold night.

The hills had been dusted again with fresh snow and the little village of Oneida lay as still, in its fresh blanket of snow, as the babe in the manger had lain in its fresh blanket of straw, that night so long ago.

In the morning Barkley and the four remaining boys (including Kevin, then a student at Oneida, the son of his dearest friends, Bill Gene and Peggy Smith) climbed into his red Cavalier with him and drove to their home in Sebring, Florida. They stayed the entire week. Those days were a balm to him!

He came back to Oneida refreshed, ready for the coming year. Soon afterward he wrote thanking them.

First of all, there are no words to express our appreciation for your wonderful hospitality for the FIVE of us. I can really think of no one who could have taken care of so many of us for an entire week with such GRACIOUSNESS and seeming ease…though I know it was much, much work on you and some strain though you gave no sign of such. I enjoyed all of it and the boys did also. As Kevin has reported I'm sure, we had a good and uneventful trip home.

1981-82
Year 10

My decision to write Oneida Journal *weekly in the* Western Recorder *is one of the most effective things I've done during the nine years of my stewardship as Oneida's president.*
—Barkley Moore

The final semester of school opened on January 7, with the highest enrollment ever, over 350 students by the time they all arrived and were settled in, with twenty-five new students. It seemed they couldn't get through January without snow and several cases of the flu. Barkley caught it that year. With no time to stop, he battled it for most of the month. Unless he literally had to lie down, he plowed on with interviews, "touring" and the "catching up" with Christmas mail, etc. There were thank you letters waiting for him to sign that took over two hours when he finally had the time to sit down.

They had received more money than the past years at Christmas and he was pleased. He wrote to Bill Gene and Peggy, "If we could have about three more Christmases, we would be caught up with our bills."

With inflation at 15% the previous year, with the second largest enrollment ever, the year had ended with the increase in expenses held to 1.9%. Gifts had been up 15.4%. For the first time in eighty-two years, the school had finished an academic year with more students than it had started with and that was with the largest enrollment ever, living on campus. The *Western Recorder* articles had been before Kentucky Baptist for just over six months now.

Barkley wrote to Jim Cox at the *Western Recorder*:

> My decision to write *Oneida Journal* weekly in the *Western Recorder* is one of the most effective things I've done during the nine years of my stewardship as Oneida's president.
>
> I make that statement because of the splendid response we've had. I have had scores of letters. Most have come from people we've never had contact with before. Many send gifts which are, for the most part, "first time" gifts. Others express prayer support.
>
> The effect of our column couldn't be better expressed than in a letter from Pauline Summers of Lexington which came in January. She wrote: "Dear Sir, until your column came out in the *RECORDER*, Oneida School was a dim, far off school, somewhere in the Kentucky Mountains. Now, it's made very real and the word pictures you have written for six months are most interesting and inspiring. I look forward to reading them every week. This way of writing about each Baptist school regularly should have been done in this manner, down through the years of the *Recorder*. I hope it continues. Each article has been a sermon. I hope to visit there one day. God bless all your work."
>
> Cordelia Hazelrigg of Owensboro recently expressed sentiments almost word for word that of many others who have written: "I enjoy your writing in the *Western Recorder*. I look forward to reading them. I wish I could come to visit you. You are doing a great work."

He found himself saying, as he had often heard Mai Mai Sparks say, "God works in mysterious ways His wonders to perform." In hindsight, one could see the divine hand of God at work. This could well have been the breaking point for Barkley and perhaps even Oneida if some of the physical stress and mental stress had not been removed. With his energy drained and physical health at risk, he could not have mounted the all-out campaign for funds such as he had done in 1972 without killing himself. This was indeed in God's timing.

Institutions like Oneida all over the country were fighting to stay open, and the economy was still in turmoil, with unemployment over six percent. The days ahead were still not smooth sailing. (Jimmy Carter lost the presidency to Ronald Reagan, and, as always when there is an administration change, everyone seemed to hold back on spending until the future seemed clearer.) In 1980 the *Richmond Times-Dispatch*, Richmond, Virginia ran a report on the problem, *Private Schools Feel Pinch of Inflation*. It reported private schools closing because of inflation: "Not a single school in the state wasn't feeling enormous financial pressure. Only the wealthiest, with the richest clients, could afford to stay open." The article said the years ahead would be even rougher. Only the older, more prestigious schools that appealed to the upper and middle classes would ride out the economic increase from the past year's increase in tuition.

The mere fact that Oneida had come through was a miracle. But Oneida had not only come through, Oneida was growing in every direction. That bespoke the fact that God's hand was on Barkley Moore and on Oneida Baptist Institute. His blessing was on the Oneida Baptist Church as well!

Barkley's plans for the coming year were to sit tight, hire no new staff, and wait to see what happened with the economy. He was still thrilled with how much money volunteers had saved the school. It had amounted to tens of thousands already. They were being lined up every day now to help all the way through summer. That year instead of adding to the campus he had plans to start a major over-hall of different facilities and their use; get classrooms in better locations for their use; re-arrange the gym's locker rooms. In the next few weeks he planned to convert a large room to a commissary for students and staff and enlarge the concession stand; convert the print shop to a space six times larger by removing walls; build two more classrooms in the gym; enlarge the art room, build offices for two coaches. All this to be done with volunteers.

By March, with all the best efforts to cut back in every way possible, the school was behind with the bills by $116,000. It was frightful to him but not nearly as overwhelming as it used to feel. At this point that was only one month's operating expense. He had faith to believe the Lord would send the money. Instead of panicking and jumping into action, he waited patiently and kept on with what they the Institute could do for itself.

During the year before the Oneida Baptist Church had called a new pastor, Rev. Joel Rackley. Barkley had already decided that Joel was the "finest and most like Brother Lyn Claybrook", whom he put at the top of the list. His wife Betty was an Oneida alumna. Barkley was overjoyed at the work they were doing. The church was growing. Much had been added to the program. There were special services for Christmas Eve and a two hour service for Good Friday. There were church suppers and the choir was going again. Perhaps the most wonderful change was the chimes playing again all through the day.

March was the time for spring revival and everyone had been praying, led by Brother Rackley's efforts at the church and on campus as he ministered to the students and staff. They had asked Rev. Denvis Rush, a pastor in the county for more than thirty years, to lead the revival.

Already that winter and spring the Lord had been moving in the hearts and lives of Oneida's students. Hardly a service went by that there weren't decisions made. Barkley and the staff had seen tremendous changes in lives of students for whom they had been praying. By mid March there were sixty five baptisms. Then they had special revival services—the formal revival had ended—but the revival did not end. On Saturday evening they had a "Billy Graham" movie and more decisions—and then more on the Sunday morning services—a total of twenty five more making professions of faith.

The revival continued on campus and in chapel. In chapel a group called Sacrifice of Praise sang. More decisions were made. Then a drama group that traveled all over the United States came and performed in chapel. More decisions were made. Mary Ratliff was one of those kids who made a profession of faith. She described sitting beside Mrs. Rackley and holding hands with her, as all the kids held hands across the pews, singing *We Will Know That We Have Been Revived When We Leave This Place.* She also remembered all the Christian girls in the dorm holding hands and walking around the dorm singing *The Walls of Jericho Came Tumbling Down* again, with Mrs. Rackley leading the girls as they marched.

April 5, 1981 would always be a special day in the memory of Barkley Moore and Brother Rackley. It was the day they had the largest baptismal service ever held at Oneida. More than eighty souls were baptized!

With the dogwoods blooming, the redbuds spreading their dazzling branches as a canopy over them in the moonlight, with the chimes ringing through the hills, the kids walked to the little Oneida Baptist Church. They walked in file, as in an army for their Lord, to a candlelight coronation service that the Girls In Action performed. Afterward the Lord's Supper was observed. Brother Rackley's sermon gave wonderful meaning to the bond they had in the Lord; a testimony that He, Christ, wanted them to always remember Him. It was such a significant service that they walked quietly back to their rooms, feeling the awe of what it meant for them that Christ had come! They would surely remember it for the rest of their lives.

The difference in the lives of the students was visible in its effect. Some of the kids for whom the staff had prayed for four to five years turned around completely, surrendering to the Lord. Without any one even suggesting it, a tremendous number of the kids destroyed their "rock" tapes. And the growth in their faith continued as Brother Rackley and the teachers worked with the kids. More would be saved in every service for the rest of the year.

On April 30 the work awards ceremony in the chapel saw many receiving "outstanding" and "good" awards. On May 3, a beautiful balmy day, the seniors had a steak dinner at the home of their sponsors, John and Hannah Sanderson, followed by ice cream and punch at Barkley's home on the hill. They sat under the towering trees with a million stars shining brightly in the Heavens above them.

On May 5 there was the annual Academic Awards Day ceremony in the chapel. The last chapel service was stunning—with the seniors in attendance and the Baptist Chorale, composed of music ministers of the Baptist churches of Kentucky, there for a special performance.

Sunday, May 10, Mother's Day, was Commencement Day at Oneida. Dr. Bill Hurt, pastor of First Baptist Church, Frankfort, Kentucky and father of one of the graduating seniors, preached the baccalaureate sermon. The graduation ceremony was in the afternoon where forty graduating seniors walked to the platform in the Melvin Davidson Chapel to be honored by President Barkley Moore as he handed them their diplomas. No one was left out—everyone was honored in some way—by Barkley as he told family and friends gathered in the chapel—many wonderful things they might never have known about their own sons and daughters!

To that euphoric climate, the precious volunteers were arriving by the day to join in the work of the Lord at Oneida all that spring, summer and fall—offering multiple thousands of dollars of labor so the school would be able to go forward with its programs, better prepared to handle all these young people's needs. And their presence would be desperately needed just days from then!

God had brought Oneida though another academic year. The students, including the sixth and seventh grade children were all safely home. Just a few days later, a fire burned down the younger boys' dorm, Hensley Hall. It was a $375,000 dollar loss. It had been in use just two years. The fire broke out in the night, and burned for hours before anyone knew it. Apparently it was caused by a short in one of the fluorescent lights that was left on in the shop below the upstairs boy's rooms. Had the fire occurred just a few days earlier, the building would have been filled with sleeping boys. Yes, God had worked once again; He had spared the lives of Oneida's youngest boys and girls. This reconfirmed his belief that miracles still happen. And what of those dozens of volunteers, already there, ready to help!

It was time to rebuild! While Barkley disliked having to ask for help so frequently, there simply wasn't enough money to begin to cover this loss, even with insurance. It was time to speak up!

It was imperative that the building be rebuilt and as quickly as possible. With camp season and summer school both starting in just a few weeks, they had to start turning down students right then.

The school had lost thousands of dollars worth of maintenance equipment and supplies. He had to call on Oneida's friends for help. But, now, because of his weekly *Oneida Journal* and the mailing list with 34,000 names, he was prepared to take immediate action and he did, both with a letter and an article in the *Western Recorder*. It seemed a miracle that he could communicate to so many, that very week, their need. It was with a great sense of God's timing once again that he wrote a cry for help! God's people started responding immediately. They showered the school with help of every kind. It was a time to love your neighbor as yourself—and neighbors of Oneida from the four corners of the land reached out to help.

So what could have been a disaster turned out to be a time of PRAISE for all the good things that came from the flames in the night. "God knew the plans He had made (for Oneida and its tired president)... plans to prosper, not harm."

The summer session went on almost as though nothing had happened financially. However, to say that it wasn't one busy, hectic place would have been the understatement of the summer!

In the middle of camps, summer school, restoration, and building going on all over the campus, Barkley and a busload of Oneidians embarked on a fun and restorative mission, to help Barkley rejoice and celebrate. It was a time to receive acclaim. Everyone was proud to celebrate with him as Cumberland College bestowed on him the Doctorate of Law. He had said of himself that he was a drop-out! But of what had he dropped out? He had dropped out of a promising career in the Law or an important position in the political who's who of America. He had dropped out to be in the service of the poor, the drop outs, the unloved, the helpless, the lost, the bright, the not-so bright boys and girls of America and lands beyond! He had dropped out to cultivate the "diamond fields" he saw in the faces of boys and girls, looking up to him, pleading for the chance to be "somebody"!

But depend on one of the kids to set the record straight. One of his former students, now a smart-mouthed college kid, said he had earned an "ornery degree". That had been said in front of over 200 who had come to celebrate the new Dr. Moore's fortieth-birthday party, given by the College for his friends, former students, family. They all laughed uproariously! Dr. James B. Graham, State Auditor and former State Superintendant of Public Education, led the group in singing an uproarious Happy Birthday! (Which leads one to ask, did any of those believe he never had any fun while working all those sixteen-hour days, never taking time away from Oneida work?) With his family, his mother, father, sister Gloria (she received her degree from Cumberland that very same day), and his friends there beside him, *his work was his fun*!

The weekend before that, Barkley and all the Oneida staff had had a wonderful twenty-four-hour retreat on the campus of Chilhowee Baptist Academy in Tennessee. The morning session would have been hard to describe except to say that most of the group had been in tears several times.

Theirs was a great, difficult, frustrating, challenging, thrilling, effort, working with hundreds of great, difficult, challenging, thrilling, frustrating teenagers filled with all the energy of youth! They deserved this time of retreat.

They came back to the opening of school, refreshed, ready to meet the challenge of 425 boys and girls waiting to be enrolled. It was the largest enrollment of the school's history.

Barkley, ever upbeat, thought it was the finest, smoothest opening he had ever seen—fewer problems, with only about five leaving in the first month because of "home sickness", when normally it would have been about twenty five in the opening month. It seemed odd to him that this should be. But it was! They were all thankful!

And then they were at it again—teachers teaching—cooks cooking—maintenance guys mending—the office staff humming away. Barkley was giving the "Tour". Everyone on the farm was busy digging bushels and bushels of potatoes—nursing baby calves—feeding rambunctious piglets. They had so many more mouths to feed. And those young people could and did eat—three times every day!

October 10—Homecoming was upon them once again. The sun rose over Little Bullskin's hills bright and clear. The morning air, crisp from a heavy frost, filled Barkley's lungs as he rushed here and there upon first light. It was one of those days one can almost see to forever! The sumac was crimson, the dogwoods clothed in deepest purple, their berries red as blood, the oaks a blaze of majestic gold, the maples clothed in bright yellow, splashed with orange. The dewy grass was still a carpet of lush, deepest green under his feet. He could see the low valleys of the farm, with the rows of brown corn stalks still standing in the fields, hear the pigs oinking, the cows mooing in the distance. There could not be a better day than this one, he thought. For just a moment he stood looking at the glory of it all.

In just a few hours hundreds of Oneida's family members would be coming back home to attend the Homecoming. Former Governor Bert Combs, a Clay County boy; Mrs. Margaret Brenner Burns, widow of Oneida's founder, a noted professional musician, still very active at eighty-six; former principal Hugh L. Spurlock (1932-47), who retired in 1976 after twenty-five years as manager of the multi-million dollar East Kentucky Electric Co-op; Mallie and Baxter Bledsoe and the family of Ezra Webb, who would be recognized for their forty-eight years as superintendents of the Clay County Public Schools; and James Benner Burns, the only living son of Oneida's founder, recently retired after thirty years of service in the U.S. State Department, performing diplomatic missions in many countries. All of these would play their different roles but the thought of Mrs. James Anderson Burns giving two piano concerts gave him the greatest joy.

The aroma of slow-roasting pigs in the huge fire pit (built just for this purpose) under the largest, shadiest trees, with space enough for hundreds to gather, was wafting all over campus. He knew the barbecue was underway! He could see the tables and chairs already in place.

He stopped by the kitchen next—there was food enough to feed an army being prepared and made ready to be served all over campus. Tea and cookies by the hundreds were ready and on trays to be whisked to Anderson Hall for the reception tea that was to be ongoing all through the day! Satisfied that no one would go hungry, he went to Sylvia Russell Hall, where his staff were busy setting up tables, including a sign-in table with name tags, programs, etc. Separate tables were being stacked high with the new book, *Dawn Comes to the Mountains.*

He was ready as the first guest arrived to begin his now famous "TOUR". He knew at least for this day he could still leave all his guests out of breath as he gave the "TOUR" over and over and over!

They sang, played, cried, ate, hugged, loved, remembered, read *Dawn Comes to the Mountains* from "kiver to kiver". This was the "right time" to do each.

As Homecoming came to an end, the hectic pace of finishing up all the projects begun in the spring made one think of a grandfather clock that had been set in motion by workers at the North Pole who were running behind—with Santa leaving so soon, they ran back and reset it to Zoom Mode. For that was how it was that year for all the busy volunteers. The clock went tick, tick, tick, tock!

By Christmas every project they had started was finished. They had built two new classrooms, moved the weight room and all its equipment to a new location, moved the wrestling and fencing equipment to a new room, expanded the concession stand, tiled, put up fireboard, added a wash basin, in general made it pretty fancy. They had converted the student center into a temporary boys dorm with all new beds and mattresses, redecorated the girls' lobby, added speakers and music system to dining room, landscaped the stone prayer chapel with stonework, torn down the inside walls of the burned dorm, and were in the process of putting a roof back on it. Yes, these volunteers had the right to be proud of themselves. By the end of the second week of December they were all gone—and right behind them all the boys and girls flew away "home for Christmas".

The joy of the Christmas season was dampened on Christmas Eve when Barkley's assistant for the past eight years, James Boswell, had a severe heart attack. He was taken to the hospital and it appeared he would be all right with lifestyle modifications. Mr. Boswell would comply faithfully, of that Barkley was sure. With nothing more he could do at the moment—Barkley heaved a sigh of relief, happy to climb the hill home—this year to find his mother, father, and sister all gathered around a glowing fire. How he treasured their presence! God had brought his parents to be with him in their retirement years and Gloria, having graduated from Cumberland, had also come home.

Barkley was surrounded by the people who cared for him most deeply in this world. His parents would be there, in the background; aiding him, upholding him, maintaining his home, tending it, turning it into a serene retreat not only for Barkley but the hundreds of guests he would endlessly bring to their door. Mrs. Moore would gladly entertain hundreds of guests he perfunctorily brought "home", cooking, washing bed linens, towels, by the boat load, every day for the rest of his life.

But for this Christmas, for just a few hours, it was just the four of them! How they enjoyed those hours together.

1982-83
Year 11

I turned 40 in August…and still haven't quite grasped that. I still think I'm 16. Don't know where these years have gone. Every day of them all has been packed with things to do. Don't think I would change too many of them if I had it all to do over. Just wish there were more hours in the day or that I could be two or three people.
— Barkley Moore

O n January 4, 1982, Barkley wrote to Dr. and Mrs. Furman Daniel, in Greenwood, South Carolina:

It is hard to believe, but we are into second semester with many new students arriving after Christmas. I have never seen a school year go by so very rapidly.

Well, 1981 is past and we are now in 1982. I pray for our boys and girls, and for each of our staff. My devoted assistant of the past eight years, James Boswell, had a severe heart attack on Christmas Eve. Please pray for him and his family. Speaking of Christmas, it was the busiest I can ever remember. The mail was quite heavy and we were busy mailing out hundreds of copies of our newly published book, *Dawn Comes to the Mountains.*

He thanked him for a generous $1000 gift and wished him a "HAPPY NEW YEAR".

They had been frantically busy and still were the rest of January transitioning into the spring semester. There were 425 students, seventy-five more that the year before. The trustees had voted in the fall meeting to build a new boys' dorm that would house ninety, to replace the one that burned; the old building would be converted to a maintenance/industrial arts facility. Work had already started up again on that and the new boys dorm, started back in September, with much volunteer help (and no paid contractor) was now two months ahead of schedule. It would be named for Preston and Ruby Baker, long connected to Oneida the school and to the Oneida community.

But no matter how busy he was, Barkley continued to write beautiful letters of sympathy when an extended-family member (he considered all who had given any size of gift to the school to be a family member) lost a loved one. Barkley's life in letters was an affirmation of his deep, compassionate, spiritual inner man, though unknown to any, except those who received them and were blessed by them. There were so many of these warm, caring letters interspersed with all the other letters that went out daily—letters that could have easily been handled by a formal card or form letter sent out by the school. All his life back to a six-year-old boy, who himself lost his little brother, "Babe", would be marked forward with compassion for the heartbroken. He knew the compassion of his Master and ever shared it—he knew the hope of Heaven from firsthand experience and with that hope he continued to comfort others.

It is in that life of letters one gets to know the real saint of God; his daily triumphs, dreams, hopes, struggles. It is in those deep moments when he was alone with God, alone with his thoughts of his friends, that one sees into his soul. For there he pours it out! He was quick to admit his failures, ask forgiveness for being late or overdue because his ever pressing duties to: students, teachers, staff, community, guests, were always present. (Most times he wrote those letters somewhere between midnight and 3:00 AM.) Who among us wouldn't have been sleeping soundly? And yet the pages were filling up his life, a silent testimony of who Barkley Moore was. There are thousands which cannot be shared for lack of space. But God was recording each in His book of Barkley's life and someday they will be on display for all to see! Barkley loved to sing, *When We All Get to Heaven, What a Day of Rejoicing That Will*

Be. He grasped, like John the disciple, who saw a vision of Heaven, that Heaven was a real place! It was as natural for he, who had studied history and the law, to see that Heaven would hold recordings of man's time on earth. He was writing volumes of heavenly books and one day when he got to Heaven, he would have the time to re-read them. He would have time to read to his heart's content *In the Garden* lit by the *Heavenly Sunshine* of his Savior.

He wrote to Frances and Andy Clark, dear Oneida friends of many years.

> Here I am at midnight Sunday answering your Christmas letter. That is about how far behind I am with everything! I spent all of 1981 plodding around the Oneida Campus trying to nudge things forward a bit more. I just dart out and back for speaking engagements…made no other trips during the entire year, often getting back at 3:00-4:00 AM and another day at dear old OBI
>
> I turned 40 in August…and still haven't quite grasped that. I still think I'm 16. Don't know where these years have gone. Every day of them all has been packed with things to do. Don't think I would change too many of them if I had it all to do over. Just wish there were more hours in the day or that I could be two or three people.

And then he gave them a written version of the "Tour". Think what it would be like if you were jogging behind him and he added all the present buildings and gave you their history, and should any boy, girl, or any of the staff happened along, you also hear of their glowing present and future potential. Go along at your own risk! If there were seventy present you'd need to find your spot. If you happened to be there by yourself, you'd better really put on your jogging shoes. You'd be in for the fastest forty minutes of your life, jogging to keep up—but no, there wouldn't be a test at the end, but you would know a lot about Oneida Institute, its program, its young people, and its campus. You'd start at the entrance to the campus, from Mulberry Street, at Hensley Hall where the maintenance shop used to stand. Let's assume you had last visited nine years before.

We lost our newest boys dorm and maintenance shop three days after school was out by fire. Lost the second story of the building completely, the first floor was gutted though we managed to salvage the outer walls. We lost about $150,000 in equipment. But have a roof back over those first floor walls. In the next three or four months plan to move our print shop to that building and have a five times larger shop, to have our own laundry and dry cleaners on campus, and restore our own barber-beauty shop that was lost in the fire. In the meantime, we have converted the Student center into a dorm for forty. Also, we are building another dorm that will house 100. It will be our first air-conditioned, carpeted dorm. It will have a large recreation room, four study room, four restroom-shower-laundry rooms, and two staff apartments: each with two bedrooms, living-dining-room-kitchen combination and bath. This new building should be finished in about three or four months. Since I last recall your visiting with me...about eight years ago...we have added nine larger or smaller buildings and much, much housing.

We now own the entire two blocks stretching from the main campus to include the lot where the old hospital used to stand. We own everything in that except for six houses. Also, we own all of Mulberry Street on the other side (where the new Chapel is) except for one house and barn. We have a staff of 70 this year, 425 students, and operating expenses will run about $1,400,000 ($150,000 of this from the Cooperative Program) as compared to $200,000 when I first came here. Much of that is inflation, much is growth. In the past year and half we have had nearly 250 professions of faith. We now have a daily service 30-40 minutes each morning year round with everyone attending, and since last March have had a nightly service, seven nights weekly, just before bedtime with 50-150 attending on any given night. The Lord is blessing in many ways.

In the past three years, our kids have been in 16 state tournaments, winning 3 state championships, runner-up in three others. We printed 3,000 copies of *DAWN COMES TO THE MOUNTAINS* and we are already preparing a SECOND printing. People seem to like it. During this year, we hope to get another book printed for

which we have the manuscript. It will be quite different from this one. Also, I hope to reprint the *CRUCIBLE*. This latter two will be done in our own shop here…
Letters, 1982

And you and I know the plans he had for 1982. Barkley once said to someone, "If you know what the school is doing, you pretty much know what I am doing." So we know he was very busy, and that he was right there at Oneida—never taking a day off for himself—never getting eight hours of sleep.

And it was right there at Oneida while doing everything he could to show the love of Christ that he had to defend his methods at times, to other saints who thought he shouldn't be doing things the way a saint ought to be doing them.

He was in a right good argument with a Christian lady who thought Christian girls and boys ought not be placed in rooms with non-Christians. He wrote:

I disagree with you, Mrs. —, about having no Christian girls with non-Christian ones. I often do that trusting that the LIGHT will blot out the darkness—.that the Christian can win the non-Christian by word and example. The POWER that the Christian has IS greater than that of the non-Christian. If the non-Christians are to be shunned or isolated just with themselves, I think we are going to be greatly handicapped in winning them. You state the Bible is very plain about not having Christians and non-Christians rooming together, but I have not read it that way. I know that the Christian and the non-Christian should not marry thus entering into a permanent relationship together. But we are to WITNESS and we can live in the world without becoming of the world. There are kids here today who came loving their rock music…who have nothing to do with it today. If we had strictly prohibited their having such music, they would not have stayed a day. Had they not stayed we could not have, would not have, had the opportunity to witness and win them to the Lord. Now, you may disagree with that approach, but it has worked in many instance and the "angels of heaven would have rejoiced over each one reached." We cannot MAKE people believe as we do. They can only be won by the reflection of that love God had for us in sending His son, and the love of Jesus who died for us. He often associated with those despised by the religious…the woman at the well, old Zacchaeus in the tree. Because of his love, his concern, his willingness to so associate…His being able to see beyond what each one was to what they MIGHT be—that each came to a saving knowledge of the Lord Jesus. We accept "potheads", "hard rock lovers", "cussers", etc. for the same reason. The Gospel is then shared DAILY. We can only sew the seed. The Holy Spirit must reap the harvest. Sometimes, oft times the seed is fallen on hard ground. But, we must continue to sow.

Letters, 1982

And that they did, through a beautiful mild winter and early spring, a real relief from the past years of bitter cold, ice and snow, never missing a chance to mentor these boys and girls.

By March the ancient tulip tree that usually bloomed too early was in glorious bloom, but this year its blossoms would survive through April. It was a joy to walk the campus with dogwoods, redbuds, and now hundreds of tulips, planted by Mr. Cooper, in bloom everywhere he looked. He wrote Dr. Franklin Owen, "Now would be a wonderful time for you and Miss Muppet to get away…and head for the hills." In other words, come and speak in chapel!

On a serious note, he was thrilled that Dr. Owen planned to recommend the amount of stateside funds for Christian Education be upped to 38%. He expressed his great appreciation for his efforts and his friendship to Oneida:

> You have taken much more personal interest, have visited here far more frequently, than any previous Executive Secretary. In fact, I suspect you have made more visits to our campus than all the others put together in the history of the Convention.

And in this lovely month, he was to hear from someone who would serve the school many years after he was gone. Mrs. Kay Underwood, a graduate of Oneida, sent from Loveland, Ohio a gift of $300 in memory of Miss Wilson, Harlan Woods, and Rev. D. Chester Sparks. He said in his letter to her:

> God doeth all things well…and I know you are thankful for the years He shared these friends with you. Do keep our Lord's work in this place in your prayers, as you will be so remembered in the days and weeks ahead.

It was spring and all the activities associated with spring sports started. Nearly 500 students were active all over campus. The baseball, softball, tract, and the tennis courts were humming with activity all day long. When he looked toward the farm he could see the tractors turning acres into fresh plowed ground, being made ready for planting. It was a wonderful time to be alive!

During that April, he was in communication with Berea College about documenting Oneida's records. Ever the historian, it was critical to him that the files he had carted around, stashed in his parents home, and protected in general ever since he was a high school student there twenty some years ago be permanently protected. In the months ahead that documenting would be accomplished through 1982. Mrs. Myrtle Webb Cooke, an Oneida alumna, had come to be guidance counselor, and he would also hand this over to her, knowing she was the one both capable and interested enough to want to help him in preserving the schools records.

The month of May began with his sister, Gloria, marrying Ronald Bowling, a fine young man from Twisting Sourwood Creek in Leslie County. Their wedding was on the fifth anniversary of their graduation. It was in the same chapel where they had graduated, the Melvin Davidson Chapel, right above his office in Sylvia Russell Hall.

It was indeed a wonderful year for Oneida and he in almost all respects. The choir sang in May at the World's Fair in Knoxville, Tennessee. Barkley was so proud of that year's choir. They traveled far and wide to perform—and everywhere they sang they amazed people—"they are that good."

He hosted the senior "cookout" at his home, with his mother cooking up a feast, the grill's smoke wafting over the hills. The next evening the drama group presented Agatha Christie's *Ten Little Indians*.

It was hard to contemplate letting go the most "remarkable class we have had in many, many years in terms of academic, athletic, extra-curricular achievement and CHARACTER." Many had been at Oneida five-six-seven years—but "that was what it was all about."

Hard as it was to let them go as soon as the kids left, everyone else was soon busy with farming, construction, maintenance, getting ready for summer school and camps. They were swamped with applications for summer school and the fall semester. Barkley wrote:

> Things are just HAPPENING. I am a little amazed at times... have a stronger faith in God than I had ten years ago even though I wasn't exactly weak-kneed in that area then.

By August they would have new computer courses in place, with $17,000 worth of new equipment. There would be two new staff with their doctorate degrees—and work would have begun in the community on a new million dollar bridge. They would have the Double-Creek one room school painted with two fresh coats "administered to those ancient poplars and the building gleaming white again". There would be new drapery hanging on every window in Burns Hall (girls' dorm) and also in Carnahan Hall and Marvin-Wheeler Hall (boys' dorms). They would have added eight new seventy by fourteen foot wide custom trailers for staff housing. They would have totally refurnished Anderson Hall, the school's stateliest house with the school's own furniture, rather than that of the staff, as it had been done in the past. And they would have built a cyclone fence around Burns-Wells Hall, a faculty facility where so many small children played on the lawn, could play with less danger of one of them darting into the street.

One could almost hear Barkley say:

We mustn't forget that in the middle of all this, the largest summer session of classes ever were going on…also a large Mountain Missions Conference with several hundred in attendance for a week, RA-GA camps, several large work camps…one from Alabama and one from Pulaski Association. It was like a bee-hive. Nor must we forget all the farming, acres of grass regularly mowed, flowers to be cared for, cooking, *etc*.

Homecoming was Saturday, October 9, with over 1200 alumni, friends, parents, students and staff on campus during one or more events. The new Baker Hall dorm for boys was dedicated at 4:00 PM on Saturday. There were so many back that Barkley and others hadn't seen for years. They came from as far away as California, New York, Florida and so many states.

The day was filled to the brim with activities. The October weather was delightful! Cool nights and a crisp snappiness in the air tinged the days. The pungent fragrance of fall filled the golden leaves floating through the air and every one was caught up in the exuberance of the seeing old roommates, singing 'til their lungs nearly burst at the hymn sing, hearing Dr. George Redding preach, watching the student drama production of "Harvey", listening to an Oneida Band Concert, watching exhibition games of the varsity basketball, soccer, swimming, diving teams. When they weren't sitting, eating or singing, they were playing: alumni players against the younger generation. Barkley was even busier than the guests, as were the staff, serving in the background. During most of this, he was in warp mode zooming around campus, conducting the "Tour" at least a dozen times, in groups of dozens at a time, talking a mile a minute!

The fall revival came right on the hills of Homecoming. There were forty-two professions of faith and many re-dedications. Life at Oneida that year was not only "life preparing", but "life changing".

There was still much going on late into the winter months as they continued trying to prepare housing, fixing up rundown buildings, fencing areas that needed to be fenced. He was over come with pride when he saw his beloved farm manager, Mr. Zane Fraker, along with four volunteers and four boys working in a drizzling rain all day one Saturday, cutting enough poplar trees to make 300 fence posts. Where else but Oneida could one find such dedication to the cause?

While many private high schools closed all over the country, Oneida grew and flourished! While the country weathered out the worst recession since the Great Depression; while businesses faltered and many failed, while unemployment was at its worst, Barkley marched on ahead, knowing God had his backside! He never faltered nor failed in his duty to his boys and girls, the staff under his care, or his Lord. He kept the faith and kept on keeping on! While he may have quivered in his boots a few times, waiting for funds, he expected God would be along shortly. He didn't throw up his hands in panic nor let fear be seen on his face, nor heard in his voice.

At the beginning of December the school had $165,000 in bills, accumulating since August, and he had $3,000 in the checking account on the morning of December 3. His faith was still strong but he couldn't help being concerned. He wrote the trustees informing them of the situation and asked for their prayers.

In the middle of all these trials, in his spare minutes he was working on a book. Maybe the book was writing itself in his head as he counted the times they overcame enormous barriers. Its working title, *More Than Conquerors*, must have repeated itself in his thoughts as he daily saw real miracles take place. If anyone could write such a book, telling real stories, it should have been Barkley. It was to be a history, right up to the present day, of Oneida—not "dry" but full of human interest and inspirational, he hoped. He wanted to have it done in those "spare moments", to be finished by 1984-85. As far as this researcher has found out, there weren't enough spare moments, but the rough draft is probably tucked away somewhere—waiting to be discovered!

Christmas Eve was a beautiful sunshiny day after a night of rain. With the students gone, the campus was very quiet. But there were about twenty staff still around doing this and that. Mr. John Stidham, was virtually rebuilding the health clinic, during the holidays, making it ready for the new doctor. Barkley was already very impressed at how much he had accomplished and what a fine carpenter he was!

Barkley had so much on his mind, as he walked over to take a closer look and thank the men, he was barely able to think of all he wanted to thank them for doing. As he walked back toward the office he was thinking of what bills he must pay. Paying the bills was his ever present problem that fall and winter and one that preyed on his mind, when there were "moments" for doing so. Having an ever growing number of children from "poverty level" homes, parents who thought or said they could pay in August but hadn't, had left the school behind about $80,000 in the past four months—but that wasn't the only reason; with the deep recession and layoffs, giving had also been down for the same reason. He had been very pressed in the past four months with bills.

However, just before the Christmas break, he gave everyone his normal check. He had told the book-keeper to write checks for every nickel they had in the checking account. In fact, he had told her to write checks for a little over $5,000 for which he yet had no money and he had told her he would hold them until the money came. Now he sat in his office on December 24, having no idea when or how he would receive the money. The mail came. He opened a letter from Dr. Franklin Owen. With the letter was a check for $5,297, the last distribution of the Kentucky Baptist Convention for the 1981-82 budget year.

A tear or two must have fallen from his eyes! He immediately started a letter, his last for 1982, to Dr. Owen. In it he told him of the events of that last two days. He wrote:

> In the very next mail, your letter and your check came taking care of those checks written in faith, almost down to the very dollar! I was struck by the amount and also having no idea that we were to receive this. Some would call it coincidence. But you and I know better.
>
> I am grateful for what Kentucky Baptists do for us month by month, and I am grateful for the strong leadership you have given us the past ten years. I wish you and Miss Muppet the happiest of Christmas seasons and that 1983 will be filled with blessing for each of you and your loved ones.

For just a moment that Christmas Eve he walked from his office and looked up to the ancient hills, dressed in their bare gray robes, gnarled and old, wise, and weather-worn—their uplifted branches declaring the glory of their God. Yes, he would look up to these hills, not for help, but to be reminded by their towering peaks, their ancient age, that he served a majestic, powerful God, that He was just over the mountain where he could not see Him directly. But, he saw Him with the eyes of faith that Christmas Eve! He had a "mansion just over the hilltop, and one day yonder", he would "walk the streets of gold".

It was Christmas Eve! However, there was so much work to do, that he returned to his office, stayed there until 3:30 AM, went to bed on campus, and was back in his office at 9:30 AM Christmas Day. He worked until 2:30 PM, then wearily trudged up the hill to home where his mom had a wonderful Christmas dinner waiting, one my family and I were privileged to share. The house was aglow with fires lit in the hearths on two floors. We ate around an old round oak table in the dining room to the right of the entrance hall with a small cedar tree lit with red, blue, green, gold old fashioned lights, It was draped with an antique lace table cloth and lit with red candles and holly. From the kitchen behind the dining room Mrs. Moore served country ham, fried chicken, green beans, okra, mashed potatoes, fried corn bread pone with molasses. On the side board were cakes, pies, cookies, and chocolate covered cherries. And from the kitchen Mrs. Moore kept bringing hot, stout black coffee which everyone drank, especially Barkley's father; but not Barkley. Afterwards the guests went down to Professor Burns' old den, now Barkley's, a room richly paneled room with beans that stretched horizontally across the ceiling. At one end of the long room were books shelves filled to overflowing with history, law, philosophy, biographies, literature books, the books of a very well read and educated gentleman. The room's English style windows flanking the fireplace looked onto the west lawn and the forest beyond, where towering pines, laurel, oaks and a vast number of native American trees and scrub trees flanked the house and wound round the driveway coming into the property that Barkley owned.

There were Sheridan rocking chairs in deep red needlepoint, by the fire; a Classic Revival sofa on the inside wall in a rich brocade, and a big round coffee table laden with scrap books filled with Barkley pictures and articles on his years in Iran. On the antique walnut tables were hand made crocheted lace doilies, antique lamps with red crystal shades and more framed pictures. On the slabbed wood floor were Persian Rugs of silk and wool; Turkoman rugs, deep blood reds, the patterns woven into the rugs by the hands of Barkley's friends in Gonbad, Iran. Each Persian rug lying on the floor had taken months to weave; one or two of them would have taken over a year. Each rug was made of totally different pattern even though it might appear to be like another. Every Persian rug is like a song, each has a rhythm, cadence and tone. The person who made it might have observed things in nature or their imagination or surroundings that she then conveys into the pattern. (Information about Persian rugs was obtained from VaheedTaheri.com.)

One couldn't help but wonder what joy went into the weaving of those poor women in Gonbad as they made their beloved Barkley those thirty two rugs. For sure, their love was in those rugs in every knot they tied and there were hundreds of thousands of knots on that floor woven by the hands of poor Turkoman women sitting on the dirt floor of their small mud abodes or on the bare ground looking up to the vast mountains covered by trees in the distance high above Gonbad, many with peaks that rose out of sight into the clouds. Or were they looking into the plains at miles of arid near-desert, with endless blue sky above? We stayed for hours lingering by the fire, drinking hot chocolate and hot cider from warm mugs—long after Barkley and Dr. JoAnn Seymour left to return to the office where they worked from 7:00-10:00 PM on Christmas night.

Barkley Moore (dark shirt) as a grade-school student, with Preston Baker, Principal of Oneida Elementary School, and other students.

Barkley Moore, as a high-school student, with Rev. D. Chester Sparks, President of Oneida Baptist Institute.

Barkley Moore as a college student, working at
Oneida Baptist Institute as a volunteer.

Rev. D. Chester Sparks, President of Oneida Baptist
Institute, and Mrs. Sparks, Dean of the Institute
("Papa" and "Mai Mai"), 1948-1962.
(Reprinted from 1962 year book)

Mary Nancy Wilson (1908-1977), Barkley's dearest friend.
Devoted Servant of Christ
50 Years an Educator
In Life She Ever Refused Praise,
In Death She Is Too Great For It.
(Reprinted from author's 1962 yearbook. Note
partial signature of Miss Wilson.)

Barkley Moore, 5,000 miles from home, alone on a mountain range in the Turkoman area of Iran. He compared it to the mountainsides on Little Bullskin, in Clay County, Kentucky; although he was about eight hours by jeep from the Russian border, he felt at home! Note the nomad in the background looking at him—this stranger whom he would come to love and respect—this stranger who would be made an honorary citizen of Gonbad, Iran before he would leave—this stranger for whom "a thousand eyes would cry" six and a half years later.

One of Barkley Moore's adopted boys, Hamid, and Barkley, on his horse, "Oneida", taking a trip to one of the Persian villages, Dozane, a village of 1,700 on the mountain ranges outside Gonbad, Iran. There had never been a school there; he would start one. Barkley Moore, a Kentucky Baptist and a Royal Ambassador of the highest rank, was on a mission to love the children of Iran for his King, the Nazarene, who had traveled paths just as lonely, had walked deserts just as forbidding.

Barkley with kindergarten children in Gonbad, Iran.

Barkley (third from left. back row) on a
field trip with a group of students.

Barkley Moore, age 29, received the Algernon Sydney Sullivan Medallion on May 9, 1971 from the President of the University of Kentucky, Otis Singletary, for his service to the poor and needy children of Iran. The Sullivan Award is the highest honor given to a citizen for service to humanity. He was the youngest person to be so honored.

"He had gone there to live, but he had no furniture. He had gone there to be a community development worker, but he had no tools. All he had were two suitcases, three months of Peace Corps training, and the philosophy that 'with love all things become possible.' Apparently they were enough. For from that inconspicuous beginning has come one of the most inspiritng stories in the history of the Peace Corps." (David C. Swanston, *The Texas Baptist Standard*)

In Washington, D.C. on March 1, 1971. Vice President Hubert H. Humphrey celebrates the Peace Corps' Tenth Anniversary with Barkley Moore, "The Legend of the Peace Corps", along with 300 volunteers and other dignitaries, including Secretary of State William P. Rogers, Mrs. Sargent Shriver, and Mrs. Ethel Kennedy.

Barkley Moore and Senator Edward M. Kennedy at the celebration of the Peace Corps' tenth anniversary in Washington, D.C. in 1971. The story of "The Peace Corps volunteer who couldn't come home" because the citizens of Gonbad, Iran loved him so much they couldn't bear to let him go, nor could he bear to leave them, was retold many times.

Sargent Shriver (brother-in-law to the late President Kennedy), head of the Peace Corps, former Ambassador to France, and Vice-Presidential candidate, speaks to graduates at Oneida on May 26, 1974. (In photo, Sargent Shriver, Barkley Moore, and Rev. D. Chester Sparks.) "The reason for my coming here was to find out the reasons for his success."

Barkley (light shirt) and E. Gaines Davis Jr., Chairman,
Institute Board of Trustees, at groundbreaking
for one of Barkley's many new buildings.

Barkley with Preston Baker, a longtime friend of Oneida Baptist Institute and Chairman of the Board of Trustees. Barkley is wearing his Sullivan Award medallion, and holding the gavel used by James Anderson Burns on such occasions.

Barkley receiving an honorary doctorate (LLD) at
Cumberland College. Left to right: Dr. Joseph Early,
Academic Dean; Dr. Paul Estes, Trustee; Barkley; Dr.
Michael Colegrove, Registrar; Dr. Jim Taylor, President.
Dr. Taylor was one of Barkley's closest allies and friends.

Barkley with his family, Mrs. Evelyn Moore, Gloria, and Mr. Elwood Moore, shortly after Barkley's return from Iran.

Barkley at banquet, with Betty Hasty (left) and Lucy Bond.

Barkley Moore gives "The Tour" to a large group at a "Homecoming". This is the Allen Trail, named in honor of Ethan and Leah Allen. It winds up the mountain behind the chapel and leads to Cemetery Ridge. The founder of Oneida Institute, James Anderson Burns, and more than 300 other Institute people are buried there.

Barkley presenting diploma to happy graduating senior.

Barkley Moore speaking about Larry Allen Gritton, Jr., a straight A student and an outstanding Christian athlete, before handing him his diploma, at the graduation ceremony in 1993. In 2013 Rev. Gritton became Oneida's twelfth President.

Barkley with "Amir", one of his best Iranian students

Barkley with Rev. Devis Rush, Chairman,
Institute Board of Trustees.

Barkley, praising one of his students, declaring,
"This is what Oneida is all about!"

The monument reads:

GLENN BARKLEY MOORE

BORN AUGUST 8, 1941, DETROIT, MICHIGAN
DIED JANUARY 25, 1994, ONEIDA CAMPUS

ONEIDA VALEDICTORIAN 1958

GRADUATED, STUDIED LAW AND RECEIVED
SULLIVAN MEDALLION, UNIVERSITY OF KENTUCKY

HONORARY DEGREES CONFERRED BY
CUMBERLAND COLLEGE AND GEORGETOWN COLLEGE

PEACE CORPS IN IRAN, 6 YEARS, 4 MONTHS

PRESIDENT, ONEIDA BAPTIST INSTITUTE, 1972 – 1994

STUDENT BODY GREW FROM 100 TO 600
STAFF AND FACULTY GREW FROM 25 TO 150

SON OF
ELWOOD AND EVELYN PONDER MOORE

"HE EXERCISED GREAT FAITH
IN GOD AND PEOPLE"

Barkley's mother, Mrs. Evelyn Moore, beside the monument to Barkley in a memorial garden near Anderson Hall on the Oneida Baptist Institute campus

Barkley's mother, Mrs. Evelyn Moore, at Barkley's grave in Hensley Cemetery. The tombstone of the former student whose body was unclaimed is in the right foreground.

1983-84
Year 12

We have begun WITHOUT A DIME or THE PROMISE OF A DIME on this project…but we MUST have it. The Lord knows that we do, and we are moving forward with perfect confidence that He will provide, somehow, someway the needed money as we must have it.
—Barkley Moore

In January 1983 the doors of Oneida Baptist Institute opened to an even larger family of students and faculty and an ever growing cost of operating the school. It was now at over $1,700,000—starting at a mere $200,000 just eleven years ago. Forty more students than had left came bustling through the doors to be registered when the second semester opened. This brought the total to nearly 500, plus ninety staff. He was responsible for all of them.

Barkley was so thankful for the quality Christian people the Lord had sent him. He was also acutely aware of his responsibility to them. There were now added to their number Dr. and Mrs. George Redding. Dr. Redding had been Chair of the Religion Department at Georgetown College, and there were two new teachers he hadn't even known a month before. But, as he said, "Our blessed Lord has promised, '*Ask and ye shall receive, seek and ye shall find.*' It is exciting to see how God works out His purposes." Each day was an adventure with God at Oneida.

The number of classrooms had been expanded, in many cases by just rearranging or finding a better use of a space. Much of this had been done during the break between Christmas and opening of the new semester. He never knew for sure just how many more might just appear, but he could forecast pretty accurately by the inquiries being made. He would step out in faith, preparing the way for more boys and girls to have the opportunity to come. How could he look even one of them in the eye and say, we don't have a bed. And that was literally how he decided, if the student was a qualified candidate in his eyes. His standards for qualification basically meant answering the question: what would Christ do in this case? Oneida wasn't prepared for the seriously, mentally retarded or emotionally unstable or true delinquent who might bring other students into harm's way. Those he had to turn away, but that was a rare situation.

Opening day found Barkley sitting in his office with carpenters putting up a concrete wall through part of it to make it into two offices, the first one for him, the second one for Dr. JoAnn Seymour, who had come in July, to be his assistant, and was working in a cubby hole. She had worked all through the holiday break, helping him answer over 700 letters. It was surely a sacrifice to give up the big presidential office, but he didn't consider it so.

Dr. Seymour was soon appointed to head up the new curriculum study that Barkley considered at the top of the list for the coming years if they were to stay on the cutting edge academically.

With Barkley's help, the village of Oneida now had a doctor's office and a new doctor. How desperately both the village and school needed them! Whenever any student became ill, someone on his staff usually spent most of the day, on the road to the hospital emergency room or doctor's office, then sat for hours waiting to be seen—and this wasn't infrequent, with 500 boys and girls to be taken care of twenty-four hours a day. The village of Oneida also now boasted the completion of a large firehouse that had been built the year before—the finishing touches put on during the break and finished in January. During the month he would also finish up another efficiency apartment and purchase another seventy-foot by fourteen-foot specially built mobile home.

On the academic side, they added three more courses and a new study was begun to evaluate how to make the program even more effective. He hoped to have this done by August. The computer program had really advanced and now had more than $50,000 worth of equipment—and was open ten hours a day. By the end of January so many gifts had come that he had been able to miraculously pay off over $165,000! On January 30, 1983 he had only $32,000 accumulated bills on his desk. He wrote to the board of trustees, "What a difference from just two months ago." Yes, they were MORE THAN CONQUERORS through Christ!

It was no wonder that the *Western Recorder* was not getting the weekly articles on time! He was frustrating the poor assistant editor, James Cox, half to death. He got a snappy letter from him in February. "By the way—I wish you would do us a great favor and write eight or ten of these in advance and send them along." He continued, "I hate to have disturbed interns and a fiery typesetter breathing down my neck every week, but I am fast becoming accustomed to it. Please help!" If he ever got caught up in the next ten years it wasn't apparent to that poor assistant editor. He was praised every week for his contributions in making the column one of the most widely read and one of the best—but they continued periodically crying for "help". They couldn't not print it and he couldn't help being late.

Oneida's basketball team was making news all over the state with coach and principal Larry Gritton leading the team to victory with a 22-7 winning streak. They were praised by the *Lexington Herald-Leader* for "running and gunning" their way out of obscurity! What pride the whole school felt as they cheered their team on to victory. What pride Barkley felt toward his team. He could boast to every one of Mr. Gritton's success. After all he had had the good judgment to hire him.

He was soon writing his best friends Peggy and Bill Gene Smith of the success, just to rub it in as he had gotten a lot of teasing from time to time from them about his own, ah, let's say, lack of ability certainly as a player, but even as a team manager. They loved to keep him in place by telling the story. From 1954-55, while Barkley was in high school at Oneida he was the team manager. Well, let's let Peggy tell the story.

Barkley was never an athlete but he always enjoyed sports and participated in the OBI basketball program by being manager. He was working as a manager when the Mountaineers got to play their first game on the new hardwood floor of the D. Chester Sparks gym. He had been issued new mops and a special solution that he was to use to clean the floor prior to the first game. Not knowing exactly how much of the solution to use he saturated the new mops with the solution and proceeded to mop the new gym floor thirty minutes prior to the first game. As the Mountaineers ran onto the floor for their pre-game warm-up, they began to slip and slide and fall to the floor. Obviously, too much solution had been used and the game could not proceed until the excess was removed. What a sight to see the Oneida boys using quilts and blankets they had retrieved from their dorm rooms to get the floor in playing condition! Their efforts were successful, the first game on the hardwood was completed, and Barkley's career as a manager was salvaged!

(No one enjoyed telling this story more than Barkley himself!)

The Oneida Mountaineers gave the school a great deal to be proud of—and a lot of fun; in fact Barkley declared them to be "the-most-fun-to-watch" team ever seen. Whenever they played, people (including him) really enjoyed the team even if they went down to defeat. The girls' basketball team was doing a great job as well, even though they lost at Regionals. They ended the season with a record of 22-11. According to him it was the finest girls' season they had had.

One member of the wrestling team went all the way to state tournament in the heavyweight division. But for the first time in years the swim team didn't do so well; no one qualified for the state competition. The fencing team won the State championship again. The soccer team had an all-state player, Reza Cohan. All in all, that year Barkley could really boast that Oneida had the best athletic program in Kentucky.

A lot of things happened in March each year. The third quarter ended and the fourth quarter began. They would be able to see how many would be graduating. They were looking at 100 to graduate in May. (Ten years ago, twenty had graduated.) Also, the seniors took their trip to Washington during the final nine-day spring break. This would be the fourth year the seniors would also go to Colonial Williamsburg.

The print shop was very busy. They were setting the type for another book. It was *Mountain Rising* by Dr. Darrell Coleman Richardson. He had written a wonderfully readable book on the life and times of founder James Anderson Burns. Dr. Richardson was a Baptist minister, a bibliographer, and author of forty-four books.

In the early seventies Barkley had actively pursued Dr. Richardson when he learned he had many years before been to Oneida and trekked around the mountains with Mr. Britton, collecting data for a future book, yet unpublished. The two became corresponding buddies, with Dr. Richardson finally coming to Oneida to meet Barkley. It all culminated in the book that was about to be published. In May of that spring Richardson was at Oneida. He was every bit the "Old Tiger", dressed in the hunt khakis, safari shirt, and sun helmet as he and Barkley headed back to Bullskin looking for all the world as if they were on a hunt.

The spring semester ended in a whirl of activity and a flame of glory. They had the first Junior-Senior Banquet in many years. It was a beautiful occasion in an amazingly decorated gym. The juniors had worked for weeks raising money with a "slave" day, arm wrestling contest, a "gong" show and a spring carnival that lasted all day and included many, many fun activities. There was the end of year honor roll trip, and the last senior outing of the year at a home on Bullskin. Graduation ended for the eightieth time with ninety four young men and women going forth, many having been there from one to seven years.

Perhaps the most wonderful thing that happened that graduation weekend was that during the baccalaureate sermon one of the boys rose to make his profession of faith. The same boy drowned one week later at Frankfort trying to save his younger brother. He was from a Catholic background but the family asked Barkley to give the eulogy. The place was packed with hundreds standing in the aisles; in the audience were former Lieutenant Governor Waterfield and many other dignitaries.

Of course Barkley was involved with all of that for many weeks after graduation—answering many sad letters with encouraging words of hope.

But as the school year ended there were many, many more needs. There was a great need for at least six more classrooms. Barkley asked the Methodists who operated the Red Bird Mission some miles from Oneida to donate a used temporary-type building that would give them just that. He estimated it would take $7,000-$8,000 to move it, set it up, and repaint it. A $100,000 staff housing project was started on Bullskin. He needed to add twenty-five people to the staff. He wrote to many that spring on the mailing list, telling them of the needs—letting them know:

> We have begun WITHOUT A DIME or THE PROMISE OF A DIME on this project as we must have it. The Lord knows that we do, and we are moving forward with perfect confidence that He will provide, somehow, someway the needed money as we must have it… Come and see for yourselves what God is doing!

He was counting on the standing promises of God through his people to meet their needs.

On top of all that, by June the school had the largest enrollment for summer school ever. Over 200 young people and a staff of thirty-one working with them in the classrooms besides the support people—cooks, house parents, office, maintenance, *et cetera*. The 35th Annual Mountain Mission Conference, which lasted five days, saw several hundred there. During the summer months there were several other camp groups as well: work groups, a string instrument camp sponsored by the University of Kentucky and many others.

The Methodists did indeed give him the building and volunteers were busy getting it moved and converted into classrooms. It was all done by the opening of the fall semester.

In October Barkley reported to the many thousands of friends of Oneida:

> As you read this we are in revival services at Oneida. It was on a beautiful autumn Thursday morning 32 years ago that I accepted Jesus as my personal Savior and Lord. Pray that the lives of many of

our boys and girls might be secured for eternity this week. You are our partner in this ministry.

Homecoming is over and our first academic quarter has ended. This 84th year has gotten off to a very good start. Our Oneida family numbers approximately 600 souls. We have slightly over 100 staff members and nearly 500 girls and boys. That is the largest number ever on our campus. We are so thankful for each one.

We have had to make a conscious decision to add no more beds. With a nearly five-fold increase of enrollment in the past ten years, and a greatly accelerated increase in the past two years, we have had to look hard at the question: "Are we to be just another BIG school?" Our decision is "no". We think we have reached the right size. We are BIG enough to have a tremendous program, SMALL enough that both students and staff can KNOW one another. We live and work together as FAMILY.

You have helped us before. We hope you will be able to do so again. Over 300 of our young people are from poverty level situations. Can you help us to help each of them? Today?
Letters, 1983

At Christmas time that year he wrote to the hundreds who sent gifts:

Christmas is a wonderful time! We are reminded of the greatest gift the earth ever received, the coming of the Lord Jesus. God loved and He shared.

You have honored Him in this season of His birthday with your gift to his work here at ONEIDA.

The season got off to a special start with a fine concert in the chapel by the Cumberland College choir. There were activities right up to Homegoing for the students on the December 23. The festivities continued right up to Christmas day for the Oneida family who stayed behind including Barkley. The Oneida church, under Brother Rackley, put on an annual Christmas dinner in the church basement, honoring the international students, with the customs of differing lands shared.

There was a sweet Spirit in that place called ONEIDA as the little Oneida Baptist Church's chimes pealed through the cloudless night, "O little town of Bethlehem, how still we see thee lie, above the sweet and dreamless night the silent stars go by"—as the curtains of Heaven draped them in for the night!

1984-85
Year 13

Each child is somebody special. Each is potentially an Abraham Lincoln, a Mary Lou Retton, a Billy Graham. Whether such potential is realized, and the world blessed, depends on what others do. Yes…might even depend on what YOU do. Or fail to do.
—Barkley Moore

King Solomon wrote, "Then I observed that the basic motive for success is the driving force of envy and jealousy." (*Ecclesiastes* 4:4) Of Barkley Moore that could never be said. There is not one word in thousands of letters comparing himself to other ministries—nor wanting to be anywhere other than where he was, doing what he was doing. The standards he set for himself were to do the very best of which he was capable in everything to which he set his hand: in work, in word, in faith, in love, in forgiving, in generosity, in play, in humility, in suffering, in comforting; to lead by example. His abilities in all of these areas, perhaps with the exception of play, far exceeded, by any standard, by any expectations, anyone who ever knew him!

With every outgoing and oncoming year he grew in stature. With trials and tribulations, vexations of the spirit, tests of faith, and weariness in body and sometimes his very soul, he continued to put it all on the line for his Master's call to tend his Galilee, which was Oneida Baptist Institute. He continued offering up to God every thing in his might: to succeed not because of what others thought, or what others achieved, or any comparison of himself to others. His only question was: What Would Jesus Do? His only comparison: his Lord's Example.

The school year opening was so smooth it was weeks before they even had to have a faculty meeting. They were all in such one accord—living together, working together. It had taken $1,700,000 to operate the school the previous year and they were just about $40,000 behind when school opened, with all the bills paid from the past year, including a $100,000 bank note they had taken to secure 100% ownership in the gas well on the school's property, thereby saving a tremendous amount on the heat bill; the note had been repaid in less than four months. The building given by the Methodists at Redbird Mission to provide classrooms for the seventh and eighth grades was in total working operation, completely insulated, anchored to a concrete slab and bricked, for only $25,000 spent. It would be called Cardinal Hall in honor of the Red Bird Mission.

Work! They were working like beavers. The maintenance department had been working all during the break and had almost completed adding an addition behind and attached to the 140-year-old Burns Museum. This would house a 1,400-square-foot gift shop, where students' work—crafts, pillows, art, pottery, artifacts, aprons, *etc.*—as well as books printed by the school, books on Appalachia, color post cards of scenes on campus, stationary, and suitable items donated to the school would be for sale. The Museum curator was continually finding items, such as a bed that had belonged to James Anderson Burns, and many artifacts, furniture, and implements of the period.

The Friendship House, a new- and used-clothing store, would be opening January 25.

> We have made a beautiful 5-room used clothing store, carpeted, 4000 feet of shelving built, everything SIZED, organized into departments, everything with a price tag, a more organized way of taking care of student clothing needs, *etc.*
> *Letters*, 1984

It was named Friendship House in honor of all the friends of Oneida who gave in friendship their gifts of clothing to Oneida.

Barkley had hoped for a complete new facility for a central building to house the main offices, more class room space and also a complete new kitchen and dining facility, but that had not come to fruition. That spring he made plans to remodel the dinning and kitchen facilities. It was the greatest need the school had. The kitchen and dining facility were totally inadequate for meeting the needs of over 600 on a daily basis. The situation was almost intolerable. The kitchen and dining room, housed in James Anderson Burns Hall (girls' dorm), had been built in 1960, during the Sparks era, when the school had 130 enrolled. Barkley was going to completely overhaul both areas, expand the dining space to include two separate dining rooms and add a covered porch-walk the length of the kitchen to keep the waiting lines of students and guests in the dry, and he was going to add a student grill!

In no time at all he made the announcement in chapel that someone had offered the school a $50,000 gift toward the kitchen and dining room project, if the school could raise the same.

Never doubting that the funds could be raised for what would be a $450,000 addition, he sent the interior designer off to Lexington to consult with an architect. And while she was at it, "Look for bricks." On February 29, 50,000 pounds of bricks would arrive, and be kept on site until ready to be installed.

There were so many miracles in procuring the funds, from the reduced cost of materials, such as bricks at little more than half cost—to volunteer help to build it; a book could be written.

Barkley was calling, writing, sending the message out for help. The offerings for help came from many sources starting with those who lived close by, who knew the needs most. From the Horse Creek Baptist Church in Manchester came $10,000 and Manchester Baptist gave $5,000. From Mr. Saul Goins, former trustee in Manchester came another $1,000. From Oneida came many offerings. From Preston and Ruby Baker came $1,000. From the faculty of the Oneida Baptist Institute came offerings; from Dr. and Mrs. George Redding came $1,000; from David Cooper, the gardener, came $250; from the J.L. Burns family came $150; from Jim and Mary Ann Mallard came $500. (Mary Ann was sick with cancer.) All of the faculty were working for salaries thousands under those they received before coming to Oneida. Barkley wrote beautiful thank you letters to each—saying in part, "It is far beyond the call to make such a large contribution while you give so generously of your time already." For everyone who worked even a short time on the project, God provided a replacement when his or her service was over!

That same year Bud and Kay Underwood, Class of 1963, returned—Bud to be the new work supervisor and Kay to assist in the office. Myrtle Web Cooke, valedictorian of the 1960 class, returned as the fulltime guidance counselor. Tim Erwin, a graduate of Oneida, and his wife Barbara came that year. Tim had his college degree by then and had worked in a bank for about four years. He was to teach in the middle school program and his wife would be assistant dean of girls.

Volunteers arrived in groups ready to help as well. On June 8, a group arrived from First Baptist, Orlando, Florida, Rev. Bill Curl's church, while the graduation ceremony was in progress. Others arrived several days after that. None of them had ever seen Oneida, but had heard of the work. Fifteen of them devoted two weeks of vacation time to working nearly ten hours a day in volunteer service. They did much work on the restrooms, shower rooms, pluming, plastering, ventilator fans back in operation, electrical work—and several other jobs around campus. Some of the students were in between the close of the year and the start of summer school. They fell in love with the Orlando folk, and those people fell in love with the students. There were tears shed as they left.

At the same time, other volunteer groups were doing much work in the girls' dorm. Each room was cleaned thoroughly in preparation for summer camps and the start of summer school. Every room was carefully mopped and waxed. Barkley declared, "It has never looked so beautiful."

The spring revival was one of the finest ever. Barkley wrote to Mr. and Mrs. Cicero T. Ayers in Winston Salem, North Carolina and many others:

> We had two services daily. Everyone attended each morning's service in the Chapel, and we had a church building full every single

night at the evening services. Our evangelist was able to really get our students' attention. 21 of our girls and 17 of our boys made professions of faith. Only eternity can fully measure the benefits of that special week. There is hardly ever a week on our campus that there aren't some soul-changing decisions. Every day there is some spiritual growth on the part of many. Some progress steadily, others in spurts, but the growth is there.

Aren't you happy to have a part in such a work? SEEING true changes in so many lives is what keeps those of us working on the campus enthused and willing to work so hard. It is a daily challenge and privilege.

In March he had a letter from Dr. Bill Marshall, the new executive director of the Kentucky Baptist Convention, in response to his invitation to speak in chapel. Dr. Marshall wrote back. "It is always refreshing to get a letter from you, and even somewhat painful when I realize how busy you are and what a massive correspondence you carry on these days.

"I am delighted to take you up on your invitation to preach in chapel."

Barkley was always asking the most prominent leaders to come speak to his boys and girls. And more often than not they felt privileged to do so. He personally wrote hundreds of letters monthly, probably more than anyone could really imagine. They are there today, as Ebenezer Stones (remembrances) in the schools archives, stacked side by side, date by date, letter by letter, literally thousands of them, for twenty two years. On June 2, Barkley wrote to thank Dr. Bill Curl for speaking in chapel.

The group left this morning. They worked hard and got so very, very much done. Several told me it was the most satisfying mission trip they had been on.

Of course, I hope that your people might keep coming to us. The Kelseys and several indicated that there are other times in the year when people might possibly come.

Please review the enclosed letter I have just written the Kelseys with many possible dates for MAJOR work.

In fact, as I point out in the letter, we could use up to three couples, or even one, ANYTIME, ANY day of the year. ANY week that would be suitable for them. There is ALWAYS MORE to do here than we can get done. We are ALWAYS behind.

Note…the last paragraph. Maybe our group can join in a worship service with you there in Orlando early in January.

God bless…and THANK YOU for ALL you have done in putting this project together.

Barkley never missed an opportunity to call for more help!

In July the George Redding's implored him to take a Bible cruise with them. He filled out the forms, sent his $100 deposit! So many of the people to whom he wrote took beautiful vacations and wrote to tell him all about them, suggesting he too take a trip or come visit them and they would see to his having a good time—a rest, *etc.* He always wrote back with glowing letters of enthusiasm, sharing in their joy while on their trips—trips to Africa, Europe, Hawaii, the Alps, the Grand Canyon! "By the time you receive and read this, you will have had your trip to Austria and other points. I hope that it will have been a wonderful and inspiring time for you."

But some of the letters he read and wrote brought much pain. For instance, he wrote to and carried on correspondence with dozens in Iran. During the hostage of Americans in the American Embassy in Tehran, many of his friends, high ranking soldiers, doctors, teachers were imprisoned, their families murdered in their presence. When Khomeini came to power, they were even more endangered, in ways Americans could hardly imagine. In one letter, he said:

I'm still in touch with Iran. Many of my very finest students have been murdered by this government. I hope someday it may be possible to go back for a visit…yet so many of the ones I was closest to are now dead that I don't know if it would be bearable. We have one Iranian boy enrolled at this time…he lost his parents

205

at age 10…escaped from there at age 14, and came here knowing no English. He will graduate this fall…two weeks from today. I have a Turkoman boy at college now, who finished here last year. We have students from all parts of the mountains and I have students from all over Kentucky, and 26 other states. In the past three years I have had students from Israel, Japan, communist China, Iran, Thailand, Guatemala, Ethiopia, Brazil, Ghana, Germany, England, Germany, Sweden, Venezuela, Zambia, Jordan, Korea, Laos, and Nigeria.

Barkley himself had been all over the state of Kentucky, speaking on behalf of all these. Traveling thousands of miles to Ashland, Lexington, Owensboro, Morehead, Simpson Association near Franklin outside of Bowling Green, Russell, Hawesville, Three Forks Association in Perry County, Booneville, Middletown, *etc.* And groups had come to Oneida where he had entertained them, fed them, given them the "Tour"; groups from Cincinnati, Bardstown, Richmond, Somerset, Lexington, Cynthiana, Pikeville, Paducah, Greenup, and many others.

While Barkley was gone, his beloved staff of dedicated souls had carried on in the manner he had showed them by his life. By the time he returned work was started in earnest on the girls' dorm and dining kitchen project, having been delayed by rain and floods that also destroyed most of the potato crop. The projected completion date was delayed to Christmas.

In his absence much landscaping and reseeding had been done. A new two story building had been started for used clothing, so many people had heard of the new Friendship House. In the Carnahan Store, the shelving space had been doubled and two teller windows added. New electric poles had been added throughout the campus. The pumping capacity of the water system tripled. Several more vehicles had been added and a large new church organ was installed in the church. It had been given in memory of Henry Corum, who lived in Manchester and had come to Oneida in 1914 as a schoolboy.

He returned on September 26, just in time to help his friends, the Preston Bakers, celebrate the retirement of Ruby from directing the Oneida Senior Citizens program that Barkley had started soon after his return to Oneida. Ruby was loved by all of Oneida. She had begun work on the Oneida Institute campus and was the only cook for the school for ten years. During that time her husband Pres was dean of boys, coach, and teacher, and the Bakers had lived on campus. Ruby fed the campus community three times daily year round. Then she became supervisor for the Oneida Elementary School lunch program for twenty-five years before managing the Senior Citizens Center. During these years she was also a wife and mother, and for thirty-five years helped her husband manage a large farm.

Homecoming was just around the corner, and there too the staff were busy preparing the campus and preparing for all the activities. It was October 6 and the campus was filled with hundreds, not a bed empty anywhere on campus. There were alumni and friends milling around everywhere, every one looking around at what had been done, was being done. On Friday night the drama group presented *Papa Was a Preacher*. Saturday morning saw the usual hymn sing in the Oneida Church. Saturday afternoon there was feasting on hamburgers and hotdogs grilled under the trees.

Homecoming was climaxed by an evening meal and a country music concert afterwards, by Joey Hensley, son of Omer "Blue" Hensley, and his band. Joey had performed on the Grand Ole Opry and his band had come all the way from Texas. It was a real hoedown!

By Thanksgiving it became that apparent the new dining facility couldn't be finished by Christmas, but work continued. Sparks Hall did have a new $30,000, heavily insulated sloped roof over the old flat roof that had been leaking for years, and work could continue under the roof through the winter months. The Thanksgiving-Christmas letter was ready to go out. It read:

Dear Friend:

On a plaque marking Abraham Lincoln's birthplace near Hodgenville is recorded this scrap of conversation:

"Any news down to the village, Ezry?"

"Well, Squire McLain's gone to Washington to see Madison swore in, and ol' Spellman tells me this Napoleon fella has captured most of Spain. What's new out here neighbor?"

"Nutin', nutin' a'tall, 'cept fer a new baby born over to Tom Lincoln's, Nutin' important ever happens around here."

The Bible tells us we have entertained angels unaware. Often we are unknowingly associated with "great" people, significant events without understanding the significance at the time.

More times than we ever know, SOMEONE might have gone on to do great things IF we had just given a word of encouragement, a bit of help just at the right time.

Abraham Lincoln had only nine months of education. Have you ever thought of how different the world would be (for the worse) had there been no school for Lincoln to attend? No teacher to teach? Even those few months made the difference.

Each child is somebody special. Each is potentially an Abraham Lincoln, a Mary Lou Retton, a Billy Graham. Whether such potential is realized, and the world blessed, depends on what others do. Yes… might even depend on what YOU do. Or fail to do.

Some events, whether birthdays in Hodgenville (or Bethlehem), or spiritual rebirth in a person's life, may not create much earthly splash…but ultimately can be of great importance if WE do our part.

We have 516 girls and boys today to teach, feed, house…in many cases to clothe…medical bills, day-by-day necessities to provide. Our young people help themselves through work, their families help to the extent they can. But there are many who have only US and we can do little without YOUR help or the help of people like you.

As we honor the birth of the Christ child, will you make a birthday gift to Oneida so that we may continue this life-changing, life-preparing, life-sustaining work so NEEDED in the lives of so many?

The formal Christmas season began with the hanging of the greens and putting up a twenty-foot Christmas tree in the chapel, something that had not been done since 1964. The students were filled with anticipation as they decorated the tree. They all attended the county wide community choir performance of *The Messiah*, led by Jeff Minor, Oneida's 1978 valedictorian, now back as music teacher. Then there was a beautiful reception in Anderson Hall. However, Barkley didn't stay for the reception; instead he hustled out the door to get to Cordia, in Knox County, where his girls and boys were playing in the championship basketball invitational games. He just missed the girls defeating Buckhorn, and the boys were into the second half when he ran into the gym, just in time to see his boys win the championship game.

The following Thursday night, the drama class presented *Her Majesty and Miss Jones*, an amusing play, directed by Miss Debbie Sizemore. The Oneida Baptist Church had their annual international student banquet the following Monday. After dorm parties all over campus, the students all set off toward home on December 20, eager to be home for Christmas!

The year 1984 was about to come to an end. It found Barkley in his office, alone. There were no checks written but kept in the hold box on his desk. There were no celebration fire works. There were no boys and girls or staff standing at his door. He was content to sit alone and contemplate how they had been blessed that year. He still had letters to write and an important phone call to make. He called Dr. and Mrs. George Redding first. And then he began the letters.

> With all of our students and most of our staff away for Christmas-New Year 'break' between academic semesters, I am having the chance to take care of a lot of 'housekeeping' type things. I've sorted through my desk drawers throwing away quite an accumulation! Also, I've located some things long misplaced and have gotten them back in their proper place. In the 'busy-busy' of everyday with the phone constantly ringing, many visitors each day, much to oversee, decisions to be made, and all of it done "on the run", it is good to be able to catch one's breath and "catch up" on many things left undone.

One of those things left undone! He wasn't on that cruise ship with Dr. and Mrs. George Redding right then, sailing into soft breezes!

1985-86
Year 14

But statistics, personal data, do not really tell you about these special young people, or who they are. Each is a unique personality. Each was created by God for a special work. Jesus died for each. Their abilities vary, but as a little boy said, "God don't make no junk!"
—Barkley Moore

D uring the holidays anyone left at Oneida, and that meant Barkley, the office staff and the farm and maintenance staff, was playing—not so! They were working like there was no tomorrow. They reorganized the administrative offices, first throwing away barrels full of outdated files, then doubling the number of file cabinets for future use. The same thing was going on in the print shop, with other staff tossing away, organizing files, *et cetera*. Here they added a new Heidelberg letter press to the two they already had. Then they set about preparing and equipping a classroom for a full time drafting program.

Over across campus at the dining room, men were busy bricking the inside walls of the dining room and hanging a new ceiling with all new light fixtures; in the new grill they were scraping up the old vinyl tile off the floor so the brick masons could begin bricking there as well. How proud Barkley was that they were using the same brick as many fast food chains used for their restaurants! It would eliminate painting for a lifetime and it could be scrubbed down with a hose. It was meant to hold up to the constant wear and tear 500 teenagers would give it. It could outlast the building. Six of the men had worked every day except Christmas to have it all done before the students got back!

It was a real accomplishment that all of this had gotten done and he kept telling everyone what a wonderful job they had done.

It was January 10 and the students were returning. All over campus there were the happy noises of giggling teenage girls, and teenage boys with changing voices; there was hugging and kissing parents goodbye and girls hugging and kissing their roommates and best friends and boys too awkward to do either! It was always a sight to behold—and one Barkley loved more than eating apple pie!

He always declared this was the best group ever, the teachers, the staff, one and all the best ever! And the opening was of course the smoothest, the best ever!

The bills were also the highest ever! By now it was going to take, by his calculations, over $2,200,000 to run the school for the year, 1985. When all the calculations for Christmas giving were totaled, he realized they were down by $52,520. He had seen it coming. Daily, for months, the world had watched with horror the news that Ethiopia's famine, a famine that had been ongoing for four years was about to end in disaster. Experts were predicting the death of at least 900,000 by the end of the year with over eight million at risk. Over 200,000 had already died while the Western world watched—live pictures of starving men, women and helpless children. Every relief organization was pleading for money!

He was very concerned. He understood why Oneida's friends had let down on giving. But he was also responsible for feeding over 500 boys and girls. He had to let the extended family and friends of Oneida know how desperate the situation could become.

On January 29 he sat at his desk contemplating what he should say. He began:

Dear friend:

We are bordering on a financial crisis in the work here. I know that you CARE because you have invested in Oneida before. You have received printed appeals from me. But this is the FIRST time

I have written a direct and <u>personal </u>letter asking you for <u>whatever</u> help you can give us.

Why am I forced to take this extraordinary step? What has happened? Since early fall, our day-by-day donations, on which we rely for nearly three fourths of our operation expenses, have been down sharply. In November things were so bad we were not able to pay one dime toward <u>food bills</u> which amount to approximately 30,000 dollars monthly…besides what we raise, and we raise most of our own beef and pork, potatoes. Christmas giving is normally a time to 'catch up' on accumulated bills. However, in December, our deposits were down $52,520 as compared to the same month the year before. In the weeks since, we are seeing this same trend.

For the most part, it is people of average means who maintain the work of Oneida. They are people who care about children, who care about Christian education, people who want to HELP others. Daily for months all of our people have seen the starving children and adults of Africa, and I'm sure many have sent donations there. Certainly those people badly need help, and we are thankful for every dollar sent these desperate people. In fact, we have helped scores of Ethiopian refugees since the revolution eleven years ago. We have Ethiopian children now, as well as from other lands, and hundreds of children from inner city areas, our mountain boys and girls, etc.

I am directly responsible for over 500 girls and boys here. Approximately 60% of <u>these</u> come from <u>poverty</u>-level homes. We have more to feed, house, and to teach than ever before. Everything costs more as you know. Also, we must clothe and help with the medical needs of many. We must assist several score even with bathing soap, shampoo, and such articles. I am VERY concerned. With the accumulation of bills we already have things could become critical for us in the next several months. The coming months are those when donations are normally the lowest of the year. We must reverse that this year.

You have helped before. Can you? Will you? Help us now? I am counting on you, but, we only want your help if you can feel good about it.

In a letter to friends he confided that through three recessions and the continuing inflation, the receipts had always been higher than the year before. He truly was counting on the friends of Oneida to help!

By the middle of January the spring-like weather of December had turned to severe weather with frigid cold and freezing temperatures; both snow and ice covered the streets, and Goose Creek froze over.

A siege of devastating flu broke out. There were over one hundred seventeen cases in a five-day period. Fortunately, Oneida had a new doctor at the clinic. He thought he was retiring when he came to the clinic, never dreaming what might await him. Dear Dr. Tim Schroeder, who had been a physician in a large University Hospital, rolled up his sleeves and set to work. He didn't leave the clinic, not even to step a foot out of it for that five day period. He slept there and meals were carried to him. Sick boys and girls had to be isolated, given medicines on schedule and carried food three times a day.

Next a giant water pipe burst. The noon meal had to be eaten off paper plates. Some of the men worked frantically to repair the pipe and had it done by dinner time. The biggest worry, on top of all of this was that some boy or girl might decide to act "foolhardy". It was so cold that Barkley had made the decision to keep the students in doors. As much as they loved to slide down the front of campus hill, and would have done it by the hour, he and the staff feared "frostbite" or that some one would venture out on the frozen creek. While the staff would threaten everything, he could just imagine seeing one or more give it a try anyway. No wonder Barkley was getting gray hairs!

With several sports in full swing, games were cancelled and rescheduled. No matter how much ice there was, the cattle and hogs had to be fed. Sometimes that meant carrying slop across the swinging bridge covered with icy patches. "Imagine that!" he wrote. Valentines Day came and went and Homegoing had to be postponed a week. Roads were blocked with trees down. One day the mail didn't even run. One block from campus a fire burned a house down.

Barkley wrote to friends Bill Gene and Peggy Smith, in Sebring, Florida, telling them about these events, concluding, "Otherwise, we are carrying on the normal routine." Well, they did eventually get back to normal, but not before Barkley and several staff working in the office one morning were nearly killed.

He was working hard at his desk and didn't see the truck coming. But had he looked out of his window, he would have seen the garbage compactor truck reach the top of Mount Moriah, the hill with the road that went pretty much straight up from his office. The truck was loaded with 12,000 pounds of garbage. As it reached the top of the hill, the hydraulic brake line broke. The truck kicked out of gear and began to roll backwards directly toward his office. Joe Scott stayed behind the wheel trying to avert going right into the building's corner—right where Barkley was sitting at his desk. He managed to steer the truck, while going down hill and backwards right into an old tree, which fortunately held. The truck came to a jolting halt just a few feet from where Barkley was sitting.

In his weekly column, *The Oneida Journal*, he wrote about other near-death experiences:

A Narrow Escape

I am so thankful I made preparation long, long ago…Praise God for his watch care in so many life-threatening situations since…

I have lived through and survived a 45 day cholera epidemic in the Turkoman tribal area of Iran where I was serving in 1965, and a devastating earthquake in the same area three years later in which many of my dear friends died. Shortly thereafter, a deranged Moslem fanatic attempted to kill me one noontime near the courtyard of Karvous school, as I was leaving from a morning of teaching.

On a speaking trip in 1971, my plane had to make an emergency landing on a foam covered runway, and in 1976 I survived a serious van wreck near Oneida with only minor injuries, vehicle totaled.

Since the cholera epidemic 20 years ago, I have considered each and every day of life a bonus gift from God.

In the earthquake to which Barkley gives a mere sentence, 15,000 to 20,000 people died all around him. Over 120 villages in the mountains near the Russian border, in the very region where he had climbed the mountains on his horse "Oneida", or walked when the way became too steep, were completely devastated. He helped drag bodies from collapsed mud brick huts. The poorest of the poor on those mountain ranges lived in meager hut dwellings perched on mountainsides, in poverty unimaginable to us in the Western world. Like soldiers who can never bring themselves to speak of the atrocity of war, there is a sacred brotherhood of silence that is observed among those who experience tragedy too great to voice!

In the same manner he describes living through a cholera epidemic. Cholera is one of the most feared diseases in developing countries because of lack of proper sanitation of water and food supplies. It is caused by a bacterium called vibrio cholera. After a deadly earthquake, cholera stalks the poor victims of third world countries as remorselessly as falling buildings. It can strike with a deadly force within two hours of being infected. "It is a severe disease characterized by profuse watery diarrhea, vomiting, and leg cramps. In these people, rapid loss of body fluids leads to dehydration and shock. Without treatment, death can occur within hours. There is no general vaccine." (MedicineNet.Com)

Barkley was aware that one's life hangs by a thread. Under the most trying circumstances he "looked at life with a positive attitude". He knew that "the key to every situation is attitude…not letting anything get you down in your outlook." That was one of the reasons he could comfort the grieving folks who was surrounded him that winter.

Barkley had other children dependent upon him, besides his Oneida boys and girls; he was supporting several students he had brought from Iran. He considered them his own, since many were totally dependent on him. He also supported several mission projects outside Oneida. In March one of his Iranian boys wrote, asking for money. Barkley wrote back,

> I am enclosing $50. I am sorry you have to go without sometimes and wish I could give you more…I am nearly 44 years old and have not saved one penny…not a lot I've ever made…never have made much by choice…every dime has been spent, most of it given away.

So don't think I am mad or that I get mad because you ask for money. I know, under the circumstances, that you must ask someone. If I appear mad at times it is not at you but rather frustration that I don't have the money sometimes when you ask.

If his parents hadn't taken over the running of his house, using their own retirement income, he would have been unable to help so many of those boys. He was blessed beyond measure that he had them. Their generosity was probably the least known fact to the many hundreds of guests they entertained for Barkley.

Spring finally arrived and the entire family of Oneida students, faculty, staff couldn't have been more excited. By April every living green blade of grass looked beautiful. The dining addition was nearing completion and the furniture and fixtures were being installed. The athletic field had been "limed" with twenty three tons of lime, had been re-sown, and was turning emerald green.

Early one spring morning Barkley took a walk toward the farm. There was a beautiful cove on the school farm surrounded by three hillsides, filled with towering beech trees and the north side faced toward the campus with a magnificent view up and down the mountains. It was comforting to him as he thought how steadfast these hills were. It had already occurred to him that this would be a natural setting for an outdoor drama, staged there with that view of those hills behind the stage. He thought it could be called *Mountain Dawn*, a dramatic story of Oneida's early days. As he looked over the valley he could see there was plenty of space to park 300 cars. He stood for another few moments under the dazzling blue sky as the sun melted away the midst of the morning dew. He knew just who to ask to write and direct such a drama. He called Russ Mobley, a 1951 Oneida graduate and a University of Kentucky drama graduate, who was then drama professor at Campbellsville College. There was no way Mr. Mobley could turn him down.

Invigorated just thinking about it, he walked briskly back to his office and made that call. Between them they decided on two productions that Russ would stage and direct. But that was a future dream. Today he had men all over campus busily working to get the dining room ready for by graduation weekend and certainly by the Mountain Missions Conference which met the second week in June.

Everywhere he went, crews were as busy as he had ever seen them. Later that day he grabbed Jeff Minor, the band director, and Bud Underwood, the dean of boys, eager to show them the view. He wrote about it in the *Oneida Journal*.

> Late yesterday after noon I went walking on the tip of the hills on our school farm. The view is especially beautiful from there.
>
> Equally beautiful is the fellowship of kindred minds and hearts. Walking with me were two of my former students…both are dedicating their lives here as are so many others.
>
> From that distance students and staff looked a little larger than dots as they moved about campus. The tractor and large disk moving across the athletic field looked like toys…
>
> Boys are working at the edge of the (athletic) field clearing away materials from an old barn we recently tore down. A fence row is being cleared…Five other boys are busy improving a drainage ditch, using muscle power and hand shovels…
>
> Spring plowing and planting is going on…Principal Hawkins is spading his hillside garden.. after such a difficult winter it is a delight to be out in the warm sun….Some of the men are bricking the porch of the 4500 sq. ft. addition to the dining room. When complete the whole project is going to be far more beautiful than we first envisioned…
>
> It reminds me of a colony of ants. Active. Busy. Organized. Purposeful. Things being done…
>
> *Western Recorder*, April 9, 1985

Barkley was thrilled to have Bud and Jeff serving alongside him at Oneida. He felt restored just being with them. It was one of the busiest springs ever and one of the most pleasurable. He promoted Bud to dean of boys and this gave him a great sense of peace. Bud's wife Kay was serving beside him in the office and between them they gave multiple tours of the campus to visitors every day, Kay taking visitors when Barkley was already out on campus. Kay was so much like Mai Mai Sparks in her mannerisms, he felt right at home with her there!

When Kentucky Baptists had their annual convention in May, Barkley had some good news to report: A.B. Colvin, Mr. Kentucky Baptist, would become his special assistant. (A.B. Colvin had rightly earned the title, as he was the Convention's chief historian. His personal collection of approximately 35,000 books, manuscripts, and periodicals directly related to the history of Southern Baptists would later be given to Campbellsville College.) One of his roles at the Institute would be to assist Barkley with speaking engagements on behalf of the school.

Commencement weekend was the most magnificent weekend of the year. The Choir performed the *Sound of Music*, staged in the chapel three nights. Barkley told every one it would be talked about for years to come. "The singing was excellent, the cast did not miss a line. Betty Hensley Bowling, Class of 1954, did a masterful job on the piano, the set was outstanding the costuming was perfect."

Dr. George Redding preached the baccalaureate sermon in the morning. Aunt May Bishop got a standing ovation in the afternoon's graduation session. She was Oneida's oldest alumnus at the time. At ninety seven she still operated Aunt May's Motel at Beattyville and personally checked in all the guests. She stole the show!

In July, with funds still coming in slowly, he sent out another letter to the "partners" of Oneida. He began:

> In a few days I will begin my 14th year as your servant in this place. There have been no easy days nor any dull ones! It is thrilling, however, to be a part of God's work with "even" the least of these. Nothing is possible with out the goodwill, prayers, and active physical help of people like you. We have built on a foundation of faith, labor and love of the thousands who have had some part since 1899.

Barkley fully counted on his supporters to come through. He continued in every way as if the funds would come. Probably no one on his staff knew the pressure on him that summer and fall. He made it a point not to have everyone frantic and worried if they would have a job. That was God's job to take care of them. By now he had learned to just keep on walking the walk. His staff was getting many things accomplished even while camps went on through the hot weeks of summer. The student grill was finally finished, and then the biggest problem was keeping it stocked with food. The students were so thrilled to have a place to be after school hours. It was supervised and the girls didn't have to have permission to go there as it was right in their dorm. It was working them to death, according to Barkley, but they would get the hang of it.

One of his greatest losses from the staff that year had been the Frakers. Mr. Fraker's ill health had forced them to leave. He still kept in touch by letter and wrote in August to fill them in on all the details of the summer.

Barkley went on about the 477 students that year—the 100-voice choir—how Jeff had built the beautiful risers for the chapel with his own hands—how they were using the choir frequently in chapel—the piano lab with about fifty six practicing an hour per day—the art area just beautiful—the home economics area really nice—the grill going 'great guns', its wares better and cheaper than anything in the village— the new dining room in use—just a totally different atmosphere, the smooth traffic flow with the new 1,000-tray-per-hour dishwasher, etc. Mrs. Banks, back as dean of Baker Hall, has those kids stepping—at the same time Bud is doing a great job in the dorms, as well as supervising the work program.

Barkley was always in touch with the volunteers. Mr. Hiram Campbell was one of those. Barkley wrote him in September, giving all the updates and thanking him for all he did for the school. He also told him the Gritton attic was finished, two beautiful bedrooms, four much-needed closets. He also told him how surprised he was to find the state highway department blacktopping the gravel road leading up the hill to where his house was and continuing on up to two more houses. He had been completely unaware that they were coming. He had never even thought of such a thing. They were in the preliminary work towards building a new potato house and right then they had a bumper crop. Also they had a new farm manager. Mr. Jack Tillman doing great job.

Homecoming was just days away. The Oneida choir would give their first major concert. Everyone was getting really excited as the big weekend approached. It was to be a glorious weekend. On Saturday, October 5, hundreds arrived to meander on the freshly mown campus. Mr. Cooper's flowers were blooming profusely. The campus had never looked better. At noon they ate barbecue under the trees. After the evening concert all dined in the new dining facility, which was fully operational. Everyone got an opportunity to see the new J.D. Embry Grill as well. The dedication and naming of both facilities would be held in the dining room during the banquet.

Julius Hacker had graduated from Oneida in 1933. His family had moved to Oneida in the 1920s so the children could attend Oneida. He was a lifelong teacher. Mrs. Hacker had preceded him in death. They willed their estate to Oneida, the largest amount ever willed by an alumnus to OBI, approximately $75,000. The board of trustees had voted to honor him by naming the new dining room complex, the Julius Hacker Dining Room.

The other person being honored was Mr. J.D. Embry. He was the father of one of the students and his wife, Martha, was a teacher and hostess of Anderson Hall. Mr. Embry was a burly river-man, working on a river boat between Pittsburgh and New Orleans. He was on the boat a month and then at Oneida a month. He would work hard in maintenance, painting, whatever needed to be done. He never took a cent from the school. He had died of a heart attack on the river just that spring. The life preserver now hanging in the Grill was from his riverboat.

At 8:00 PM they all returned to the chapel for the drama group's performance of *You're a Good Man, Charlie Brown!* Charlie Brown, Peppermint Patty, Linus, Schroeder, and Snoopy had been hard at practice, according to Barkley.

Fall was beautiful. The mountains turned more glorious in their display of color than Barkley had ever remembered. The riot of color in the woods, the scent of rosemary, oregano, and sage growing near the sidewalks, the carpet of golden leaves under foot, the crisp chill in the air, were all stimulating. The "Tours" went on during every day, with church groups, and incoming students. Whatever he was doing, whenever anyone showed up, if he was there, he stopped, received them, as if he had just been waiting for them to arrive...and they got the "Tour", which was growing longer by the year. There were more buildings, more people, more flowers to show and talk about. And he knew, whether any one else did or not, that this was the one thing he did for the health of his lungs, for the health of his body. Filling them deeply with the fresh air forced them to keep functioning. He always felt better for the walk—and besides he loved to be out walking, out talking with the best of them. At the same time he was embedding Oneida's history and his own time on earth deep into their memories, "For Time and Eternity".

He loved to think what was going on at Oneida, every action taken, every prayer given, every soul saved was impacting the world for Christ.

He preached it to everyone:

Oneida is state missions. There are young people whose homes are in Louisville, Lexington, Winchester, Russell Springs, Frankfort, Lebanon, Walton, Independence, Ashland. Five are from the mountains including three from Clay County, and one each from Leslie and Harlan counties.

Oneida is a home mission field, why look at these boys and girls... four are from Ohio cities...four are from Chicago. Others are from Naples, Fla.; Mt. Clemens, Miss.; Bloomington, Ind.; Nashville, Tn.; and Appalachia, Va.

Oneida is foreign missions. Three are from Ethiopia, and one is of Korean descent whose home was Singapore.

But statistics, personal data, do not really tell you about these special young people, or who they are. Each is a unique personality. Each was created by God for a special work. Jesus died for each. Their abilities vary, but as a little boy said, "God don't make no junk!"

When the leaves had fallen and the cold snap of November air greeted the Kentucky mountains he and his boys and girls were just getting a good start. Wherever he went he boasted that his students were "three times champs"!

The boys' varsity cross-country team ended regional play with a 39-1 record and were regional champs for the third year in a row. Coach Larry Gritton had nurtured sophomore Bill Gibson and junior Willie Bowling into top runners for the state in one year. The girls' cross-country team came in third, qualifying them for the state tournament.

The same weekend coach Tim Erwin's varsity girls' volleyball team left for Lexington for regional play and defeat—but even that was a victory because, as Barkley explained, "the season's record of 5-9 was the best the school had ever had in this sport."

"Coach Tom Jenken's soccer team defeated Boyle County in regional championship play before being defeated by Lexington Catholic. The best soccer season we have ended with a record of 10-2."

And the best was yet to come. The second week of November found the seventy-member choir, the directors, and several faculty members heading out to the Kentucky Baptist Convention's annual convention. It was the start of a 2200-mile odyssey. Fifty of them gave a performance that brought the messengers' to their feet in a prolonged standing ovation. They didn't know that twenty were missing, stranded on I-75, the bus broken down. Those twenty made Barkley just as proud as the ones that sang.

While they were disappointed, the chaperones reported to Barkley that "There was no moaning and groaning, no bad spirit, no complaint. They talked quietly. As the moment approached when the choir was scheduled to sing at the convention, the bus group fell silent. Ten minutes later they burst into applause just as the group who made it to Lexington were acknowledging their ovation." Another bus was dispatched from Oneida to get them safely back home.

On Thursday afternoon seventy-one of the choir members, four staff members serving as bus drivers, and four others acting as chaperones, boarded two buses to begin a long journey to Orlando, Florida. There was some slight apprehension, according to Barkley. But they had prayer and were off. They drove through the night, maintaining communication between buses with C.B. radios the drivers had rigged up. The following is paraphrased from letters and *Western Recorder* articles of 1985:

We had breakfast just across the Florida line at a fast food restaurant. The management, finding out that we were a choir, asked the group to sing. The patrons warmly applauded each number...

We arrived at First Baptist, Orlando, about 11:00 AM. There was no time to unpack, change clothes, or even to find their toothbrushes. We quickly washed our faces in the church restrooms, combed our hair, and were off to Epcot, the newest section of Disney World. Our tickets were provided by Disney to the Magic Kingdom, as we were to perform there...over $3,000 in value.

We just had to let the students go their own way through the vast complex but every child including the youngest seventh graders showed up at the buses at 8:00 PM no one lost! [Only a man who was pretty sure of his boys and girls would ever have had the nerve to do that.]

We went back to First Baptist and each of our students met the families that were to host them for two nights and provide breakfast each morning.

At 8:00 AM Saturday everyone met back at the church and boarded buses and were carried to a portion of Walt Disney World the next morning, they again loaded onto buses that were to take them to a part of Disney the public never sees...the back stage areas. We were shown the dressing room area where our students were to prepare for the concert they were to give that evening at the Dock Stage in Walt Disney Village.

Then everyone scattered for another day of delight in the Magic Kingdom.

Hundreds gathered at the Dock Stage at 6:00 PM for our students' performance. It was a beautiful Florida evening, a crescent moon hanging overhead, a floating riverboat restaurant in the background.

Our boys and girls, dressed in appropriate costumes, sang a "hit" song from each decade of the 20s. *Ain't She Sweet* began the program followed by the 30s *Over the Rainbow* with Dorothy, the Wicked Witch, the Cowardly Lion, and the Scarecrow.

The girls then appeared on the stage dressed up as WACs singing a World War II number. Then eight of the boys appeared on stage dressed in white pants and white shirts, wearing OBI royal blue sweaters, and did a rousing rendition of *Mr. Sandman* from the 50s, the entire choir chiming in. Three of Oneida's black girls then did an impressive medley imitation of Diana Ross and the Supremes from the 60s.

The performance was climaxed with the entire choir singing *We Are the World*. In the front row were six of his foreign students, in the native dress of Ethiopia, Korea, Japan, and Thailand. Each sang solo parts in their native tongues, and then the English version.

The audience gave them a great round of applause. Some Kentuckians were in the crowd and went up to speak to them. They knew of Oneida but were surprised to find them performing at Disney World!

Costumes, band instruments, and ourselves were all soon loaded on the buses. A count showed once more that all were present…we were off for a meal at the end of another long and exciting day. Then back to First Baptist where host families were waiting to take each of us back to our beds for the night.

Sunday morning we all met at 8:00 AM in the magnificent $19 million complex of First Baptist Church, which seated 6000 people. The choir, standing in the orchestra pit, found themselves to be in tune for the morning service. The orchestra pit then descended to the floor below, his students riding same. There they rested in a waiting area until the service began. Orlando's robed 450-voice choir slowly came into view again standing on the rising orchestra pit as it came up from the floor below. You can imagine what a kick our kids got out of that! But they all looked very dignified, just as though they rode orchestra pits daily and sang before congregations of 5000 people routinely.

With an estimated 70,000 people watching the televised service, the choir sang *Climbing Up the Mountain* and *Every Time I Feel the Spirit*, two of the songs they had sung so effectively a few days before at the Kentucky Baptist Convention. Again they thrilled our hearts and the congregation.

It was a tremendous service with former Kentuckian Bill Curl leading the singing, and pastor Jim Henry preaching a missionary message. Hundreds came forward at the end of the service committing themselves to various mission projects in the coming year.

Afterwards we rejoiced to visit with former Oneida teachers, Mr. and Mrs. Lynn Gritton and visited with many others who wanted information about Oneida.

Then we were off for another two hour drive, an afternoon "Cookout" in a nearby state park hosted by Sebring First Baptist. A volunteer group from Sebring First Baptist had recently spent a week at Oneida, painting, doing carpentry, papering, picking beans were among the group that had the grills going. They had prepared enough hotdogs, hamburgers, and all the trimmings for a bunch of seventy-nine hungry teenagers…we made short work of the delicious meal…

We had a good time of fellowship with the boys kicking around a soccer ball with young men from First Baptist.

Much of the state park is a carefully preserved swamp full of alligators and water moccasins. They have built a narrow boardwalk through the swamp with a rail on one side. Guidance counselor Myrtle Cooke clung to the rail for dear life. She enjoyed the alligator walk about as much as I had enjoyed the railroad car on Thunder Mountain at Disney World. I promised the Lord if I wasn't flung into orbit, and instantly killed, I wouldn't take such a "ride" again. I think Mrs. Cooke made a promise not to tempt the alligators again. She also feels the Florida park system should add another rail…

We were off to a local college gym where Bill Smith, professor of physics, and of course an Oneida graduate, had made arrangements for us to use the gym to shower before we headed out again to perform another concert that evening… They were also part of the Sebring group who also did volunteer service at Oneida this summer…

We drove from the gym straight to Sebring's First Baptist to perform another concert. The sanctuary was filled with an estimated 500 people. The choir was once again in great form. We had the entire worship service except for the opening hymn and prayer. They even gave us the offering! They also insisted that I speak and of course it didn't take much encouragement to get me going…

Afterwards the Sebring folks took us all into their homes for an evening meal, the night, and breakfast just as the Orlando people had done…

The following morning we began the twenty-seven-hour trip back to Oneida, going by way of the Kennedy Space Center where we saw a film and exhibits…

The only sleep we had from Monday morning to bedtime Tuesday night was "catnaps" on the buses. Upon arriving at Oneida at chapel time Tuesday the students showered and went to class. That night some of them played in two varsity games while others played in the band.

Oneida Journal articles; *Western Recorder*, November 26, December 3, 10, 1985

It was a great trip—with two buses and 4200 miles driven, hundreds of meals, thousands of new friends, memories for a lifetime and—almost every dime had been paid for by their hosts. While Barkley had never taken a real vacation—even put off the one on a cruise ship—God had virtually sent him on one of the most thrilling ones of all, along with the best companions he could ever have had, his children!

Barkley's home, Burns Mansion, high on a cliff overlooking the campus had a front porch stretching the length of the front of the house, with screened windows on three sides. From those windows, in the late fall and winter, when the leaves had fallen, he could see the Red Bird Creek and Bullskin Creek mingle with the waters of Goose Creek to make the South Fork River.

It was always a thrill for him, when he occasionally slept there, to awaken and look out those windows onto the campus—to thank the Lord for another day of life—the opportunity to serve. He could see the eighteen major buildings and staff houses. They were a testimony to the love—faith—hard work of literally thousands of people over the years.

It was the second week of December—Homegoing. He had slept on the porch. Awakening early, he stood gazing out the windows, composing an article for the *Oneida Journal* in his thoughts. He noticed something different. The lights were on in the smaller dining room. That reminded him it was Thanksgiving morning. But, he wondered why the lights were on because the students normally ate in the interior dining room.

As there were only 115 left on campus, Mrs. Celichowski, the food supervisor, had the lights on and was setting the smaller room's tables into a u-shape around the room. Arriving at the dining room shortly before noon, he found all the students and staff gathered in their Sunday best seated around tables covered with formal white cloths—fall leaves and pumpkins gracing each table. The sunny window ledges glowed with baskets of small colorful gourds. What a wonderful surprise!

They had so much to be thankful for that Thanksgiving Day! They all bowed their heads and waited patiently as Barkley prayed. He thanked the Lord for the abundance of blessings—but most important—the blessing of the Holy Spirit in the lives of 200 who had found the Lord.

In less than three weeks everyone would go home for Christmas. All the festivities would be over: the cutting of a 20-foot tree by the farm manager and school boys hauling it to the chapel—the merry fun decorating it—the carols sung—the gifts given—the holiday ham eaten, and at least a thousand cookies devoured! Every one at Oneida would have helped the clock tick down the hours—doing their part perfectly on time! The year 1985 would draw to a close!

1986-87
Year 15

The widow's 'mite', the little boy's two fishes and five biscuits, given in love and with faith, are the substance of miracles in the hands of a God who knows every heart. Come visit us this beautiful spring and see with your own eyes what God is doing here.
—Barkley Moore

"Off and running" was how Barkley described the opening of the school year 1986. Classes began that January with mild weather. With over 525 enrolled, even with a few students deciding not to come back and a few who had completed their requirements for graduation and would not be back until commencement, they still had a full house.

Barkley was better prepared than he had ever been before. Behind him was a vanguard of over 100 dedicated, talented, educators—the best in the State of Kentucky. They were loyal—totally devoted. It took men and women of stout heart and faith—Barkley continually stretched the limits of both. The board of trustees bore up to Barkley's dreams with grace, though they must have quaked in their boots at times.

Dr. A.B. Colvin's appointment to be his assistant had been a tremendous blessing. He brought with him twenty-seven years of experience, stature and leadership among Kentucky Baptists. His role as speaker for Oneida across the state was just in time—God's perfect time—to give Barkley more time to spend at "home" with his "children", and all the guests who came his way. He was thrilled! Of course he would still speak as well, but it was a real blessing to have Dr. Colvin.

Behind Barkley at the beginning of 1986 was also a solid support team of forty. He had a remarkable farm manager in Mr. John Tillman. Mrs. Bud Underwood, Kay, was now in charge of admissions and his administrative assistant. Mr. Bud Underwood, her husband was dean of boys. Bud had taken an enormous burden off Barkley's shoulders. He was the first to arrive on campus in the morning, and except for Barkley, the last to leave at night. No matter how late a bus load of his boys and girls arrived, Barkley was waiting for them.

The men and women under Barkley were all more than conquerors! To the man, to the woman they were ready to lay down their lives for the cause of Christ, to lead these young people to the greatest source of knowledge, to impart their years of wisdom into the least of these young charges. With a team like this behind him, Barkley was ready for 1986.

The number of guests coming to Oneida went up daily. It took both Barkley and Mrs. Underwood running their legs off to keep up with them. After all, by now he must have invited tens of thousands to come for a visit. And, they were doing just that!

The beginning of January 1986 was the first time on record that Barkley wasn't pleading for financial help—not that they had any funds left over or that he didn't have more dreams, more plans for the new year.

He had gained an even greater depth of faith in God in the past year when a crisis—the specter of hundreds of thousands dying from starvation in Ethiopia, starred the free world in the face. He and every one else dependant upon voluntary contributions suffered as funds were diverted to Ethiopia. But, Oneida's growing extended family of friends and Kentucky Baptists would come to his aid!

In the year just beginning, when obviously Barkley had slept no more than in years before, nor worked less, his letters barely mentioned his eighteen-hour days, his being tired! One can only conclude that God must have been sustaining him, giving him supernatural strength. As usual, he was making plans for coming year. By June he hoped to begin construction of a vocational classroom building. It would be a two-story concrete building. The building would include a large shop to teach carpentry; a vegetable preparation area with walk-in freezers; rooms for storing rakes, hoes and other work program tools; space for computerized drafting and teaching crafts; two restrooms; and a multi-purpose classroom where agriculture and driver's education would be taught.

He also planned to have a well-equipped shop to teach auto mechanics and welding with adjoining classrooms. He wanted to make sure everyone who graduated from Oneida, including the 40% who would not go on to college, were prepared in a practical way to earn a living. While Oneida had a tremendous college-prep program, he felt it was time to devote more time, attention and resources to better prepare those who were not college bound. He had most of the staff; with a little re-organization he could implement the plan with ease. Doing the construction themselves they could complete the building for $100,000. Barkley used the Oneida journal to announce his plans and ask for help.

> It isn't much money compared to the cost of buildings. Yet it is a fortune when you don't have it…You can have a part in another miracle at Oneida. Give what you can as God moves and has blessed.
>
> The widow's 'mite', the little boy's two fishes and five biscuits, given in love and with faith, are the substance of miracles in the hands of a God who knows every heart.
>
> Come visit us this beautiful spring and see with your own eyes what God is doing here.

He was inviting all 2,300 churches of the Kentucky Baptist Convention to "Come and visit." No wonder he was walking several miles each day taking tour groups around the campus.

Some of these plans were not to be realized that year, but the school would make do as it always did, with what they did have. The Bob Halcomb-Joe Barnes Athletic Field would be finished along with a modern track, baseball, softball, and soccer field and there would be a dedication.

Barkley's plans also included the writing of several books, for which he would have had to use his precious few hours in the middle of the night between 2:00 and 6:00 if he were to write even one more word than he was already writing. God was recording the stories Barkley meant to write someday! They were also being written in the blood, sweat and tears of his life! They were being written in the sands of his time on Earth!

And what was now filling up the files of his letter boxes, were no longer his pleading letters, begging for help, but answers to letters that were pouring in to him from his growing family of former students who considered him their spiritual father, or at least a big brother looking over their shoulders. In many cases he was the only father many knew. The girls always referred to him as Mr. Moore, but many of the boys, whether they had graduated, dropped out, or were still in high school, simply began with "Sir". They wrote to him for many reasons: to ask for advice, to ask for forgiveness, to tell him of their jobs; their lives, their girlfriends, to ask him to come to their weddings, to thank him, to praise him, to ask him to pray for them, their families, their friends. He answered everyone personally. And there were always stories to tell about his boys and girls.

Longtime pastor and friend of Oneida Brother Lyn Claybrook died at the end of January. Barkley wrote to their daughter:

> I just wanted to write this note to let you know you are in our thoughts and prayers...I was only a second grader the year you graduated. While I remember you, I was too small a boy for you to have known or to remember. It is a fact that your father and mother laid much of the spiritual foundation undergirding the labors of today....We had a special remembrance honoring your father in our daily chapel service earlier today.

The letters were pouring out to friends. In many he referenced ongoing and new work: the continuing renovation of Goins-Hounchell Hall, housing the swimming pool and student center; the farm manager and boys, excitedly preparing for the garden season, studying the catalogs, ordering seed, getting plants ready; the first year to raise gardens on the campus side of Goose Creek allowing many of the girls to participate in the gardening program for the first time.

Periodic letters went to one of his Iranian boys away at college. On March 1, he sent him the usual $100 per month and advised him to

> Spend it carefully and make it stretch as far as possible. This is hard earned. I haven't accepted a cent pay raise in over ten years, so am actually making much less than ten years ago and working as hard as ever.

Aside from special things that needed doing, the daily feeding, housing, teaching (and, in many instances paying for clothing, medical bills, *etc.*) of nearly 500 girls and boys made for a real financial struggle. The cost of running the school was now $7,000 a day, around $2,555,000 per year. However, the tone of the letters wasn't desperate. His confidence in the Lord's provision was rock solid.

Oneida might have hung out a sign saying: ALL GUESTS WELCOME. On May 3, four men from Clinton Baptist Church Brotherhood arrived and spent the night. They were at breakfast the next morning, along with seven ladies from the state WMU who were already there for a training meeting for Oneida's region. Along with these two groups, another group came from the Brotherhood of the Pikeville Baptist Church. Before long another group also showed up from Henderson, Kentucky. While the kitchen staff was feeding them a wonderful breakfast Barkley went between tables playing host. After breakfast he began with the "Tour". Just then a family with a new student showed up. Before the day was over he had walked miles and talked hours.

Barkley should have hung a sign saying: ONEIDA CLOSES AT MIDNIGHT. Maybe they would have all gone to bed. Ha! They were never all in bed—not even close! Take the day just ended. Barkley and two of his staff worked until after midnight. After they left, Barkley continued working another forty-five minutes. Finally leaving his office at nearly 1:30 AM, he ran into dean of boys Bud Underwood, making his nightly rounds of the campus. They talked until 2:00 AM reviewing the events of the day. Who knows when they went to bed? Barkley was back up at 5:00 AM to leave at 5:45 AM with the choir for a concert in the morning service of Hurstborne Baptist Church and an evening concert at Farmdale Baptist, both in Louisville.

On Monday morning he was "on the road again" to Cedarmore, the conference facility of Kentucky Baptist, at Bagdad, Kentucky, for the spring meeting of the executive board and back to Oneida late Tuesday afternoon.

Graduation weekend was at the end of May. It was worth recording. In an article for *The Oneida Journal*, Barkley tells the tale:

Beautiful Girls, Handsome Boys

What a wonderful week we have had! The 1986 Commencement events are over and another school year is history.

We had four different honors assemblies to recognize, perhaps, the most achieving group of students in history. In the first year of statewide academic team competition, our Oneida students won the high school district academic championship, and our middle school students won the second place award.

Sophomore Troy Miller, who came to us in the 7th grade four years ago from Floyd County, advanced on to state tournament and ranked third in language arts. One of our middle school students advanced to the state in science. Many of our students this year did college level work in English, American history and other subjects.

Our valedictorian, with us four years, made so high on nationally given PSAT test last year that Yale University, Stanford University, and many other leading universities have written her with scholarship offers.

Our athletes were also honored. With the exception of three of our varsity teams, each team set school records. Varying championship trophies were added to our shelves this year including our first in tennis and our third straight regional championship in cross country. Several of our students have taken first place in their track events and have advanced to the state tournament.

We also honored our achievers in choir, band, piano, art and drama. For the first time "arts" sweaters were given for outstanding participation. Even as our assembly was being held, 16 pieces of art done by OBI students were on display in Louisville's Center for Performing Arts, having already been on display for weeks in the Old State Capitol.

Percentagewise, considering high school enrolment, we had the largest number chosen by audition in the all-regional and all-state choirs this year. In the past two years our choir traveled over 8000 miles. About 50 of our students got in five hours of piano practice a week with a teacher supervising. Some made remarkable progress. Last spring in drama, *The Sound of Music* went to a three night performance, but last fall we had 12 performances of *You're a Good Man, Charlie Brown*!

Also we had an assembly honoring those of our students faithful in our daily work program on the farm, in the kitchen and dining hall, maintaining the grounds and cleaning the buildings.

The juniors gave a beautiful dinner for the seniors after Wednesday evening prayer service. The girls were so beautiful, the boys so handsome in their finest clothes. The food was excellent and the fellowship so wonderful that it was nearly midnight before we finished.

Friday night was an evening of three one-act plays-poignant, hilarious and thought-provoking in turn. Also our fourth quarter art show was on display in the library. I never cease to be amazed at the talent of some of our students.

And Saturday evening was pure enchantment. Students of the class of 1926 with accompanying family members had come from as far as Texas and Florida to celebrate their 60th anniversary. From Florida and Alabama and Kentucky were students of the smaller 1936 class back for their 50th. A total of 68 special invited guests for a two hour dinner in beautiful Anderson Hall, the only building remaining from their gathered school days...

Our dean of girls, Marty Hatfield, and her mother, Mrs. Janet Miller, had sewn for weeks. The result was stunning. Each youth had on shirts or blouses with a blue bow-tie or bow, wide blue cummerbunds, black trousers or skirts…

Then the group moved to Davidson Chapel for a two hour concert by our 92-voice choir… They sang all of it from memory, much of it a cappella. They moved from the 50s hit *Mr. Sandman* with the men's octet to the eight-part *a cappella Shenandoah.*
Western Recorder, June 3, 1986

Dr. A.B. Colvin preached an unusually good baccalaureate sermon on May 18. This last service for the graduating seniors was always held in the Oneida Baptist Church. It was an intimate service limited to the class member themselves, their parents and loved ones, staff, alumni and other guests.

The invocation was followed with the singing of *When We All Get to Heaven* by the congregation. Prayer followed, led by Gifford Walters, Oneida pastor and Bible teacher fifty years ago, who was back to help the Class of 1936 celebrate their golden anniversary.

Many eyes brimmed with tears as the class and congregation sang the haunting *Blest Be the Tie That Binds.*

Three hours later the colorful academic procession into the Melvin Davidson Chapel began. Nearly one hundred Oneida staff, trustees and invited guests were in academic regalia. The service would last at least four hours. Every parent, every graduating senior waited for their name to be called. As he or she stepped onto the stage, Barkley Moore would honor each: telling something wonderful about that young man or woman or their family. It was worth the wait for it was a sendoff filled with such high expectations, such high praise, you would have thought you were in C.L. Lewis' Narnia land, where each of them were kings and queens being commissioned to conquer the Empire!

Ten Glasses of Milk

Father's Day morning. The phone was ringing again at 8:55 AM, It had already rung three times. This time I hear the broken voice of a young man. "Hello, Mr. Moore. Do you know me?" I do not recognize his voice. "No, who is this?" He tells me. It had many months since I've last seen him or heard his voice.

He shares with me personal things. Several times he paused between choked words. I can hear him sniffling from time to time. I visualize the husky young man on the phone. He so often seemed assured, the body of a man, yet, just a confused young boy. His mother had never married. He had no brothers or sisters. Suddenly he reminds me that this is Father's Day. "You know, Mr. Moore, I've never had a father. I'm told he is a school principal, but I've never seen him in my life. He has never written or called me. I don't know what he looks like. But he must be a good man to be a principal."

As he considers that, he continues, "Mr. Moore you are the nearest to a father I've had." I am a little startled. The boy goes on to relate to me a conversation that he had with me once in the laundry room as he washed his clothes. I don't remember that particular conversation, but the boy said, "You'll never know just how much that meant to me." I don't tell him that I don't remember. He cries some more.

We never know when we are saying something that sticks with someone a lifetime. Sometimes it is for good, other times for ill. I am reminded of what Brooks Adams wrote a century ago: "A teacher affects eternity; he never knows where his influence stops." That is true, of course, of every teacher, how much truer it is of the Christian teacher, how much greater even is our challenge, our responsibility, our opportunity...

Standing on the church porch visiting with the farm manager that Father's day as I was getting ready to go to the dining hall for lunch, I noticed a car pull to a stop. A young man strode toward me. I suddenly realize who he is. I had last seen him three years before in a Marine Corps uniform.

It was lunch time...so of course I invited him to lunch. On the buffet was beef from the farm, smothered in gravy, boiled potatoes from last year's crop, cooked carrots, lettuce and other vegetables are on the salad bar. Hot rolls and freshly baked blueberry pie...

While I was eating with the young marine, I watched a new boy, only 13 and already 6'3". He downed 10 glasses of chocolate milk!

I made a mild comment on all he had eaten. The boy admits to the start of a tummy ache. He says he got up too late for breakfast. It is great to see healthy young people eat. I am grateful for good appetite as well as good food.

Western Recorder, June 24, 1986

Barkley had already gotten his own father a special gift. Now he was anxious to walk up the hill, sit down in a rocking chair and have a long visit—and just once take a short nap on the front porch. More than likely, on that Father's Day afternoon, you would have found Barkley stretched out on one of the long sofas, dozing; the screened windows wide open, the sweet fragrance of honeysuckle, and the fragrance of old fashioned Sweet William growing all over the hill side, wafting through the air as the fans turned lazily in the warm breeze!

Barkley himself received several beautiful Father's Day cards and a letter from David Allen Barker, Class of 1985:

> Greetings to you with all the joys of Christ. I hope God has blessed you with many surprises. I would like to thank you again for all that you have done. I owe OBI my future. Because of OBI, I am now attending Northern Kentucky University. Because of the love there, I have chosen teaching as a career.
>
> Thank you again for everything. I owe you so much. Please feel free to call upon me to help in any way. I may be small, but my love for Christ and you will see me through.

He signed it "In God's deepest love."

On June 20, Barkley wrote to his Iranian "son" again:

> Thanks for your letter....I don't have any idea what your "very important news" might be; however, if it is anything that would interrupt your work towards a college degree, it is a mistake. You have done so well, gone so far. Don't let anything interfere with your finishing college. Whatever else you want to do can be put off until your college is finished. It is always good to finish what you start.

September arrived and with it brisk autumn mornings. Homecoming came on Labor Day weekend. It was a glorious day! The second addition of *Mountain Rising* went on sale as well as *Dawn Comes to the Mountains*. Both hardbound books printed by Oneida's own printing press had taken thousands of hours of labor. The resulting sales were gratifying, as hundreds waited in line to purchase them.

Barkley and the staff were back at it, and in full swing as November approached. In the classroom and on the athletic field, things couldn't have been busier or more exciting. On this particular day almost the entire school was on the athletic field—standing to their feet, shouting, screaming as the Oneida soccer team, played in the second game of the regional tournament.

Having defeated Clark County in the first game of the regional with a score of 8-1 and having won all thirteen of their games in the regular season, they came up against Montgomery County, Mt. Sterling, who also had a winning season. It was a battle from the first second. The teams played forty minutes without interruption, no huddles, no time-outs, had a twenty-minute break and went at it for forty more intense minutes to tie 1-1. Then they played a ten-minute overtime, still tied, and a second ten-minute overtime, still tied. Then they went into a five-minute "sudden death" overtime and still tied. The exhausted teams went into a "shootout" where five boys from each team attempted a goal one on one. On the last round their man made one, Oneida's missed. It was over!

Barkley had never been more proud of an Oneida team in any sport at anytime even in state tournament victory. In fact in their defeat he was more proud of them than he had been in most victories. He declared them all heroes!

That fall and winter Oneida had to be one of the busiest places on earth. During the last two weeks of December before the students left for Christmas break, Barkley's head was spinning. Pastor Joel Rackley conducted three usual morning services, each well filled. Following lunch there were at eight major activities. John and Hannah Sanderson, teachers at Oneida for fifteen years, were hosting their annual Christmas open house for the senior class which they sponsored each year. While that was going on, the junior class sponsors were chaperoning a Christmas party in the new dining room. During the same part of the afternoon a Walt Disney movie, *Where the Red Fern Grows*, was being shown to many of the other students.

Prior to the evening meal the Fellowship of Christian Athletes had a Christmas party in the newly renovated home economics department that had been doubled in size last year. During the evening worship service, approximately thirty of the middle school students sang a special Christmas musical they had been practicing for months. Many sang solos to the surprise of Barkley who was unaware of just how much wonderful talent these pre-teenagers possessed.

After the evening worship service, the Baptist Student Union went caroling in the village. It was a bright night with a ring around the moon. Barkley had gone over to the farm manager's home for tea and fellowship. He could distinctly hear the carolers a half mile away in the quiet evening. The last major event of the evening was the annual girls' dorm Christmas party, hosted by Deans Hatfield and Garrett.

In the dining room the evening before they had welcomed nearly one hundred pastors, wives and other guests to the annual Booneville-Irvine Association Christmas dinner held on campus.

Monday was the usual busy day, beginning the last week of the quarter and final exams before Christmas. After school the wrestling team was off to Lexington Bryan Station and a wonderful 36-30 victory over that very large school.

In the meantime, senior Debra Thomas who had been at the school for four years, was delivering a speech at the Governor's Mansion, in Frankfort, one of only two of the past summer's Governor Scholars, statewide, invited to share in a dinner of approximately sixty corporate supporters of that annual academic program. Governor Collins gave her a warm hug and later quoted Debra several times in her own speech.

At the same time all that was going on, the Middle School Academic team was away in Bell County winning their fifth academic competition of the season. The high school academic team record had been 4-1 including one televised win.

Closer to home things were not going so well. The girls' junior varsity and varsity suffered losses on the home floor, as did the middle school basketball team away. The girls' varsity record was 6-1, the middle school boys' record 14-4.

Other Christmas events that year included boys' dorm parties, the church choir concert, the student choir singing two differing programs, and the second of four major drama programs for the year. Then home for Christmas for the Oneida family!

That year Barkley was named a Kentucky Colonel by then-Governor Martha Layne Collins. Being named a Kentucky Colonel is the highest honor bestowed by the Commonwealth of Kentucky by the governor. According to the office of the governor of Kentucky, "Kentucky Colonels are unwavering in devotion to faith, family, fellowman and country. Passionate about being compassionate. Proud, yet humble. Leaders who are not ashamed to follow, gentle but strong in will and commitment. The honorable order of Kentucky Colonels, as a brotherhood, reaches out to care for our children, support those in need and preserve our rich heritage." (I've never known a Kentucky Colonel who from his appointment onward didn't refer to himself as Colonel. Yet there it was buried in the letter files—not mentioned by him, but in letters from Kentucky gentlemen who addressed him as such.)

1987-88
Year 16

The calls are daily, pressing and, in many situations, heart rending. Just last week three brethren brought an 18 year old boy to us whom they discovered had been sleeping in a car for two years, even on the coldest nights of winter.
—Barkley Moore

January 1, 1987 found Barkley and twenty of his staff finishing up the work done in the computer lab during the Christmas break. They had repainted, carpeted, and assembled twenty new computer desks, added two large sections of cabinets, added new disk drives, printers and software. There probably wasn't a better computer lab in the state, certainly not one more used, as Oneida's lab was open twelve hours daily.

Major work had also been done in the office. While the overall physical plant had tripled in the past ten years, the office space was basically the same. During the break some of the staff re-organized the space once more, getting rid of as many things as possible. Almost all the records were now computerized such as: the mailing list, payroll, accounts payable, student accounts.

The sixty-member academic staff and house parents arrived back on New Years day along with four additional staff. A new apartment building for faculty had been completed on Little Bullskin, the ancestral home of President Burns, where the school owned more than eighty acres in various coves and hollows. In all eleven families had moved into different housing to better accommodate everyone.

The following afternoon they all gathered for a seven hour meeting. Every student's name was read and discussed in detail. The next morning they continued the meeting for two more hours reviewing the past semester and making plans for the new one.

As the students arrived the following day, as much as could be done had been and they were "off and running". Barkley wrote:

> As we enter upon the New Year, we are thankful for the blessings of God. We are mindful of the truth of the text of the first sermon preached on the Oneida campus, New Year's Day, 1900: "Except the Lord build the house, they labor in vain that build it.

There would be more building going all the coming year. Work was under way on the 3,000-square-foot Craft House being added onto the back side of the 125-year-old historic log cabin, the James A. Burns Museum. That year they would finish a new 3,000-square-foot agriculture center, which would be named for J.B. Henson. A 4,000-bushel holding bin for shelled corn, needed for the corn from Oneida's fields, would be built. Oneida's farm was an enormous operation, and growing yearly. Its produce, beef and pork were the mainstay of the schools food supply. The labor provided to run it was primarily Oneida students.

Again there were no direct mailers going out, but Barkley did use the *Oneida Journal* to let Kentucky Baptists know how thankful he was to them.

Sleeping in a Car

> Many of you who read these words contribute to our work. But the great majority do not. Those who do are more than contributors or benefactors to us. We think of you as a friend, a dear friend of girls and boys, one who puts your money where nearly every cent goes to feed, house, care for medically, teach, and, in many instances, clothe more than 500 young people.
>
> We are reminded that our Lord picked out the word "friends" to

characterize those choice souls who had come through all the tests and stood before him at the last, trustworthy and beloved. Sometimes people comment on the friendliness that is a part of Oneida. We like to say that it is friendliness reflected from all our wonderful friends.

Daniel Webster once said, "If we work upon marble, it will perish; if we work on brass, time will efface it; if we rear temples, they will crumble into dust; but if we work upon mortal souls, if we imbue them with principles, with the fear of God and the love of fellow man, we engrave on these tablets something which will brighten all eternity." And so we do together at OBI.

The Lord has blessed in so many ways this past year. Yet it remains the struggle it has always been to keep on day by day, and to try to improve. There are as many, and perhaps more, today in our school on full scholarship, not paying even a penny, than any day of our history. We care for nearly four times more children than we did for 70 years of our history.

The calls are daily, pressing and, in many situations, heart rending. Just last week three brethren brought an 18 year old boy to us whom they discovered had been sleeping in a car for two years, even on the coldest nights of winter. Often he went hungry. Occasionally he would steal to eat. Sometimes he would do something to get arrested, just so he might have a warm meal and a bed in the county jail. They brought some clothing articles, and we have since gotten more clothes for him. He has been out of school several years, but is now happily going to class each day. We are very impressed with him. His smile has brightened several difficult days.

How can we turn such a one down? We cannot while there is a bed.

But to be able to minister to all we care for, and others who wish or need to come, we must have the help of people like you.

I cannot bring myself to come and high pressure you face to face. In 15 years as president of this school, I recall directly asking for something, face to face, one time. I do present our cause when speaking. I do present our needs when writing like this.

What we are doing is as worthy as any, much more worthy than most, for we get a lot more done, dollar for dollar than most. We invite any doubters to come and see for themselves.

We feel the Holy Spirit will direct those in whom he dwells. Yes, he will direct you to share with us if that is his will. If he moves your heart to help us, please do not resist. Do not quench or grieve him.

If he does not lead you to help us, he will surely call you to some other work of his. We can only let you know our needs, about $7,000 per day.

It is, and has always been, a struggle at Oneida. We are never satisfied with anything short of our best for the many boys and girls who seek only an opportunity. We are not willing to give up this effort.

If Oneida is God's work, and the evidence of every day of every week of every month, for 87 years, gives testimony that it is, then it must be that God is well pleased with this kind of struggling, this approach to fundraising. Our approach is to have faith, do God's work, and to daily proclaim his good news.
Western Recorder, January 20, 1987

While January was more typical of early spring, February was back to wintry weather. In the first week, snow banks piled up all over campus which brought the boys out with shovels. As soon as they got them cleared it snowed some more. The men put large blades on several vehicles and plowed the road on campus and the streets where faculty lived, which meant a good part of the village. There was no excuse to miss a single class.

One Friday morning, the sun finally broke through the snow clouds. Barkley had come to the office as burdened down with the weight of responsibility as the heavy snow on ground. He found himself unable to stay in his office. Not a kid anymore but still taken in by the beauty of the sun beaming through his window, he let his feet take him for a walk! He checked in on classrooms filled with working students. He went to the classrooms where the younger children were singing. This always lifted his spirit. They sang out to him, "Good morning Mr. Moore" and several went over to him or gave him a wave. He went from there to Britton Hall, built just a year or so after the founding of Oneida. The old two story house with its large white columns and second story balcony porch, was where the kindergarten for staff children, were busy playing with Mrs. Buckner and Dot Burns. Walking back up the street he checked on the progress of the Craft House. He was fully restored as he paced at a fast clip back to his office, just in time to open the morning mail. He no longer seemed to carry such a burden! Soon it was chapel time, and his heart was full as he went in to lead the students in praising the Lord.

In March Oneida won three regional championships and one of the coaches won "Coach of the Year." That was also why he was at Oneida. He loved cheering on the various teams.

Oneida swimming and diving coach Rick Coffey had earned the title with eighteen of his coaching peers voting for him at the regional meet. He had been with Barkley nine years by then, along with his wife Jennifer, an outstanding middle school teacher. Barkley was so proud of him, knew he richly deserved the honor. Rick had come to Oneida because of Bob Halcomb, an Oneida principal, back in Ohio where Rick attended high school. Senior Stuart Brice had won the diving championship under Mr. Coffey's excellent coaching.

With sixteen teams competing in regional wrestling, Oneida's Paul Brewer, a senior from London, won the championship in the 145-pound class. His wrestling coach was Daryl Hensley, an OBI graduate, back after college to teach. Paul wasn't all brawn. He was also an excellent speaker. He played a key role in Oneida's winning "Most outstanding delegation" in the 1986 Kentucky Youth Assembly.

The "Oneida Players" drama group had won the regional drama championship…the sixth in the past nine years. The group had presented a one act play, by Allison Spitz titled *Broken Sentence*. Tom Jenkin was the drama coach and also the soccer and baseball coach that year. With all that was going on in athletics, Oneida was also turning out spelling and art champs.

Oneida sixth grader Gary Goodman won the 1987 countywide spelling championship, ranking first among nearly 5,000 county students. Barkley smiled when he thought back to the letter he had received a few years ago in which a donor had rebuked him for a letter that had gone out with a misspelled word. He planned to take Gary and Troy Taylor, who had also won the award when he was in seventh grade, out to a steak dinner.

The art work of two Oneida students won awards in regional competition that same spring and had been sent on to state. One of those artists was Stuart Brice, a senior. He also was outstanding in drama, writing, and athletics. The other artist was Willie Akidil. He had been there since seventh grade. He had been brought to Oneida by his great aunt, a psychologist with the Manhattan Board of Education, who had raised him. Barkley had practically raised him since then! Willie was also extremely talented in weight lifting, and had a beautiful voice. His aunt had written just recently thanking him.

Oneida faculty and staff were hopping as well as Barkley that spring. But, it wasn't all work. Especially that glorious spring morning in April when the Greyhound's engine was cranked up, along with one other bus. Sixty-eight young people piled aboard, along with band director Richard Burns and Barkley. They were off to the "Dogwood Festival" in Knoxville, Tennessee, for an overnight excursion where the band would march in their second competition public parade.

Arriving just in time to dress quickly, get their instruments, flags etc., they found themselves in a group of 367 other bands lining up to march. They were just a short distance behind Grand Marshall Willard Scott, NBC *Today Show* weatherman.

Afterward it was a half-mile walk back to the Greyhound. They all piled into it, instruments and all, including Barkley. It was a tight squeeze, even though all their uniforms, band equipment, flags, were stashed in the luggage compartment. They all rode together, stuffed in like sardines, to find their other bus.

Since they had left early that morning, they were all starved. Bob and Pat Key of Central City, whose son was in the band, met up with them and brought food. Then they were off to find restrooms where the band members got out of their hot uniforms and ate.

From there they were off to Oak Ridge on an educational trip to a museum. Then it was back to Knoxville to the festival in the evening.

On the way back they ate a picnic supper in Cove Park. They spent the night at Chilhowie Academy, Oneida's sister school just outside Knoxville. Barkley always packed these trips with as much fun and education as possible. It had been an exciting three day trip. These were all reasons Barkley was at Oneida—to cheer these fine young people on to victory in all areas of their lives.

There was another mountain top experience that spring. Almost 250 students were loaded onto school buses for a trip to gigantic Rupp Arena on the University of Kentucky Campus. They were to be a part of the ceremony for the commissioning service of forty-nine foreign missionaries in front of a crowd of around 15,000 people from all over the Southern Baptist Convention.

This spiritual "high" was followed by the spring revival, led by A.B. Colvin, who had recently become President of the Kentucky Baptist Convention, and who continued to be Barkley's assistant. There were multiple decisions for Christ.

Barkley wrote in the *Oneida Journal* about the adventures of several teams, complete with coaches and chaperones, all out at once over the state, all in one weekend.

They all returned safely, while the hundreds still on campus had gone about the normal on-campus routines of work, study, free time, *etc*. There was much evidence that his Oneida family had not been idle on campus, while he and so many others had been away.

Two weeks before graduation, all the faculty were back in another six-hour meeting at the end of a school day. Their supper was brought to them from the school kitchen as they met in the library. That meeting was to decide who would earn the schools highest honors. Barkley was always there for that specific meeting.

Early the next morning he was off to Cedarmore for the May meeting of the Executive Board of Kentucky Baptist and was back by 5:00 PM at his desk working.

The days flew by. When guests arrived he always stopped to give the "Tour". During the same week he had special meetings with staff, and speaking engagements across the state. He also hosted twenty-two guests from First Baptist Church, Hamilton, Ohio to a tour and lunch.

Just as he finished that round, he found guests from Bowling Green, Central City, Morganfield, and Murray, Kentucky arriving.

He was off with the choir on Mother's Day to sing at the Prestonsburg Presbyterian Church where the church was filled nearly to capacity. Afterwards they were served a tremendous dinner. Barkley's reputation for enjoying good food preceded him every where he went as well as his reputation for speaking past the hour. Perhaps that's why he got served so many good meals right in the church—to get him to quit preaching! Anyway it was on to the Bert T. Combs highway, where Barkley noted to the students that it was named for a former student of the Institute, of course. They traveled on to Crittenden Baptist Church in time for supper and a concert that evening and back to Oneida by 1:00 AM.

On the Monday before Graduation, the Yearbook Honors were announced in chapel. The yearbook was dedicated to Rick Coffey. Right in the middle of all that excitement guests from Frankfort Buck Run Baptist arrived along with a five person film crew from New York— there to finish filming *The Oneida Way*.

The following day farm manager Jack Tillman took a group of twenty seven girls, members of the OBI chapter of Fellowship of Christian Athletes, on a six-mile hay ride up Little Bullskin Creek and back, along with their sponsors. They meant to sleep under the stars, but rain prevented that, so they all went back and slept on the gym floor.

All that led into graduation weekend, Saturday May 16. There were all the usual events leading up to graduation including the Athletic Banquet and the Junior-Senior Banquet. According to Barkley, both events were just about the best he had seen at Oneida. Then, there was a beautiful musical comedy, *Snoopy*. The next day those attending numbered in the hundreds as the Commencement service began its four hour session. All nine of the living members of the Class of 1927 were back as well. In the Class of 1987, thirty-one received the Advanced Diploma, having done an extra year of math, extra year of science, two years of a foreign language; and a year of art, drama or music in addition to the state requirements and Oneida's requirement of Bible and computer literacy. They expected about 90% of those to go on to college. During the festivities of the Saturday before they dedicated the newly finished farm building.

As soon as the ceremony ended, the campus was emptied of students in a matter of minutes. Students, having already loaded luggage onto buses, cars, vans, flew away the moment it was all over. As soon as the last guest was gone Barkley walked up the hill toward home for the night, satisfied that he had done his best for one more group of his children.

The Mountain Missions Conference would be beginning in a few days with camps running through the summer. Crops were being planted and volunteers would be working on projects all over campus as well as finishing up the new craft facility. Summer school would be beginning in a short time. He would have a few days to examine the financial situation.

While he hadn't had time to give it a lot of attention he still needed to let their friends know they needed help. It was an ever-present responsibility, and now he turned his thoughts to writing a letter, updating friends of the school on what was happening.

Dear Friend:

Have you ever walked a swinging bridge?

We have a new one across Goose Creek leading directly from our new athletic complex to the road in front of our farm manager's home. We are putting a cypress floor on it that should last for decades to come. This bridge will cut off three fourth mile walking per day for each boy and girl working on our farm.

Do you like to string and break beans? Or shuck and silk sweet corn? If so, come and visit with us and we'll let you in on the fun.

We have 17 acres of vegetable gardens planted. We have more than 600 mouths to feed three times daily and it takes a lot of food! We have been eating from the gardens for more than 6 weeks. We are raising cabbage, tomatoes, broccoli and cauliflower, lettuce, carrots, three kinds of squash, okra, lima and snap beans along with the green beans, already mentioned, asparagus, beets, radishes, onions, cucumbers, spinach. Then there are the pumpkins (wonderful pies will result) and kids love watermelon, cantaloupe, and strawberries.

Oneida boys and girls LEARN to WORK.

Come to visit and browse in the new 3000 sq. ft. addition to our Craft House. You can watch out students making beautiful craft items. You may want to take a turn at the quilting rack and help sew a new pillow!

It has been 18 months since we have written a letter like this to you. We do not hound people to death. You, yourself, know that we do not fill your mailbox with constant appeals. We do not beg over the radio or television. We have no gimmicks to sell or give you to encourage you to give to us.

Will you consider helping us begin our new fiscal year "in the black". We have many thousands of dollars of unpaid bills as I write. We do everything we can to help ourselves before we ask you for a dime. For example, I am informed that it has been a year and a half since we have bought a pound of beef or pork. We raise our own cattle and hogs and the feed to fatten them. But there is MUCH that we cannot do alone. Will you help? Surely you can spare $5, $10, $25 or $100! WILL you SHARE with Oneida's girls and boys who WORK to help themselves?

The fall semester opened with just over five hundred students. There were students from over twenty-five states and twenty-one countries, with more wanting to come. It grieved him that he couldn't take every needy child who wanted to come, but Oneida wasn't adding any more dorms for the simple reason that they didn't want to become just another large school. The board of trustees had urged him for some time to cap the number and now they had voted on it! Oneida was big enough to have a tremendous program and small enough to know and work with the students as individuals, and for each to have an active participation in the many activities, sports, music, art, and drama events.

While he was still speaking at churches almost every Sunday he was now so busy at Oneida, he wasn't looking for invitations. But, he always went when he was invited and would even offer a backup date if he was engaged on the date he was asked.

However, he stayed at Oneida during the week as much as possible doing the work God had led him to do, carrying on the mission entrusted to his care. He wrote in the *Oneida Journal* that it was his faith and belief that "when we do a good job with the boys and girls in our care, when we keep ourselves within God's will, that God will provide us all that we need".

Come and See for Yourself

God has promised to provide. We are simple enough to trust that. We practice it. We are not disappointed in how God makes provision nor in how much…The great majority of our young people are from poorer families, many from poverty. Some are refugees from communist or dictator-ruled lands. We take them first come, first served regardless of their color, religion or economic condition. We do not ask for references. It is enough for us to know that God created them. The Lord Jesus Christ died for them. If they are emotionally and physically mature enough to be away from home we will accept any child, grade 6-12 provided we have an empty bed. Why not? That is our whole reason for being. Jesus, the head of the Oneida school, commands us by His word and His example to do so.

Because we are faithful "to minister unto the least…to proclaim daily his saving gospel to our young people, to feed the hungry… clothe the naked…give water to the thirsty…take in the stranger", our God is faithful to us. He brings people to see what is being done at Oneida. Our work speaks for itself. Thousands who have been ministered to are living witnesses. Those who know go and tell those who do not know.

The "report" is sufficiently positive that we have had a five-fold increase in students and staff over the past fifteen years. Our physical plant has tripled. Our financial support is up thirteen-fold in fifteen years. The effectiveness of the program for our children has measurably increased.

This has not been done by copying the methods of the business world. It has been accomplished by ministering to those who come to our doors and trusting in God to sustain and bless us. He has mightily. Come and see for yourself.

"Except the Lord build the house, they labor in vain that build it." *Psalms* 127:1

Western Recorder, September 8, 1987

Over the next three-month period there were 133 professions of faith. Eric Rigney, BSU president, led a nightly devotional during the Kentucky Baptist Student Union Convention at the Galt House in Louisville in September. (BSU is a college and University organization. Oneida is the only high school in the nation to have a chapter.) On campus there were regular devotional services led by the BSU all through the year. And then there was the Fellowship of Christian Athletes, who were instrumental in leading students to Christ. Eighty-eight were baptized by October, with more waiting. Pastor Joel Rackley was on and off campus all through the day, working with students.

Homecoming that year was one of the best ever. The weekend began with a "Sorghum Stir-off". The whole weekend of the old-fashioned Homecoming saw hundreds return. They dedicated the new 3,000-square-foot J.B. Henson Agriculture Center. They spread out over the athletic field to watch the marching band perform. They feasted on barbecued chicken, great kettles of soup beans and onions, boiled potatoes freshly dug from Oneida's gardens with plenty of butter, corn bread and homemade yeast rolls and home made cobbler.

Before Barkley knew it, it was countdown to Christmas!

Countdown to Christmas

December 2 was a cold, nippy starlit night with the feel of Christmas in the air. The church was filled to see Mr. and Mrs. Mallard's video tape of their nearly two months in Spain last summer where they visited various mission stations and Baptist work. This is their sixth year teaching with us, he in science and she in Spanish. They are a wonderfully dedicated Christian couple who took a

$28,000 cut of income to serve at OBI. Several weeks ago we had an equally large crowd as Rev. and Mrs. Rackley gave their presentation of their three-week missionary trip to Kenya.

Dec. 5 was a gorgeous sunny Saturday with students off for six differing events in eight buses. The single biggest event was our Marching Band marching in the Lexington Christmas parade.

Dec. 6 was another beautiful Sunday. I took three of our students and spoke at Mt. Tabor Baptist Church, a few miles away from Lexington… I got to personally see our band as they led the parade.

Our Middle School Choir, teacher Patrica Schmittendorf leading, did an excellent job at evening worship singing A Gathering at The Manger. Scores of those involved with the Fellowship of Christian Athletes went caroling afterwards in our community.

Dec. 8 our Marching Band reportedly did a superb job representing Clay County in the Governor's Inaugural parade. I saw them on film tonight over TV while visiting with our hardworking farm manager, Jack Tillman, and his wife who teaches our piano classes. Besides those 70 being away all day, nearly 40 swimmers and divers had to leave for Covington right at chapel time. Unfortunately these 110 missed a tremendous message at our daily chapel by Dr. Tal Bonham, executive secretary-treasurer of the Ohio Baptist Convention. His son is one of our students. Tonight 57 of our international students and Baptist Women had a wonderful meal at Mr. and Mrs. Rackley's with food representative of some favorite dishes of the ten foreign countries our students come from. Such a dinner is held annually to share some Christmas cheer with many who are thousands of miles from home and family.

Dec. 9 several were baptized, the church monthly business meeting was held, and the Baptist women had a fine presentation on foreign missions. A reception was held in the pastor's home afterwards for the "singles" of our school staff…

Dec. 10 Oliver Hawkins, in his 11th year of service here, preached a wonderful message at chapel. Tonight our cheerleaders along with their staff sponsors, Mrs. Robinson and Miss Creech, went Christmas caroling. I became aware of this when I heard them singing outside my office door. Our business manager and bookkeeper, Tim Erwin, in his 6th year of service joined me in responding to their special salute.

Dec. 11 A fine musical group from Tennessee Temple University led our morning chapel.

Dec. 12 OBI was visited by members of Calvary Baptist Church, Berea, bringing over 1200 home made baked Christmas cookies, candy canes, etc for our 550 students. Many of these were enjoyed immensely by our girls in their annual dorm Christmas party after, "free time"…

Western Recorder, December 22, 1987

Hear the Song

On Dec. 13 the usual morning services were held in the Oneida Baptist Church, each reminding of the birth so long ago. The Clay County Choir, directed by Oneida's Choir, director Richard Burns, sang Handel's glorious *The Messiah* in the evening worship service. A reception was held for them in the historic Anderson Hall. The 14 room house with its great columns has hosted many Christmas events over the past 76 years.

Later in the evening the annual older boys' dorm party for 218 residents of Carnahan and Marvin Wheeler Halls were held.

Dean and work supervisor Bud Underwood and Mrs. Underwood and Steve Derryberry led Chapel this morning. Their voices blended so beautifully in song. Among our younger staff, each day of their lives is a sermon in love and concern for others. They have a wonderful rapport with our students and everyone.

Another busy day ended with the younger boys of Baker Hall, capacity 112, having their annual Christmas part. Each boy ate homemade cookies, received a Christmas gift, made possible by the generous provision of Mr. and Mrs. Whitehouse, who owned The Cherry House and are very active in the Ballardsville Baptist Church.

Day 15-Mrs. Schmittendorf and her choir led the chapel service today. The staff children, kindergarten through grade five, are so cute as are our sixth and seventh and eighth graders. They sang contemporary Christian songs of Christmas.

Day 16-Tim, the middle of the Mallard's sons, and his fiancée are home from New York on the holidays. They are fine musicians. Their chapel program was another Christmas spiritual treat. Even the oldest of our staff felt something of a child again looking at our beautiful chapel Christmas tree.

Day 18-Exams and the semester over, we assembled for our annual service in the chapel and listened as our Oneida Choir sang so beautifully the wonderful carols of Christmas. Many parents and other school friends present to pick up students for the holidays shared in this always special service. It climaxed weeks of Christmas activity. Amid much hustle and bustle, each heads for home. Happy, noisy, cheerful youth in their prime and glory. Happy birthday, Lord Jesus.

"Savior, make us to remember, other children near and far, who should see the star."
Western Recorder, January 5, 1988

The Christmas letter was lying on his desk ready to be mailed. He had seen the star of Bethlehem and his boys and girls at Oneida had been given every opportunity to see it as well. It was with joyful satisfaction in a job well done that he ended the year of 1987.

Dear Friends:

As the old year passes, and the new one begins, new hopes are entertained and old ones are made brighter. Faith in God and in one's fellow man, created in the spiritual image of His love, are strengthened.

Surely no children in the world have any more loyal friends, with kinder hearts and more willing, helpful hands than those who have been fortunate enough to enter Oneida Institute. Most kindly Christmas greetings have come pouring into the office for several weeks. Many checks accompanied the greetings-some large ones, and the smaller ones greatly enhanced by the kindest words of interest, sympathy and sincere prayers for the complete success of our labors.

In many ways, the holidays were the longest, busiest days of the year. Still they were the happiest of days and we were filled with gratitude for the opportunity to work under such circumstances. A truer, more genuine spirit of Christmas was relayed through reading the hundreds of letters expressing goodwill and fellowship. Such an experience is one never to be forgotten, wholesome and elevating. At times one dared to hope that we might enter the new year with absolutely no deficit. But this was not quite meant to be.

To the friends of our school, old and new, we send our final word for 1987. God wants Oneida to live...of that we are certain. He has the means to accomplish His purposes, the people to do His will...that we know full well. "He stretched out the north over the empty place and hangeth the earth upon nothing." "Five sparrows are sold for a farthing and not one of them is forgotten before God." Nothing of His is too great or too small for His care. "Blessed are those servants whom the Lord when He cometh shall find watching."

As we enter 1988, dear friends, how can we thank you? With words, yes, but they are such a little thing. We often find ourselves wishing that kindnesses and good deeds could be repaid directly, but that can be only rarely. The poor man whose hopelessness was relieved by the Good Samaritan could not repay his benefactor directly, but he could try his best to go and do likewise We pledge anew, in our one public New Year's resolution, to use every dollar given to Oneida as wisely as we know how in the education and training of these young people for Christian living and leadership.

Barkley Moore,

President

1988-89
Year 17

The great majority of American teenagers are simply bored to death at school and after school. Unable to do more than attend class, they make their own excitement. They are turning increasingly to "pot", hard drugs, alcohol and promiscuous sex. The "dropout" rate steadily increases.
—Barkley Moore

I t had been quiet. With over 550 teenage boys and girls away two weeks for the Christmas holiday, it was very quiet. That was wonderful for a few days, but Barkley missed each one of them. For his part, he liked the sound of young people at work and play. The decision to hold the bed count to 500 had many waiting to be accepted as Oneida entered into 1988. The growing word of mouth from educators, pastors, and lay folks who had now come to trust Barkley's methods and the school's reputation for an outstanding academic program was the driving force that propelled the sheer numbers of parents, educators, and those in the ministry seeking Oneida's help.

The school was literally flooded with applications. The students too had found Oneida! Why? In a word, they were "Somebody" at Oneida. America's children had long since become just a number in a system that produced sheer numbers, a system that reduced the individual to a "nobody". Barkley wrote:

On the Frontline

Ours has been a response to a genuine need, a felt need, not an artificially created one...The bigger the number, the bigger the school, the less opportunity for the individual girl or boy. In most American schools today, the sense of community has been lost. There is a notable lack of effective discipline. A proper learning atmosphere has been lost in large measure...

Unfortunately, most of American education at the elementary and secondary level is so structured today as to make the average student feel like he or she is a "nobody." Sheer numbers force most young people to be spectators, not participants. The great majority of American teenagers are simply bored to death at school and after school. Unable to do more than attend class, they make their own excitement. They are turning increasingly to "pot", hard drugs, alcohol and promiscuous sex. The "dropout" rate steadily increases...
Western Recorder, January 19, 1988

When over 500 returned and more waiting on a snowy Sunday evening for the start of a new quarter, he was thrilled to see them, hear their laughter. How could he turn down even one? He felt in his heart that if Oneida could save just one from becoming a "dropout" it was worth the effort. But, oh the joy of seeing them not only not drop out but excel! Every hour they were away was an hour too long! Potentially an hour missed in their training. Their return marked for him the passing of time.

Each day and each birthday is a reminder of the passing of time. We are grateful for each day the Lord gives us to live and serve. We are also thankful for the ETERNITY we already have by FAITH.

His mission in life was to tend to their training, to their becoming "more than conquerors", not mere dropouts. They were on the frontline and fight they would for every boy or girl who entered the halls of the Oneida Baptist Institute.

That January the weather was warmer than usual and Oneida missed out on the all too frequent flooding of the creeks and river that bounded Oneida on three sides. However, the floods would come—by February they were having beautiful spring-like days with the temperature in the low seventys and the birds twittering everywhere. It was a most unusual day for early February as Barkley began to unfold the story, of the many activities in which the students were engaged. They were off to destinations all over the state in their quest for excellence. When they returned, it would be to hit the books with equal zest.

A Victory-Filled Day

Our wrestling team was up, had breakfast and left campus by 6:00 AM one recent Saturday. They were competing at Wayne County against teams from eight other schools. Such meets are very lengthy affairs. It was a weary group that got back to the campus 17 hours later at 11:00 PM.

Jason Payne, a junior from Knox County, took second place honors in the 152 pound weight class. Two of our wrestlers took fourth place in their classes...

The freshman and junior varsity boys basketball teams left at 8:00 AM and returned at 3:00 PM. Their games were played against Williamsburg High. Our Oneida boys won their games with the exact same margin, 29 points.

Junior varsity coach David Robinson and freshman coach Greg Slade do superb jobs with all of their teaching and coaching duties. They are both Oneida graduates and were roommates several years while here in high school. They graduated together in 1982, both honor students. David's wife Bonita is also a real asset as a teacher and cheerleading sponsor.

At 1:00 PM our swimmers and divers went into action in a home meet against Paul Blazer and Boyd County High Schools.

A standing room only crowd watched the exciting meet from the bleachers of our heated pool. Our boys defeated Paul Blazer 56-22, a team we had previously lost to. Also our boys had a 67-16 victory over

Boyd County. Our OBI girls defeated Boyd 45-30 but lost decisively to an excellent Paul Blazer team.

Eric Dishner, a sophomore from West Virginia, was outstanding in diving, winning with 171.9 points. He reminded me of our OBI standout last year, Stuart Brice, who won the regional diving championship.

Hitoshi Nakamura, from Japan, won the 40 yard freestyle in 19.2 seconds. He is also an excellent baseball player.

Jeff Jackson, a sophomore from Corbin, shined as he broke our school records for the 100 yard freestyle in 52.6 seconds. He is also an honor roll student.

Mary Ratliff, with us since sixth grade, broke her own standing school records in the 100 yard and 200 yard freestyles. Mary started earning high school swim letters while still in elementary. She has six.

As soon as the swim meet was over, many of the swimmers hastened to board Oneida's two Greyhound buses at 4:30 PM for a band trip to Eastern Kentucky University. Our band was invited to play for 30 minutes before the start of the EKU-Tennessee State basketball game, during all 'time-outs' and halftime…

The trip to EKU was also special because it was our first time to take both our buses on the same trip. During the Christmas holidays, Somerset First Baptist donated to us another Grey Hound in excellent condition. Its rebuilt motor has only 50,000 miles. They are made for up to a million miles of travel. We've been greatly handicapped in having only one such bus because it takes two buses to haul our full band, our full choir, *etc.* An ordinary school bus just can't keep up with a Greyhound, and it is important to travel together in case of an emergency. Now that problem is wonderfully solved. The luggage compartments are super to store the band instruments in as well as luggage on long trips.

Meanwhile back at the campus, our middle school "B" team and our eight grade basketball teams were both defeating Owsley County teams.

Western Recorder, February 9, 1988

There was never a dull moment for sure; nor a moment when a student at the Oneida Baptist Institute couldn't be involved in some activity, whether fun, competitive, inspirational or scholastic. Barkley Moore's life revolved around and was mixed in with all of those activities. He would never have left the campus except in one of those Greyhound buses with his boys and girls if continuing fundraising hadn't been necessary. Fortunately, by 1988, his trips away for speaking engagements were usually on Sundays. So, he was able to go with his boys and girls on many of their trips. Nothing pleased him more than that; second best was cheering them on—whether they were leaving or returning home. He was there for them, making sure each one had his time in the limelight, to help each one be a Somebody.

Oneida was on the frontline of the battle; on the cutting edge of the educational and social problems—of a country in desperate need. Barkley wrote:

> Each life salvaged, each soul won to the Lord, each is important, each is precious. But there are millions who need our help. We can only minister to a few hundred at a time. But we are a lighthouse, a beacon of what can be, should be done.

In just a few days it would be time for the annual senior trip to Washington. That class that year would hold another first time for a senior class. Barkley was popping his buttons! There would be over one hundred graduating seniors in May 1988. That was a first! They would take the two Greyhounds.

The Oneida Rocket

March 17: There it sat. Blue and white. The great motor pulsating with power, built for 500,000 miles of travel...yes, half a million miles. Countdown. Two minutes to 7:00 AM and holding.

The door closed. No one could be seen about the vehicle. Though I could not see inside nor could I hear, I knew from past experience what was happening. All heads were bowed in prayer preparatory to a once-in-a-lifetime experience. Then at 7 on the nose, there were three great revs of the engine and they were off.

The Oneida Rocket?

No, just our old faithful Greyhound bus off on another senior trip to Washington, D.C. with a bunch of excited seniors and staff chaperones.

Breakfast at Oneida, lunch in Abingdon, Va. and supper in a suburb of Washington. Checking into their motel rooms that Friday night, they went bowling. then toured the Jefferson Memorial, the Marine Corps Memorial, and reportedly some wept at the Vietnam Memorial, America's own wailing wall, that has such a powerful effect on the many thousands who see it by day and by night. Then there is nothing more majestic than walking up the lighted steps and seeing the brooding Lincoln seated in his chair.

Day two began with breakfast and arrival at the White House at 8:00 AM for a specially arranged V.I.P. tour. Then the Washington Monument, where the elevator was closed but they enjoyed a tour of the Museum of Air and Space. The group afterwards picnicked at Haynes Point, an island in the Potomac River.

Then it was an evening at the theater, Ford's Theater, to see the play 'Elmer Gantry.' But as the lights dim one cannot help but look upward to the very box where Lincoln sat that fateful night.

Sunday found our group in Arlington Cemetery for the ever solemn hourly Changing of the Guard at the Tomb of the Unknown Soldiers. That ceremony is always one of the unforgettable memories of anyone's trip to Washington.

Also they visited the grave-sites of John and Robert Kennedy, saw the eternal flame, and straight up the hill is the home of Robert E. Lee.

Morning worship was at the Luther Rice Memorial Baptist Church in Siler Spring, Md. These mission-minded people warmly welcome our students each year. Several are longtime supporters of Oneida.

Then followed a picnic in Rock Creek Park where Teddy Roosevelt romped and Woodrow Wilson courted his second wife. A delightful Sunday afternoon spent with the animals of the National Zoo and a glimpse of the famous pandas.

The day ended with a leisurely supper, window shopping, and all the ice cream everyone could eat, a yearly tradition. New records were set.

Day four of Oneida's 38th annual senior trip to Washington began with watching money being printed at the Bureau of Engraving. Then followed and exciting time at the FBI headquarters seeing its many exciting exhibits, the shooting range, etc.

The afternoon was spent in the Capitol building itself. Following this the group split into four differing groups seeing either the Museum of American History or the Museum of Natural History, the National Art Gallery and the National Archives where the American Constitution is attracting more than usual interest in this 200th anniversary year...

Supper was eaten in historic Fredericksburg, Va. And then on to Colonial Williamsburg to spend the night.

Day five began with the usual morning devotion. The day was spent in touring wonderful Colonial Williamsburg. One has to have seen that old American town to understand what it means to walk the streets, visit the shops and eat in inns where our Colonial fathers lived their lives or at least visited if at all possible. This is the sixth time that Colonial Williamsburg has been an important part of our annual trip.

A side trip, a first, was a visit to Jamestown, the first white successful settlement of the English colonies. Seeing replicas of the thatch-like homes of those earlier settlers was interesting. But the most exciting was seeing the seaworthy exact replicas of the ships *Godspeed* and the *Susan Constant*. These ships have made the same voyage that our national forefathers made over 380 years ago. Our students and staff climbed around over the ship and posed for their only full group picture of the entire trip. Several thousand individual pictures were made during the week to be treasured a lifetime.

There followed shopping at Williamsburg Pottery and an evening meal of all the pizza one could eat. Then back on the bus for a trip to Charlottesville.

Day six began with a full morning at beautiful and historic Monticello, beloved home and revealing monument to the genius of Thomas Jefferson.

After a pleasant but uneventful day of travel, the weary yet excited travelers arrived at Oneida at 10:30 PM approximately two hours ahead of schedule.

Our seniors are safely back from Washington. Students and staff were bubbling over when they returned. It takes a lot to get young people excited these days.

I still remember vividly my own trip to Washington with the Class of 1958. No matter how many times one might visit Washington, there is nothing like doing so with one's classmates. Knowing that you are soon to separate along life's many differing destinies, never all again to be together, makes it singularly special.

It is heartening to know there are still young people like those who go on Oneida's senior trip year after year. In nearly 40 years of students going to Washington from Oneida we have never had a serious incident that would make us unwelcome to return to a hotel or motel or a restaurant.

The annual trip is one of Oneida's oldest and most valuable and cherished educational traditions.
Western Recorder, March 20, 1989

On March 21, in a letter to a family friend, Barkley reported on physical improvements that were being made.

We have finished a new 3-bedroom, 2-bath house with half basement behind firehouse for $32,000 air-conditioned and carpeted. It is beautiful. Last week we poured the foundation for apartments for 8 "singles" on a shelf above the farm, a gorgeous view. With the new swinging bridge that is a 12-minute walk from the office. We don't have a dime in hand or promised as of now, but going forward on FAITH as we have done nearly everything else the past 16 years. Somehow God sends us just enough to do what has to be done though always under pressure...you saw that day by day while you were here. I never cease to be amazed but watching how God works when we do our part in faith and love has made me a stronger person than when I first came now many years ago. I'm beginning to get rather gray around the fringes and recently my 3's and 5's have begun to fuzz for the first time, so went last Monday and had myself fitted for bifocals. They are taking some getting used to.

We had two floods early last month in the space of ten days to a depth of about five feet on the athletic field…the first flooding in the past five years, the first since we built the tract, etc. Many had told me for years that everything we had done there would wash away. The floods came and went, not even a hairline crack in the track or anything for which I am most thankful. Just washed off the mud with our high-pressure hose and went on. Early next March we plan to build four regulation tennis courts…We are steadily widening the opportunities for girls. When I first came here, we had one boys' basketball team and four cheerleaders.

Letters, 1989

Strawberries on the Sly

We have some of the most beautiful gardens you ever saw. When the planting is finished, there will be approximately 22 acres. This year's garden program began Feb. 15 with the planting of more that 400 cabbage, broccoli and cauliflower plants under plastic tunnels…

In early March, more of the same plants were put out plus 100 pounds of onion sets, and 200 lettuce plants. The lettuce heads are now the size of baseballs and just beautiful. Also, carrots, spinach, peas, beets and radishes were planted at the same time. They are now growing beautifully in nearly perfect rows.

In mid April the tomato plants were put out. They have been blooming for some days. Also there are pepper plants, watermelon, cantaloupe plants, straight neck squash and corn. To date about 7000 plants have been transplanted from our greenhouse with about 5000 more plants to go…

Officially we started picking our first strawberries a week ago. Don't tell anybody. I'm not supposed to know. Our boys, who weed the patch, unofficially have been picking for about two weeks. But that is the way it is when you put boys in a strawberry patch or a watermelon patch. That is why we have planted a lot of strawberries and melons. Our kids do the work. They also get to do the eating.
Western Recorder, May 24, 1988

Oneida wins statewide academic honor

Early Saturday morning another group drove to Louisville airport and took a flight to New York. These were our young people who, the weekend before, had taken part in the three day mock Kentucky United Nations Assembly meeting in Louisville. Over 500 of Kentucky's top students, representing 44 high schools, competed. Each school was assigned to represent a differing country in debate. Oneida was assigned the nation of Israel. At the conclusion, Oneida was voted "most outstanding country." The highest group award. We were the smallest school represented.

Our group then got to go to the United Nations and see the sights of New York for five days. Our students excel not just in one or two things, but in a variety of ways. It is a rewarding challenge to be involved in such a work.

In the afternoon, the half of our 60-voice choir not involved in tennis, softball, tract, baseball, the trip to New York or BSU sang at the funeral of Austin Sizemore, a 1966 OBI graduate and a former dean of boys and OBI farm manager. He died of a heart attack at age 43. Former OBI teacher and principal Harold Holderman and I led the service.
Letters, 1988

May flowers were blooming all over campus. The hills turned green overnight, or so it seemed. It felt like it was just yesterday that the school year had begun. But here they were in that seven hour faculty meeting deciding who would receive the honors for the year. May 15 was graduation and just days away. It was an upbeat group of teachers who voted by private ballet for the students they thought deserved the many honors to be given.

106 Graduate at Oneida

The largest and best prepared class in Oneida's history has just left us, a total of 106 young people...There were 95 Oneida staff members and several special guests marching in the academic procession in addition to the classes of 1928 and 1938. John Sanderson gave the invocation. Graduation this year was doubly special to the Sanderson's as their youngest son, Jay, was the class valedictorian. He was awarded a $15,000 scholarship by Vanderbilt University...

Presidents Awards were given to outstanding seniors. The top honor went to Elmer Lessa, the son of a Brazilian Baptist pastor... In athletics OBI freshman Damon Tigner was honored for winning the state Class A high jump...

Several staff members were honored for lengthy service, including Larry and Linda Gritton, 15 years, and Rick and Jennifer Coffey, 10 years. Earlier in the week Ada Abner was honored for 20 years service. (She was head cook.)...

Following student and staff honors, the congregation sang *Send the Light*. The benediction was sung that year, by graduates Willie Akikil, Anthony Pepper and Benny Williams. They sang *God Please Be Patient With Me*.
Western Recorder, May 31, 1988

As soon as graduation ended, they were into the summer program of work and camps. They were eating much fresh produce harvested from the early spring planting. How wonderfully the strawberries had tasted with fresh whipped cream on top. They continued to add to the gardens, planting more summer crops. They would have two more greenhouses by fall with a total 8,000 square feet where they would be able to grow at least 20,000 plants for transplanting, in the following spring, to the two commercial greenhouses built on the farm and named in honor of A.B.

Colvin. They would use "wide row gardening" rather than single rows. In wide row gardening plants are placed two to three wide. Officially, working on Oneida's farm was another way for students to shine and have a great sense of satisfaction. Bud Underwood's team of gardener students were dazzling Barkley and other onlookers with their efforts.

By September Oneida's eighty-ninth academic year was back in session. There was a net gain of four teachers over the last year. That meant a better teacher-student ratio than ever before. The visitors to Oneida on one particular day had seen the entire school staff, teachers, maintenance, cooks, office and house-parents gathered for the annual two-hour service in the Oneida Baptist Church held prior to the return of students for a new year. They had heard a sermon by trustee chairman Denvis Rush.

It was a dizzying few weeks until Homecoming. Barkley's correspondence glowed with the telling of it.

We are still in the glow of our annual HOMECOMING held earlier this month. We prepared for 2,000 people, both noon and the evening meal, and fed very nearly that many, the largest number of former students and staff, other friends and their families ever to be gathered at one time on our campus, along with present students and staff. Nearly all the food we served was raised here in our gardens and on our farm, including the meats, and we baked fresh bread for both meals as we normally do each day.

It was a day of hugging, kissing, talking and, yes, some tears. It was a day of song and prayer and sharing of scripture. It was a time of storytelling and remembering. It was a day of looking backward and forward. Former Kentucky Governor (1959-63) Bert T. Combs made a fine talk. He was a student at Oneida in the 1920's and a portrait of him was unveiled in the chapel to hang along with two others so previously honored in the history of the school. Two beautiful greenhouses totaling 6,000 sq. ft. were dedicated in the memory/honor of Rev. E.L.& Gladys Howerton and Dr A.B.& Irene Colvin. Their respective families were present and many friends. Alumnus Dan Davidson Jr., Class of 1956, was recognized for his outstanding state detective work now the subject of a nationwide best-seller book (a recent Book-Of-The-Month Club selection) titled Bitter Blood. Dan has been hired as a consultant on the TV series and the Hollywood movie that are to follow. Dan lived on our campus from age five through high school because his step-mother "Miss Imy" taught here for years, and his father was sheriff of the county when he graduated.

Eleven schools, all larger than Oneida, were here for HOMECOMING to participate in a cross-country run, volleyball and soccer meets. We won the soccer game 8-1, came in second in girls' cross-country and third in boys' cross-country out of eight school competing in that, and lost in volleyball. It was a beautiful day weather wise and many, many people commented that they had never seen our campus look nicer. Folks began touring our farm, the new greenhouses, and seeing our baby pigs as early as 8:00 AM. The Marching Band performed twice, the choir sang beautifully as usual, and our drama group did a good job with Our Town, two nights of performances. The Craft Shop did a tremendous business as many did their Christmas or other shopping. Our students produce many quality items, and we sell them for much less than most any other place. Four people were kept busy all day, sometimes five, in the Craft House.

In recent weeks, over sixty of our boys and girls have received the Lord Jesus Christ as their Savior, and have followed him in baptism. We have so very much to be thankful for. God is pouring His blessing upon us and you and everyone who helps sustain this work with gifts and prayer are a part of that ongoing miracle.

Letters, 1988

The first academic quarter had roared into a hot fall that all too soon turned into cool nights and crisp, cloudless days. Early in November, an alumnus, Judy Rose, made it possible for 100 members of the Band & Choir to hear the Metropolitan Opera star Roberta Peters perform at the University of Kentucky as well as a jazz concert. The choir traveled many miles in concert including: the Ohio Baptist Convention, concerts in

West Virginia, West Kentucky. Basketball season was underway. The fall sports season was over, now the wrestling, swimming and diving teams were hard at work. They had won the district soccer championship, had come in third place in the Region in girls' volleyball; and ranked second in the Region in cross-country.

The fall colors absolutely dazzled the eye that year, on the campus and in the surrounding mountains. Barkley wrote that, "Such beauty reminds us of all that we have to be thankful for." In counting the blessings of that fall there were many such as the irrigation system. They had been blessed with wonderful gardens, the largest Irish potato crop ever, thousands of bushels of corn which had been gathered and shelled for feeding the pigs and beef cattle through the winter months. Right then they had a cover crop of wheat growing on the former potato and corn fields.

He was personally busy every day with many guests and out speaking almost every weekend. On top of that there were the articles for the *Western Recorder* and hundreds of letters each week to write. And then he worked directly with the students as time permitted. It all made for a busy and fulfilling life, according to him.

Thanksgiving was well past with the students away for the break. Now the days were spiraling into a crescendo of activity climaxing one busy week and leading into another and finally to the Christmas break. During the month of December the chapel services were given by various foreign missionaries. There were missionaries from China, the Philippines, Kenya, Trinidad, and Liberia. All of these brought the reason for the Lottie Moon Christmas Offering to life for the students.

It all led down to the end of classes on Thursday before Christmas. At the final worship service, the seventy-member Oneida choir gave a wonderful program of music under the direction of Richard Burns. That was immediately followed by everyone boarding the buses and the beginning of the great exodus home for Christmas!

1989-90

Year 18

It is the purpose of Oneida to provide a climate for youth that is conducive to the development of: respect for authority, honesty in word and action and the highest moral Christian behavior; well adjusted and responsible personality and strong physical vigor; an appreciation of the value of an education and the attainment of each student's highest intellectual potential.
—Barkley Moore

Winter had come to Oneida. It came along the creeks and snuck up the crevices of the hollows and valleys lying silently below the towering grey hills. The quiet of the village belied the fact that on campus the staff that had stayed behind during the break were busier than if the students had been there. As always Barkley had plans for far more than was possible to get done during the break. While they did celebrate Christmas, the very next day, every one was busy again. The faculty arrived back in time for the first meeting just ahead of the students.

Barkley was still up at 2:45 AM on January 6, 1989. For the first time in nineteen years he was about to miss the "honors" meeting the next morning that he held with the faculty at the beginning of each spring semester. He simply had to be away! He wrote a memo for each of them to receive that morning. The memo in part read:

All that we are able to do <u>today</u> is built upon what has been accomplished in the <u>yesterdays</u> of Oneida. <u>What</u> we do <u>today</u> is the foundation on which all of Oneida's <u>tomorrows</u> will be built.

There followed a five page report of things that had been accomplished the past weeks between Christmas break and the opening of school. The darkroom had been expanded, all the offices in Russell Hall had been painted, and new carpet had been laid. Much painting had been done in the gym and the floor refinished. New closets were built in the gym, a wall had been removed in the special help department, a new road had been built from the north end of the athletic field to the south side, opposite the swinging bridge. New gutters were added on seven buildings. Space for 200 hogs had been added. The vegetables growing in the green house were a thing of beauty. "Beginning" nursing classes were to come. Changes in the Driver's Ed. schedule were planned. The update on costs of operating the school was $2,800,000 for the past fiscal year. Finally, he had a personal message for each of the staff.

I regret very much not being a part of today's "Honors" meeting. When we talk about our students, their efforts and our efforts in their behalf, we are talking about the very "heart" of our work. I have always found these meetings, and the discussion, and taking the time to consider those most worthy of honor, representative of that which makes Oneida a very special place. These meetings are always, for me, a time of inspiration, renewal, and recommitment to this very special work. I hope that Today's meeting will be such for you.

I trust that each of you know that I appreciate you each very much, care for you very much, though I seldom say it in a personal and individual way.

Barkley, not a morning person, was out the door of Anderson Hall that same morning with less than three hours of sleep. He was leaving for two funerals: that of Mr. E. Gaines Davis Jr., his former chairman of the board of trustees for seven years and a trustee for fourteen years, who had handled all of Oneida's legal matters for over twenty-five years and "never charged the school so much as a dollar". He would also attend the funeral of Mr. George Rickard, a friend of the school who contributed heavily until his death at eighty-five.

The morning's first rays of daylight peaked over the eastern ridges of Little Bullskin, long after Barkley and his student driver, John Saldaris, made their way around the big bend just outside Oneida. Daybreak found Barkley sound asleep in the backseat of the red Cavalier. When he awoke, it was to the brilliant light of a cold wintry day.

'Tis winter now
'Tis winter now; the fallen snow
Has left the heavens all coldly clear;
Through leafless boughs the sharp winds blow,
And all the earth lies dead and drear.

An yet God's love is not withdrawn;
His life within the keen air breathes;
His beauty paints the crimson dawn,
And clothes the boughs with glittering wreaths.
Samuel Longfellow

He knew "They that trust in the Lord shall be as Mount Zion, which cannot be removed, but abideth for ever. As the mountains are round about Jerusalem, so the Lord is round about his people from henceforth even for ever." (*Psalms* 125: 1-2) He thanked the Lord with his whole heart and they traveled on their journey.

In less than a month Mr. Cooper, the beloved old gardener, and Dr. George Redding, the beloved Bible teacher, who had retired from Georgetown College and taught at Oneida, both died. Barkley spoke and the choir sang at Paris, Kentucky for Mr. Cooper's funeral. The choir sang again for Dr. Redding's funeral in the John L. Hill Chapel at Georgetown College. It had become Barkley's custom over the years to attend funerals with the choir or ensemble, who would sing the hauntingly beautiful *When They Ring Those Golden Bells*, and *When We All Get to Heaven.*

By the end of January the students were well into their third quarter. It was no wonder that Barkley's thoughts were upon the use of time. In the *Oneida Journal* article on January 29, he wrote:

Make Each Day Count

One of the first things we do at the start of each new quarter is to call the honor roll for the previous nine weeks. Each student from the smallest sixth grader to the tallest senior that "made the grade" comes to the platform. There are two categories: those with straight A's and those whose overall grades average a B.

One never gets too old or sophisticated not to enjoy being on the honor roll and receiving recognition before one's peers. Those who don't make it, while perhaps slightly envious, generously give a round of applause to those who do.

Aside from the satisfaction of knowing that one has done a good job and the recognition, those whose names are called are not required to attend the evening supervised study hall in our two dining rooms. But every student must attend unless and until they do get on the honor roll. If one's grades drop so as not to be on the honor roll the succeeding quarter, then it is back to required study hall.

It is a fact of human nature of every age and clime that recognition is important to motivate people. It is one of the underlying principles of our work with boys and girls. Believe each can do something, expect them to do something, and recognize them for what they have done when they achieve it. There are few young people who are in our program for as long as nine months that are not recognized before their peers for something. We not only recognize the top but those who have made the most progress. This is true in academics, athletics, behavior, art, music, drama, vocational programs and in our dorm living.

It is also important that young people are taught and understand that a job well done is its own reward whether anyone else note it...
Western Recorder, January 31, 1989

Buildings were going up in more than one location. They were working on a new three-bedroom two-bath home for a staff family that he hoped would be finished by May. A new classroom building that would house seven new classrooms and a second gym were in progress, and he hoped they would be finished by October. A new 3,000-square-foot auto mechanics shop building was also under construction.

On the Oneida Farm winter had settled its brown wardrobe on corn stalks standing in the field even though it was warmer than usual for January. So when a fresh dusting of snow came it melted like frosting on warm brownies. Inside the temperature controlled greenhouses on the farm, no matter the weather outside that winter, rows of fresh produce and delicate strawberries were soon ready for harvesting. It was Valentine's Day and there were lots of sweethearts all over the campus, celebrating the beautiful spring like day. Barkley's joy, though he didn't have a sweetheart, was bubbling over!

Our Educated Pigs!

I just had a salad of fresh lettuce and tomatoes. Delectable! Delicious! Delightful! The lettuce and tomatoes were fresh from our greenhouse, growing in January. Also we have beautiful cabbage and cauliflower, and our own greenhouse radishes have been a part of our salad bar for weeks. It is exciting.

Also excited are many of our young people, largely middle schoolers, who are developing a 'green thumb.' One cannot measure or imagine the effects of each one for a lifetime, but certainly for the good…

Winter Turns Spring-like on Oneida's Farm

January turned into such a beautiful, sunny, spring like month. We got a tremendous amount of hill grubbing done on our farm clearing more pasture land. We average 10 students a day, five days a week, working with ax and mattocks. One beautiful Saturday we had 37 at work…

Another interesting daily sight on our campus every day except Sunday is watching our compost crew at work during their daily chore time.

All the leaves racked from our large campus last fall are in great piles near our gardens. These leaves are constantly turned over week by week with some manure and sawdust mixed in along. We also have a shredding machine that cuts up twigs and sticks through the fall and winter and is added to the compost. We also shred all our cardboard boxes to make a mulch to go around young growing garden plants. We think this natural fertilizer preferable to the "store bought" kind.

We teach our students that food comes from something other than a can...

Litter After Litter of New Pigs Are Coming On

Children and adults alike delight in seeing our cute "babies". Also they enjoy seeing our hogs drink water after they become bigger and are weaned from their mother's milk. We don't let our pigs drink out of some old trough or other container that they might step in or otherwise get dirty.

No sir! We educate our Oneida hogs to put their two front feet on a small raised platform and drink from a nipple waterer. That is a spring loaded nipple on our water system that flows by gravity from a reservoir we built some years ago in the hills above our farm. By this method the water is always fresh for our hogs, and there is very little waste...

On the Oneida Farm

Every time I think of our hog operation, I recall an episode summer before last. I took a number of visitors on a sunny afternoon to see the farm. I saw no one and heard not a sound. I assumed our students were in some field out of sight. I showed our 3000 sq. ft. farm shop building that includes our agriculture classroom. Then I directed the guests over to the hog barn. What was happening?

An old sow was giving birth to a large litter. One little pig followed another. For most of those boys, it was their first experience seeing a live birth of anything. They were in awe. No matter how many times one might see birth, of pigs or whatever, it is a revelation of the mystery and wonder of God's creation.

I will never forget that scene that afternoon. There is more to an Oneida education than books and ball games. That is nearly as awesome though as a little pig being born…

Western Recorder, February 14, 1989

Oneida's farming operation was essential to the school. In the year 1989 it would need to provide meat and fresh produce for the daily feeding of 500 students and 131 faculty and staff. In one way or another, from Barkley himself, to the farm crew, made up of staff and Oneida's student farmers, they were all caretakers of the land. Unknown to anyone, fast approaching them were swirling, churning, clouds, clouds that would produce the most torrential downpour of rain in over ten years; rains that would produce, not one but four floods of devastating proportions, one right behind the other. In the days ahead, friends of the school across the land would rise to the occasion to also become caretakers of the land, to keep the Oneida farm going and food on the table.

Oneida's boys and girls were learning the joy of work—the pleasures of a job well done. Barkley was quick to give a friendly smile, a pat on the back. He took great pleasure in sharing with Kentucky Baptists the triumphs of the Oneida farm.

A Rabbit in the Flower Bed

It is a beautiful spring day and I've just returned from showing a group of guests about our campus. Flowers are already blooming, have come up on their own, in varying flower beds. In one bed there is a gorgeous red flower different from all the others. I never saw anything so beautiful and I don't know what it is called. As we drank in the beauty, one of the guests pointed out that a beautiful fat rabbit was sitting in the middle of the bed! And so he was. He just looked at us making no move to leave. I remember the day each one came to us, the varying circumstances. Some were very difficult. But that is all past. Each has grown and matured, and each one I saw this morning is a better and happier person…

Across Goose Creek

Looking across Goose Creek, I could see some at work in the 3000 sq.ft. farm shop building. Others were busily painting our largest barn with a coat of red paint. Our farm manager appeared to say the crew was getting the job done faster than he anticipated. He had come for more paint. For a sixth grader, he is big for his age. He is very serious looking with his dark rimmed glasses. He has moved around a good bit in his life. He arrived three days ago for summer school. He seemed shy.

This Saturday morning I spent several hours walking around our extensive campus gardens. I found this young man, our newest student, working away in the garden, I thought to myself, "It's time for him to be homesick. He's probably feeling pretty sorry for himself. I'd better stop and talk with him a few minutes."

So I tentatively opened a conversation half expecting some belligerence, and broached the idea of being "homesick." His head jerked back, he looked up at me, and enthusiastically said, "Man, I love it here!"

That was wonderful to hear. We had a lively conversation. I walked on, my heart a little lighter. Twelve others were as busy as beavers also in the garden. Each gave me a warm smile, most everyone had something pleasant to say. There was a genuine pride of accomplishment with their tomatoes, melons and cabbage.

I looked up the mountain behind the chapel. Some of the boys have been busy with the weed eaters several days this week. Their efforts and the effect of daily rain showers have that grassy hill looking more beautiful than I have ever seen.

Western Recorder, February 14, 1989

Oneida Paint Shop

Walking back out of the garden, I came upon seven of our students painting beds. They had a production line going. Some carrying. One working with a spray gun. Two others touched up with brushes. Above their heads a crudely lettered sign: "Oneida Paint Shop."

Four were busy in our small motor repair shop. They were working on weed eaters and lawn mowers. With the many acres we have to mow, there is always repair work to be done.

Walking across campus I spotted seven busy on the lawn mowing crew in various areas. Two were hard at work in the garbage compound. A large number of girls and boys were breaking and stringing beans fresh from the gardens, which will be frozen for winter use.

Looking beyond the shop I found another large crew gathering watermelons, pumpkins and beautiful tomatoes. The melons have been especially tasty this summer and I could visualize the pumpkin pies. The tomatoes are being frozen for juice this winter and to be used for soups on wintery days.

A chain on our potato digger had just broken when I got to the farm. Already hundreds of bushels had been dug in the morning hours and seven of our boys were busy carting the filled wooden crates into our large underground potato cellar.

It is the purpose of Oneida to provide a climate for youth that is conducive to the development of: respect for authority, honesty in word and action and the highest moral Christian behavior; well adjusted and responsible personality and strong physical vigor; an appreciation of the value of an education and the attainment of each student's highest intellectual potential.

These goals are attained by giving proper attention to the disciplines necessary to develop the spiritual, physical, mental and social capacity of each individual.

Western Recorder, April 4, 1989

Champs All

Our middle school has proven themselves champions this year, academically and athletically.

Some weeks ago our middle school team won the regional middle school Governor's Cup Academic Championship defeating 13 other district champs and district runner-ups in the process.

Our middle school basketball team ended their season with a remarkable 37-0 record against the "best" of many counties. Winning every game in many exciting and close contests they won three invitational championships.

Chosen most valuable player in the tournament was eighth grader Larry Allen Gritton Jr. of Oneida. [Now the President of Oneida Baptist Institute] He was also chosen MVP in the same tournament last year even though the OBI team came in third place in that competition. Larry is a straight "A" student and an active Christian. All his school years have been at Oneida, his father and mother having been teachers here 16 years. His dad has been our varsity basketball coach all those years.

Larry comes by his love of basketball naturally and he has tremendous ability. Through much of the season this year, he was not only our leading middle school scorer but was also the sixth man on our varsity team which had a 20-10 season. Those "in the know" say he will be one of the state's most remarkable players in his high school years. In any event, he is a very choice young man in every way. *Western Recorder*, May 2, 1989

On May 21, Oneida graduated 116, the largest number of graduates ever. It was also the ninetieth Commencement ceremony of the school. In a standing-room-only crowd over 1,000 gathered close as all 100 of the Oneida staff, and members of the Class of 1939, celebrating their fiftieth reunion, everyone in full academic regalia, led the procession up the stairs to the Melvin Davidson Chapel. Behind them were the 116 graduating seniors. "It was the best of times, it was the worst of times." (*A Tale of Two Cities*, Charles Dickens)

The First Flood Comes

Floodwaters were all about us June 16. Looking south was one vast lake from our campus hill to near our farm manager's home. Only the tops of our concrete block dugouts could be seen on the athletic field and the second story of our concession-dressing room building.

Our beautiful gardens, the potato field and the corn fields were totally submerged and presumably totally destroyed. We had already been eating from the gardens since mid May.

Our farm manager got Walters, our civics teacher, across the new lake in a boat in time to teach his summer class. Mrs. Walters works in guidance but she didn't brave the boat trip!

Also Gilbert Samples, teaching biology, made it in. The public highway at the western corner of our campus was about four feet underwater. So he had to walk the last several hundred feet to our campus going through Homer Allen's front yard and garden to get onto our campus. Before the day was out scores of guests had done the same.

Our senior and junior English teachers were cut off by flood waters on the eastern side of the campus. The seniors were doing a research paper and worked all day in the library under the watchful eye of our librarian, James Yowell. Our Appalachian studies teacher and former English teacher, Betty Rackley, filled in for the juniors. So the school day proceeded very normally for nearly 200 summer school students.

Boys' dean and work supervisor "Bud" Underwood had been up all night superintending other staff and students in removing a tool shop, many buses, etc. to the higher ground of the campus. Spare bus tires were tied with ropes so they would not float away.

Several of our faithful cooks realizing we were about to be cut off, came to work hours early and all were bountifully fed through the excitement of the day.

Shortly before chapel, a prospective student and family climbed their way around the mountain into our campus for their tour and interview. In the group was the elderly widow of an Episcopal priest who broke her hip a year ago. She arrived with a large tobacco stick in hand looking like Moses about to part the waters!

Twenty six senior citizens from Louisville's Beechmont Church, some very senior, wound their way up and around the mountain into our campus, having found the highway blocked. Some of our school boys had spotted them and were assisting them. Hours later our boys again gave them their arms around the mountain to their bus.

Next to arrive was a Hopkinsville lawyer and his family, the daughter a prospective sophomore for the next year. They arrived on the eastern side of our village, close enough to our campus to get a picture but not to get in because of the floodwaters. One of our recent graduates led them 47 miles back around to come into our campus.

The floodwaters began to recede in mid afternoon and by dark the highways were once more open on each side. Our guests had all departed including a group of volunteers from Severns Valley Church, Elizabethtown, who had arrived the previous Sunday to work all week.

Just before dark one of our 1988 graduates arrived from Tennessee to see us. He was so anxious to get here he got a speeding ticket! On the verge of being a "drop out" when he first came to Oneida, he now has a "B" average at his university.

After midnight two of our girls, graduates in 1983, telephoned. They were visiting one another and reminiscing about Oneida. It was a wonderful end to an exciting day.

Western Recorder, June 27, 1989

July 4: Stewardship in Adversity

Whatever happens, especially when we suffer a setback, it is good to remember that God is yet on his throne. We need to be reminded from time to time that we are dependent on God ultimately. In all situations, there is still much to be thankful for.

In our recent flood, there were no injuries or deaths. No staff member's house was flooded nor that of any of our students. It was heartbreaking to see all of our gardens and seven acres of Irish potatoes under water as well as our corn fields. Most of that is destroyed. But already we had eaten much from the gardens since mid May and hundreds of gallons of beautiful strawberries had been frozen for later use.

Thousands of hours of work had gone into all this by our students with several staff supervising. Even though most of the projected produce is gone, our girls and boys learned much in the effort. Hopefully even now we are teaching them how to go forward in adversity.

We will plant late gardens. Around the first of August we will replant the potatoes and try for a late crop. We are going to replant much of our corn.

In the meantime much food will have to be bought. But please, if you want to help us in this do not go out and buy cans of food to bring or send us. It is so much easier for both you and us, and much better stewardship, to simply send us the money you would have spent in buying the food and the cost of shipping or bringing it to us.

You can be sure we will take some of the money you send to buy seed, fertilizer, etc. We believe in teaching our girls and boys how to raise food, to learn to grow things, to feed themselves in some way other than out of a can. A Chinese proverb, thousands of years old, says: "Give a man a fish, you feed him for a meal; teach a man how to fish, and he can feed himself for a lifetime." That is the philosophy of the Oneida school.

Western Recorder, July 4, 1989

An Outpouring of Blessing

Some tomato producers near Steubenville Baptist Church read of the loss of most of our gardens in the June flood. Early in August they telephoned us and said if we would bring a truck to their fields, they would have picked and waiting 5000 pounds of tomatoes. Several of our men went and had to call back for a second truck for they had picked 10,000 pounds!

We had to send for some of our cooks on "break" after summer school and before the fall season begins. For the next several days they had a number of our students working from early morning into the night preparing the tomatoes for storage in our walk-in freezers, the largest of which is 2600 cubic feet. We will have a lot of wonderful tomato soup as well as juice through the winter months.

Months ago the Lord put it into the heart of a state policeman who is director of the Okolona Baptist Brotherhood near Nancy in Pulaski county to suggest that the church raise an acre of potatoes for Oneida. Pastor Rollin Bradshaw and a group of men of the church came some days ago with nearly 100 bushels of large and beautiful potatoes for the girls and boys of Oneida. How wonderful they look in our nearly empty potato cellar built to store thousands of bushels.

While all this was going on many bushels of sweet corn became ripe. This had been on higher ground and escaped the ravage of the flood waters. The cooks were totally involved getting the tomatoes in the freezers. So our dean of boys, Mr. Underwood, drafted a student crew and he and they worked long hours blanching the corn and putting it into large plastic containers for freezing until needed.

As this work progressed, some of our large sows gave birth to 11 new pigs. There is definitely going to be meat on the Oneida table.

Many acres of corn planted after the flood are growing rapidly and are beautiful. Several acres that survived the flood are also very good. Our farm manager advised me that the late corn could most effectively and efficiently be utilized for silage. In a week's time we have built two beautiful 50 feet high silos, our first. Some professionals came to do the job and several of our boys pitched in to carry materials. They would work until it was totally dark at night.

Ballardsville Baptist Church gave $15,000 toward the silo project in memory of Mrs. Eppie Whitehouse. At the very hour her son, sister-in-law, her pastor and many friends were scheduled to leave for Oneida for their annual week-long work project, her funeral service was held. She and her husband had been a part of the first Ballardsville work group that worked a week in the summer of 1980.

284

Pastor and people, including members of Mrs. Whitehouse's family, came on to Oneida four hours later than planned. Early the next morning they were hard at work. How much more lasting will be the silos, holding 520 tons of feed for our cattle, than are flowers, beautiful though they are. Her son "Jeep" said his mother would have loved the silos as she was such a practical woman.

We are grateful to the hundreds who have sent money to help with food needs and with all the many projects being accomplished. God is so good.

Western Recorder, July 21, 1989

More Than Conquerors

I awakened this morning after four hours' sleep with a powerful sense of God's presence. That was not lessened as I looked out the window to find a dark looking, cloud- filled sky with a slow drizzling rain coming down. God is the God of the rain as well as the sunshine. As I bathed and dressed, my mind raced over the various blessings of the past few days, many so unexpected, and I felt almost overwhelmed. I cannot quite explain the sensation.

As I left the house, our campus lawns were glistening with the moisture like a smooth green carpet. The grass is still so beautiful. With all the rain we have had the grass looks like it does in early spring. Our students have freshly mowed it.

Verses from the powerful eighth chapter of Romans echoed in my ears as I walked across campus picking up a scrap of paper here and there, also one pop can. Even in the rain I can't resist doing that. The campus is so beautiful that even a piece of litter is out of place. But with over 500 boys and girls, there is always at least one or two who are careless.

God's holy word, hid in my heart, made me step even faster because of the powerful assurance that every believer in the Lord Jesus Christ can have.

"We know that all things work together for good to them that love God, to them who are called according to his purpose...if God be for us, who can be against us? He that spared not his own son, but delivered him up for us all, how shall he not with him also freely give us all things?

"Who shall lay anything to the charge of God's elect? It is God that justifieth. Who is he that condemneth? It is Christ that died, yea rather, that is risen again, who is even at the right hand of God who also maketh intercession for us. Who shall separate us from the love of Christ? Shall tribulation, or distress, or persecution, or famine, or nakedness, or peril, or sword?"

"Nay, in all these things we are more than conquerors through him that loved us. For I am persuaded that neither death, nor life, nor angels, nor principalities, nor powers, nor things present, nor height, nor depth nor any other creature shall be able to separate us from the love of God, which is in Christ Jesus our Lord."

Nearing the gym, a group of our boys headed for the farm on this Saturday morning threw up their hands with a big wave and matching smiles. They were gathered around our recently purchased used tractor-trailer truck on which was a tractor with hay-bailer I had never seen before. I was informed that these were new pieces of equipment for our school's use. Our farm manager and dean of boys left at 1:30 PM yesterday afternoon to pick them up, and arrived back at 6:00 AM. I was not even aware of the gift or their trip to pick up the equipment until early last night.

Western Recorder, October 10, 1989

October 17, the rain poured down in sheets, pummeling every blade of grass, every inch of the farm, the campus and village of Oneida. The worst of four floods that year was upon them. Unlike the floods that last for days as we often see in the flat farmlands of our country, most floods in the mountainous Clay County come and go in a very short time. However, depending upon how well saturated the ground already was, the flooded farm lands could be totally devastated in a few hours.

More Flooding

I was with our staff helping move equipment until about 11:30 AM. The single most important area that had to be evacuated was our central student workshop with its thousands of dollars of lawnmowers, weed eaters, electric saws and tools of every description. Also we had to move athletic equipment, concessions, etc. from the concession building on the athletic field which flooded to a depth of over four feet.

Dean "Bud" Underwood and son Harold, who is our auto mechanics and welding teacher, were on a much needed vacation in the Smokey Mountains when they heard the newscast that Clay County was flooded. A quick phone call to our campus to confirm the situation and they were on their way in 10 minutes.

I had gotten to go through the morning mail which had gotten in ahead of the flood waters. Then 18 folks arrived from Severns Valley Baptist Church, Elizabethtown.

We unloaded some used clothing the church group had brought and I directed them on to our dining room for lunch. The bus driver and I took their bus a few hundred feet back up the road as the flood waters were about to inundate the entrance to our campus. After lunch I took the group on our usual campus tour, flood or no flood…

Over the Mountains and Through the Woods

Several hours later I led the Elizabethtown group around the mountain, and back to the highway and their bus. It reminded me of our last flood, June 16, when I did the same thing with a large group from Louisville's Ninth and O Baptist Church.
Western Recorder, November 7, 1989

What were they to do? God made them farmers; they would do it all again. They would do what they had been doing through all the flooding of that year. They would continue to build, to sew, to reap! And in a year when the floods came down, Barkley kept right on building on the Solid Rock. He wrote of the many improvements that were finished before Christmas.

Despite Four Floods

Despite four floods in 1989 (normally average one every ten years...and that in winter), two of which came during crop and garden season, 1989 was in many ways perhaps the most remarkable of our history. MAJOR improvements (and there were many significant minor ones) include three pieces of family housing including a 3-bedroom Bedford stone one block from the main campus and a new 3-bedroom, 2 bath with basement house behind old Britton house which still stands and is owned by the school. Also SIXTEEN beautiful apartments for "single" staff were added during the year and occupied. Then we have a beautiful new second gym to complement the main gym that also has seven large classrooms and three recreation rooms: weight-lifting, billiards, table tennis, all air-conditioned. By the end of this month we expect to have a 3,000 sq. ft. auto mechanics shop building complete...we have a very significant vocational program on campus while remaining basically college prep with about 66% of our last class of 116 graduates going to college. (By the way, Oneida graduates have been in such institutions as Harvard, Columbia, University of Minnesota, Stanford, Vanderbilt, etc. during the past ten years) Also during the year we built two large silos holding 550 ton of silage...
Western Recorder, October 31, 1989

Oneida Christmas Wonderland!

A beautiful snowfall always makes the Oneida campus in the center of four converging valleys surrounded by mountains look like a picture postcard. Kids and even adults like to build snowmen at such a time and slide down the front of the campus hill. Succeeding generations of Oneida students have known that thrill. I last tried that about five years ago and decided perhaps I'm getting a little old

for such fun. Surrounded by young people all the time, I still have much of the enthusiasm of the young. I get just as excited showing folks about the Oneida campus as I did 35 years ago as a high school boy. People have always excited me…
Western Recorder, December 30, 1989

All the traditional events of Christmas, in which he would be very much involved were still to come: the marching band performing in the Lexington Christmas parade, Pastor and Mrs. Rackley's international dinner, caroling in the Oneida community, the county wide presentation of the *Messiah*, the presentation of *The Homecoming*, the dorm parties, the twenty-foot tree in the chapel, the wonderful chapel services. All led to the very last event before every student and most staff left for the holidays, a worship service, with the choir singing the cantata *Let the World Rejoice.*

Christmas excited him too! The wonderful message of Christmas, to love, to share as God shared His very best with a sinful world. Christ excited him more than anything in all the world and it was His birthday!

1990-91
Year 19

Oneida is a place where it is well understood that each soul is beyond measure or price. What happens here on a daily basis is as truly a miracle of our Lord as anyone can read or hear about. Many lives have been, and are being, transformed for eternity. There is no way to measure such things but one sees and knows it is happening.
—Barkley Moore

1990 was the beginning of a time of change. Nelson Mandela would be released from prison. Mikhail Gorbachev would become president of the Soviet Union. The Internet would come into its own. New technologies and new freedoms would change the shape of societies worldwide. The Berlin Wall would be torn down, and the two Germanies would finally be reunited. Iraq would invade Kuwait, an ill-advised act that would lead to the First Gulf War. Barkley saw clearly the hand of God in all these events. He wrote:

> God has powerfully and recently demonstrated that he still has a hand "in the affairs of men" for all the world to see, those that can see spiritually. Then His blessing of Oneida the past several years has been of such magnitude that we feel that we are in His will very directly as we labor in faith and love. What happens here on a daily basis is as truly a miracle of our Lord as any one can read or hear about. Many lives have been, and are being, transformed for eternity. There is no way to measure such things but one sees and knows it is

happening. There is repeated evidence that this is so. Then there is the "physical" that can be seen and measured to some degree even when we don't understand quite how it is possible. But ours is a God of the impossible…

Letters, 1990

In the past two years God had blessed Oneida with thirty more staff and the added housing needed. The school had acquired 200 acres, mostly adjoining the campus, and a 115-acre farm had been given to the school by the Preston Keith family. Academically, athletically, in music, art and drama, the students were excelling. There were over 600 students, teachers, and staff members worshiping daily in chapel. Month by month, year by year, opportunities were being added. However, Barkley knew the cost to so many of his very deserving and devoted staff. It had only been in the last fiscal year that any of them had been paid as much as $10,000 a year. He knew their giving up large salaries had largely financed the five-fold increase in buildings in the past fifteen years and the tremendous growth in programs and in enrollment. He wrote:

> If we did not have so many staff financially able to serve without any salary at all, and the rest willing to work at a fraction of the salary they could have in any other school situation, we would not be able to minister in the tremendous fashion that we do. Students fortunate to find Oneida are lucky young people indeed…

Barkley himself was giving almost every penny he made to students on campus, and students he still continued to support away at college, as well as Christian causes he supported. He didn't own a personal car, not that he needed one, as he was content to stay on the campus greeting the scores of guests that now came weekly. The old red Cavalier donated to the school was fine transportation for the speaking engagements he made away from the school with his student driver at the wheel. Often he rode the big blue Greyhound along with the choir. He loved being able to be in chapel with his family gathered round, even though it was reported by many students that it was occasionally a time for him to get a short nap. He would introduce the speaker, sing with enthusiasm, but the minute he got still, some days it was just impossible for him to stay awake and down his head would go, coming to rest on his chin. However, they couldn't say he was for sure sleeping as he always seemed to be fully awake if just one of them misbehaved and he always stood up when it was time for prayer or singing. The students understood but got a lot of smiles out of this enduring gesture. Maybe he was just resting his eyes!

The Oneida Baptist Church ranked second of more than 2300 Baptist churches of the state in numbers being led to the Lord. This was reflected in the student's spiritual growth. That he felt was the most important thing that was happening, the greatest of God's blessings.

Barkley found the time in between all the ongoing activities to stop by the boys' dorm, spend time with any number of boys, gabbing and just playing rook. Some days it would be after handling the most pressing heartbreaking problems. These were his boys, his family and he often came home to them at the end of a day's work. It might have been the rug rat dorm, where he would have a bowl of cereal and milk in the break room with the younger boys, or it might have been to sit and chat with the varsity boys' high school teams in the gym, or he might have gone to the cafeteria and played rook with any number of students and faculty gathered round. He often could be found in small groups at faculty members' homes where both girls and boys would also be found having great conversations. Long after they were all in bed he would be back in his office working on their behalf. Once in a while he would then show up at a faculty member's home in the wee hours of the morning needing to be fed. Of course everyone was honored to be able to serve him.

And so it was that the year of 1990 was in full swing. It would take over $3,135,000 to support his family of boys, girls, faculty and staff. He would see it done for they deserved every dime. There would be many hours spent in the days ahead, more hours than any one man should expect of his body. He would catch a few hours sleep, never getting fully rested, but on he would go, determined to do his best for these who were in his charge.

Barkley continued pouring his heart out through the *Oneida Journal* to his extended family, Kentucky Baptists, in praise of what they too were doing as they helped the children of the world at Oneida. While the school might have gotten behind even a hundred thousand or so, in a couple of months they would be caught up to date. This was largely due to Kentucky Baptists, and Baptists from all over the Southern Baptist Convention, along with the many personal friends Barkley had made in his years serving the Peace Corps, and those thousands of folks whose names he had gathered over the years, responding with $5, $10, $20 gifts over and above the Cooperative Program, $274,000 that year.

In the following articles from the *Oneida Journal*, you will read a small part of what he wrote to Kentucky Baptists. As his articles explain much of what went on, it is my opinion that they let you, dear reader, see, from Barkley's own pen what really mattered to him in 1990.

Two Homecomings in Seven Months!

We have just finished our first spring HOMECOMING. What a wonderful day! It was our second HOMECOMING in seven months, our first time to have two in the same school year! Last fall we met as usual in October and had the largest crowd back ever.

Events began at 10:00 AM with registration and the start of a five hour tract and field meet involving eight schools: Berea, Williamsburg, Clay County, Corida, Leslie County, St. Camillus, Dilce Combs and Oneida.

Oneida won the boys' meet with 147 points and Berea was second with 92 points. Junior Damon Tigner set a new record on the Oneida tract with his high jump of six feet, five inches. Ahmed Reynolds, a junior, set a new OBI track record in the 110 hurdles in a time of 15.9 seconds.

Our girls' basketball came in fourth of seven girls' teams competing. Eighth grader Samantha Cameron, competing on our high school team, was the day's girl standout winning the shot-put championship with a throw of 30 feet, one inch.

Our boys' team defeated Buckhorn, 9-6 to remain undefeated in six games played so far in the Three Rivers Conference.

In the girls' competition Oneida defeated three teams to win the conference championship.

The championship victory in baseball was an exciting 7-6 score over Cordia. September Wooten, a sophomore, hit a double, Chary Spencer, a seventh grader, came in for the tying run.

Meanwhile back on our campus various HOMECOMING events were going forward with next year's seniors selling soft drinks and fresh made cotton candy to raise money for their trip to Washington and Colonial Williamsburg next spring. They cleared over $400 for the day.

Alumni returned spanning the years before the first world war through the most recent class. Many came early and stayed late, eating both noon and evening meals.

From 4:00-5:30 PM the action moved to Melvin Davidson Chapel where the Oneida band and choir gave a tremendous concert specially dedicated to Sam Carmac, a faithful alumnus and friend of the school, and the nine children of Zilphia Campbell Keith who recently donated their 115 acre family farm near the campus in appreciation of their Oneida years.

Western Recorder, May 8, 1990

Every Day Is Special

Summer school is going full force, and we have 226 students on campus this summer and more coming. Over 60 of these are here for the first time. Tom Jenkin, formerly a teacher and coach with us five years, has been doing mission work the past year in the Amazon jungle of Brazil. He led our first four chapel services of the summer session, each day a powerful message, each day presenting the Lord Jesus Christ and him crucified and risen. As he always did, he held every student's and staff member's attention daily.

Our summer school day lasts six hours. Each level of English is taught. General math, business math, algebra I and II classes are filled. Biology, American history, political science and Bible are other summer study opportunities.

As much or more is learned at Oneida outside the academic classroom. Oneida's work program is a wonderful tool in teaching responsibility, good attitudes, self-respect and simply how to do things with one's hands. Oneida students learn how to plow and plant, to cultivate, to harvest, to put away food for winter use. Oneida students learn how to carpenter, do mechanical work, weld, purify water or treat sewage. Oneida students learn how to paint, refinish furniture, clean properly, cook, wash dishes properly, so many things as a part of our work program.

Then the spiritual dimension of Oneida is simply something beyond all measuring... What is the value of a soul?

Oneida is a place where it is well understood that each soul is beyond measure or price...

Western Recorder, July 3, 1990

The True Measure of a Man

John is the youngest of three children. He grew up without a father. There was no child support, no food stamps. His mother worked whenever she could and, somehow, made ends meet. We took him without one dime of money. Over a semester he ran up a bill of over $200 in loans for supplies, etc. He did average school work but failed to come back after Christmas. That was some years ago and he is now legal age. I have just heard from him:

"Do you remember I owe the school? My mother refused to give it to me. She says it is my debt and I must earn it. I have drifted, not doing much of anything. She still refuses to pay my debt. She said that 'the true measure of a man is being responsible for all your own actions'. I have worked and saved the money that I owe you. Also I have worked and saved up enough money to pay you $50 a month. I really need my education. You work hard to get minimum wages. I have to get an education to do better. I realize how stupid I was trying to get by the easy way.

"Please let me come back and get my education. Oneida Baptist Institute is the best thing that ever happened to me. You and your staff care about our future. You all worked with us to achieve. If you can find it in your heart to let me come back, I will be eternally grateful."

Now what shall we do about this young man's request?

You know what we are going to do. What are you going to do?

Western Recorder, July 24, 1990

Baptist Student Union

Emily came to us from a large mountain county seat town in her junior year. Her father had died three years before and she lived with her widowed mother.

She became first chair flute in our band, was captain and most valuable twirler in our flag camps, traveled thousands of miles with our choir in concert.

Most importantly she found and grew in the Lord Jesus Christ.

I recently received the following letter from Emily: "This summer I am serving as a BSU summer missionary at Russell Springs...If I had not been introduced to BSU through Oneida, I might not be here today!"

Started in 1950 at Oneida by Georgetown graduate Martha Bain, Oneida's BSU is the longest continuously active high school BSU in the United States. It is one of many opportunities that Oneida students have, unlike most of their counterparts in our nation.

Martha Bain was a tremendous English teacher at Oneida for 12 years and then a college professor until her retirement.

Not only is Emily doing summer missionary work, but countless other Oneida young people have done so through the years because of that initial spark while they were part of the Oneida family. I count myself as one of those. I served as BSU president here at Oneida several years and in my senior year had the privilege of speaking to the 1957 state BSU convention. The other day I came across part of what I shared on that occasion about Bible schools we helped conduct near Oneida.

Sir Lancelot, our car, often sat down on his exhaust pipe in the mud holes. He was loaded with six workers, a portable organ, gallons of Kool-Aid. One of our Bible schools was held in a one-room school house which had washed off its foundation in a flood. The building contained several very rough desks which had been hewn out of logs. The only light provided was from the windows, which were held up by cornstalks. How those children wanted to learn and to hear of the love of Christ! How they loved to sing, Climbing up Sunshine Mountain or I'm in the Lord's Army.

We came to the last day and found ourselves locked out of the building. There was a pickup truck nearby, and near it a log. We placed our organ on the truck bed, we sat on the log and worshiped under the sky. That is a worship service I will never forget. Neither will those mountain children. Yes, it is Christ in you the hope—the hope of such spiritually starved people. "I will lift up my eyes unto the hills, where the field is white unto harvest." That is the challenge of the mountains.

Memories. Youth. But the same Lord, the same need, the same mission today.

Western Recorder, July 30, 1990

Summer Blessings

How very quickly summer school went by. A total of 241 girls and boys were enrolled sometime during the six weeks of classes divided into four quarters...

I received a special blessing on our last day of summer chapel. As usual many guests were present from various places. We sang four hymns. Bob Hanson, pastor of the Presbyterian church in Greenview, Ill. led in prayer. He and his wife had arrived to pick up their lovely daughter Ann who came to us this summer. This young lady has a bright smile whenever you see her. Her parents were very pleased with her summer's progress and are bringing her back in the fall. Ten of our students had just completed their last required credit for graduation, and we said goodbye to each of them one by one. I shared the wonderful eighth chapter of Romans including: "Who shall separate us from the love of Christ? Shall tribulation, or famine, or nakedness, or peril or sword? Nay, in all these things we are more than conquerors through him that loved us. For I am persuaded that neither death, or life, nor angels, nor things to come, nor height, nor depth nor any other creature shall be able to separate us from the love of Christ, which is in Christ Jesus our Lord."

Listening so attentively were ten sharing with us for the last time in chapel as students and the one girl and five boys who were baptized in the last Wednesday night service of the summer session. I sensed a special reverence as coach Gritton led our final prayer. What a wonderful privilege and blessing is our daily Oneida chapel service!

Late into the evening, my assistant was also busy with incoming and outgoing calls about prospective students for the coming school year. Our dedicated business manager, Jerry Pierce, was at work writing checks, paying bills. I have a staff of people who enjoy what they do, who love their work, and I offered a special silent prayer of thanks for these special people who work so tirelessly, often to the midnight hour...

Western Recorder, August 7, 1990

Governor Combs' Surprise Visit

On the fourth day of a new year, former Gov.(1959-63) Bert Combs came by for a one and one-half-hour visit. It was a total, but delightful, surprise. He celebrated his 79th birthday earlier in the month. He was a schoolboy here at Oneida 68 years ago, a second generation Oneidian. His mother enrolled at Oneida Monday, Jan. 1, 1900, Oneida's first classroom day.

My mind raced back to other visits by this noted former student. He came for HOMECOMING in 1959, the nominee of his party for governor. Also, a 1930 graduate, Pleaz Mobley, was the Republican nominee for lieutenant governor that year. So it did not matter which party won that year, Oneida had one on the ticket. That was quite a commentary on the influence of a tiny school in the eastern Kentucky mountains in a state of over three million people.

In the third year of a very notable governorship, Gov. Combs returned to speak at our 1962 commencement. Riding with him in his car were Saul and Lillie Hounchell, Oneida graduates of 1911, and his cousins. Saul had been principal of Oneida when Bert was a boy. Having earned his doctorate in English, Hounchell was a professor at Eastern State Teachers College for 28 years. He took a leave of absence to serve as Oneida's fifth president, 1941-46. Previously he had taught a total of 18 years at OBI, and had been a principal 15 of those years.

On the night of the 1962 graduation ceremony, D. Chester Sparks announced his retirement after 14 years as OBI president. He and Saul had been baseball teammates during their Oneida school days.

Other notable Bert Combs visits included Homecoming 1981 and 1988. On both occasions Gov. Combs spoke.

This time Gov. Combs just came for a visit. Our first stop was our print shop. We gave him two of the books recently published by the Oneida Mountain Press. Then we went upstairs to the chapel where we saw the new carpet as well as in the band room and the piano lab. Our middle school choir was having its first practice of the year and Gov. Combs seemed to delight in listening to them sing. He told them he was about their age when he first came to live on the Oneida campus.

Gov. Combs then carefully inspected the five shelves filled with academic trophies for the five years since statewide academic championships have been conducted in Governor's Cup competition. Then he looked over the many shelves of athletic championship and runner-up trophies won in the course of qualifying for participation in 53 tournaments, winning 14 state championships and runner-up in four others.

Outside he looked across the valley at the 16 staff apartments built since his visit two years ago. From that vantage point he could also see the new 3000 square foot auto mechanics-auto body shop,

3200 square foot farm equipment storage building and a new 1800 square feet of storage for the student work program.

Then he went to visit the new gym finished last Christmas, seven new classrooms and three recreation rooms. He was delighted with the new student-made tables in the two dining rooms.

Afterwards we walked to Anderson Hall, the only building remaining from his own school days at Oneida. There, for the first time, he saw oil portraits of his grandfather, Lee Combs, and his great-grandfather, "Meridy" Combs, both members of Oneida's first board of trustees. Also, we have a lovely portrait of his great-grandmother, Easter Allen Combs. All these folk are buried on the mountain overlooking the school campus along with 314 other former Oneida students, staff members and benefactors.

Then we walked back through the campus to his car. All through the visit Gov. Combs had bantered and shook hands with scores of Oneida's girls and boys and many delighted staff members.

We very likely have a future governor or senator, or even a president of the United States, in our student body right now. I'm sure we have many future missionaries, teachers, doctors, you name it. We are trying to teach them the meaning of service. On this day of the governor's visit, our chapel message had been on Christ's washing the disciples' feet. Pray for God's blessing this school year.

Western Recorder, September 11, 1990

A Bagpiper at Oneida

Did you ever feel like you were riding on a cloud? Yes, everyone has a few such times over a lifetime. I have been blessed with that feeling hundreds of times. This is one of those times.

Our first Family Day is now history. What a wonderful day it turned out to be! We had never had such a day before. We did not know quite what to expect. We thought it would be a good day...we prayed for such. We worked hard to do all we could do to assure it would be a useful day, an enjoyable day. But the day went far beyond our expectations.

Much of the week was cold and rainy. There were predictions it would be so on Saturday, our Family Day. It's true that no one got sunburned...we didn't see the sun all day. But there was no rain. It was almost perfect weather-wise. It wasn't hot; it wasn't cold. It was just right.

Registration and the day's events were scheduled to begin at 10:00 AM. Many were here by 7:00 AM. Lines had formed in the registration area shortly after 9:00 AM. There was a steady stream throughout the remainder of the day.

It was almost certainly the largest number of people on our campus in the entire history of the school including graduation days and Homecomings There were cars parked in every direction for several blocks.

Grandfather Kenneth Crony delighted folks throughout the day. He fought in Europe four years during World War II with the Canadian army. Resplendent in bagpiper dress (skirt and all), a chest full of war medals, he marched back and forth through the campus skirring his bagpipes. One was reminded of the fabled Pied Piper of Hamlin as folks surrounded and followed him about.

In the afternoon, he opened the talent show playing his melodic reed pipes, and the program ended with his rendition of *Amazing Grace.*

The greatest single event of the day was the visitation between teachers and parents...I have not seen our teachers so excited in years. All the parents I overhead also seemed excited about their visits with the teachers. To meet them, to know they cared enough to stand in line even to see a teacher...it was exciting.

While all this was going on, hundreds of public students were here competing in a cross country run, volleyball and soccer. Our Mountaineers won the day in everything. Several records were broken.

Another record broken was sales in our craft house. We sold over $1,700 worth of students-made crafts.

Probably another record was the number of people who visited our farm on Family Day. That wasn't even on the printed program. But the lure of walking our swinging bride, seeing the little pigs

(Remember those educated pigs?) the cows, the greenhouses had a power all its own.

Our choir was excellent as usual and the band probably put on their most beautiful show ever. Their final number was *Cum Ba Ya*. Certainly the Lord did "come by here" Oct. 13.

Have you been to Oneida lately? Why don't you come before winter sets in. The leaves have lingered longer on the trees this autumn…green longer that I can ever recall.

Western Recorder, October 23, 1990

Eighty Souls Won

As I wrote in last week's column, more than 80 young people have accepted the Lord in recent weeks at Oneida. They have followed him in believer's baptism. Every day is soul-winning time at OBI as we worship our Lord in daily services. Sharing Christ at least once every 24 hours in worship, with every student and teacher attending, is one of the precious privileges of the Oneida experience…

Western Recorder, November 6, 1990

Cooperative Weather

A real emphasis of this calendar year at Oneida has been new roofs. We have spent nearly $200,000 in that area alone. God has blessed us with warm, sunny weather into December allowing us to do all that we set out to do. Normally much of what we have accomplished would have had to have been postponed to next spring.

The D. Chester Sparks gym and classroom building was first roofed in 1954. We have just finished roofing it for the third time.

Also we have completed a new roof for our swimming pool-classroom building. Named Goins-Hounchell Hall, it honors two former students who served over 50 years at Oneida in nearly every capacity including that of president.

During the summer months we built beautiful hip-shaped roofs to replace the previously flat roofs of our two oldest boys' dorms, together, house 218 boys along with houseparent's' apartments, our campus store, a weight lifting room, TV area and a large laundry area. Those buildings are named Carnahan Hall and Marvin-Wheeler Hall, after benefactors whose generous spirit was so crucial in those formative years of our work 90 years ago.

Also, in recent months we have put new roofs on four staff houses. That joined with other roofing of the past several years, including Anderson Hall, our oldest building, and Burns Hall, our largest building, has our roofs in the best shape in memory.

The beautiful weather has permitted us to make a large shelled corn grain bin out of a 30-foot high former oil tank and to rebuild a grain bin moved from another location. With the one we constructed two years ago, we can now store 8,600 bushels of shelled corn. During the harvest this year, our former corn picker totally gave out. After two weeks spent on one repair after another, we gave up. We now have another corn picker that can pick and shell four rows at one time. We have a new auger that gets the shelled corn from the ground into our storage bins. We have bought a new silage cutter in recent months that helps keep out silos filled with over 500 ton of corn silage.

Beautiful weather also allowed us to complete four beautiful tennis courts the last week of November that has been a dream of years. Our first tennis court, built in 1969, was covered by our new second gym, built last fall. With only one court, our tennis teams have had to have all their meets away including their practices. Each game and practice has involved traveling from 34-100 miles or more daily. We have made such effort because, unlike many sports, tennis can be played into old age. Whether in music, art, drama, crafts and other vocational skills, along with sports, we put a high priority on our students' learning skills they can use and enjoy for a lifetime.

A 1928 Oneida graduate and longtime school worker and benefactor, Preston Baker, and his wife, Ruby, allowed us to haul thousands of tons of shale and dirt from their farm, three miles away. It took us two weeks with five dump trucks, a loader and two bulldozers to fill an area eight feet deep, adjoining our athletic fields, running 250 feet east-west and 120 feet north-south. Very beautiful courts painted green in bounds and red out of bounds have been completed. Several factors, including warm weather, joined to allow this to happen weeks after such work is normally cut off. They are all-weather courts, with much space around the 10-foot high chain-link fence for seating, as well as room for aluminum bleachers at midcourt.

These courts will be in use immediately and will be dedicated at our next homecoming, Saturday, April 27, 1991. They are named for alumnus and former staff member Omer "Blue" Hensley and his wife, Sophia, both now deceased.
Western Recorder, December 12, 1990

Letters from Saudi Arabia

At least three of our graduates from last spring are now in Saudi Arabia...

Mike telephoned me a few hours before boarding the plane to leave. A letter has now come. It reads in part: "We are about 400 miles from Kuwait. I'm with the 82nd Airborne. We are pulling guard duty. In our spare time we watch movies, play football, volleyball, read books, lift weights. We eat two hot meals a day and one meal ready to eat. We have outside showers and the temperature is about 80-85 degrees. We have to use our sleeping bags at night. We live in a building they built like a warehouse. We sleep on cots, and there are about 200 of us here at this post.

"We have to keep in mind that we could go to war at any time. Everyone thinks something is going to happen. 200,000 more troops are coming. There will be rotation of troops until this thing gets settled or we go to war. Many are stressed out, but I'm doing good.

"Tell me what you have done this school year. Tell me your changes. I have to go guard right now. Hope you will write. Do me a favor and send the Oneida Mountaineer."

Many memories of Mike come back to me as I think of him there in the desert sand many miles from home and Oneida. He came to us nearly four years ago. Today he is a muscular man, nearly 6 feet tall. Then he was a young teen-ager, somewhat withdrawn and could be belligerent.

He matured considerably as we worked with him. He was away from us twice for extended periods. Once was by his choice, one was by ours. So I accepted him in the school three different times. He learned discipline and responsibility. Looking in his file this morning, I find this letter from him in August 1988: "I just thought I would write to see how the place is doing, and how are you doing? Well, Dr. Moore, I hate to say it, but you were right about being away from school. Even though you want to get away, something always wants to come back. I really miss the place a lot. I really do. I learned a lot that I couldn't learn in public school. I learned more discipline than I ever had in my life. I'm grateful that I had a chance to come down and meet people I really loved. I would really like to hear from you."

Mike came back and went on to graduate. Who could have dreamed where he would be just six months later? Or could have foreseen the situation he and hundreds of thousands of others are facing. We must pray for each of them, and daily. I am sure that Mike is one that will do his duty. I thank God that we had the privilege of working with him. At the time it did not always seem a privilege. But it was and is a privilege to minister to precious young human souls in a very formative and difficult time in their lives, and teen-age years. We never know what trials each is to experience in life. But we know that Mike and Steve, possibly Carol and others now serving or about to serve on Saudi Arabia, are more spiritually prepared for what lies ahead than they would have been without Oneida. We are grateful that each was ours for a little while.

They and many others were remembered as nearly 170 of our Oneida family shared a family style Thanksgiving dinner together in our beautifully decorated dining room. Nearly 500 others were away from us that day, with their individual families or elsewhere.

No one in the land had a more bounteous or more delicious meal than did we at Oneida...

Western Recorder, December 11, 1990

1991-92
Year 20

If ever there was a need for educated people and for strong Christian character, today is the day. Christian education gives hope to the hopeless, power to the weak, and ambition to follow the ray of hope.
—Barkley Moore

T he year 1991 began differently than the years before with the staff and students taking a shorter Christmas break. They were all back and ready for class on the last day of the year. It was a good start with every one in class following the normal schedule. The weather had been spring like most of the winter, turning wintry in mid-December. But it was again spring-like, and everyone was in an anticipant mood as it was New Year's Eve. While some had resented having to return a few days earlier, by now their mood was happier. Barkley Moore was wont to feel that any day away from Oneida and studying was a day wasted for the students. It was his practice to give the same lecture every spring before the students were to leave for the summer break. That lecture always came down to the value of time, and Oneida students, in his opinion, should use every season to advance themselves. Summer breaks spent loafing were anathema to his way of thinking. If he had his way, they would all be studying year round; if not studying, then at least working. His favorite song seemed to be *We'll Work 'Til Jesus Comes* and sure enough those students sang it over and over again. Sometimes he gave them a lecture at the end of the singing of it. It was his new idea that if they started earlier in January, then all those not staying or returning to summer school, would have the jump on other students looking for those illusive summer jobs. He reported in the *Western Recorder* the results of his new plan.

Why Do We Give Our Lives?

On New Year's Eve all students and a portion of the staff assembled to see the classic movie *Ben Hur* for three and a half hours. Some had seen it before, but the majority had never viewed this wonderful movie. Of course it was the kind of film one could see many times and still enjoy as I had over the past 32 years. The students liked it.

Then many students and staff went to the Oneida Baptist church for a 75 minute candlelight "watchnight" service. There were congregational hymns, prayers, individual testimonies. Three former Oneida teachers were visiting. One spoke. Another sang. The French teacher played several hymns on the saxophone. The service ended with the singing of *Blest Be the Tie.*

In the meantime, all other students and many staff saw in the new year playing in the new gym.

Both church and gym groups then met in the two dining rooms for nearly an hour of eating and fellowship. They had various kinds of meat and everyone fashioned as many sandwiches as he or she wanted on fresh-baked buns and all the trimmings.

By 1:30 AM everyone was in bed with the understanding he or she could sleep an extra two hours and then go to third period class. The first classes ever held at Oneida were in New Year's Day, 1900. So it was very fitting to have classes the first day of the new year, 1991. As on that first day so long ago, and most days since, Oneida had daily chapel worship.

No girls or boys anywhere in America could have been better behaved or had any more wholesome fun than did Oneida's during the 48 hours from their return on Sunday through New Year's Day. Yet they also had two days of school, a variety of activities, and were lifted to spiritual heights several times. There were no "hangovers."
Western Recorder, January 11, 1991

So, yes, indeed, they were all back and all sober-minded! But, given his sense of protectiveness for his charges, one had to think that he was also glad that they were safely back. It had been his practice since day one, to remain up and waiting, for every bus group to return to campus, whatever the reason for their being gone. He may not have been the first one up, but he was always the last one to bed.

Barkley had said before, and repeated again as 1991 began to unfold, "If ever there was a need for educated people and for strong Christian character, today is the day. Christian education gives hope to the hopeless, power to the weak, and ambition to follow the ray of hope."

This was plenty of reason for him to map a course that both kept his kids out of trouble and prepared them for the future roles he expected each of them to take in the world. He was planting Christian character and Christian education in their hearts as well as minds. He may have taken the idea of work just a little too far in the minds of some of the students. However, he also had the idea that play, and playing hard was important as well. Play they did and he was always looking for ways to improve their opportunities to play for the fun of it and in competition. After all if you were playing, then singing and smiling was much easier and so was working. The students had been playing on the new tennis courts, completed in December every day the weather permitted.

Homecoming was set for April 27 and he was busy with planning the events that would take place. Plans were to dedicate the new 3,000-square-foot shop on the farm with its new hydraulic lift that could lift 24,000 pounds. The Greyhound buses weighed less than that. Now they would be able to work on them when it was necessary to have them elevated. Oneida had made over $2,000,000 in improvements on the campus and farm over the last two years and he was thrilled, even with donations down. The bills were paid and up to date. What a difference from the days just two years ago when he had the constant worry of making it through every month.

He still implored everyone to pray for the school and himself. "Keep us in your prayers as we fight the good fight minute by minute, hour by hour at Oneida...as real a battlefield as is the Persian Gulf." Souls continued to be saved and every one was precious to him. But, as with every year there were plenty enough problems.

Many students had come back for a visit during the break at Christmas. One of them that had been back was Glenn (name changed), a graduate from the year before. Glenn had joined the Air Force, had completed his Air Force training, and had ranked second out of hundreds. He looked great and Barkley had been pleased to hear that he doing so well. Mike Showalter, Jeff Hasty, Bruce Williams, all recent graduates stopped by as well. Mike, on his way to Germany for three months, along with many college classmates and professors planned to be back in time for Homecoming. Jeff's wife had given him a roundtrip ticket to Oneida. Jeff was in college as well and he came along to be with his old roommate, Bruce Williams, who was a sergeant in the military police. Bruce and Mike had both spoken in chapel. Bruce gave a beautiful talk on what Oneida meant to him. His theme was "Our Common Ground—the Lord Jesus Christ." Barkley considered each of these young men to be his boys.

In just ten short days he would lose one of them. On January 16, Glenn (not his real name) killed himself. This was a real blow to Barkley. Glenn had done so well his senior year and been on the honor roll. Barkley needed to feel His Heavenly Father's ministration of mercy! This was one of "his" soldier boys but it wasn't on a battlefield in the Middle East that he had lost his life. Some other deeper enemy had defeated him. In a long essay written just the previous year he had reaffirmed his faith in Christ, noting his many failures along the way.

Glenn was brought back to Oneida to the chapel by Barkley. There was never a more reverent group of students gathered there. Knowing that he knew the Lord made his committal service very special. Sitting on the platform facing the casket, Barkley thought back to when Glenn first arrived at Oneida. He had come from a broken home. Looking out into those attending the funeral, he saw mostly students and staff; he could see only one from Glenn's family. Glenn had seven half brothers whom he hadn't seen for over nine years, although they all lived in Kentucky. His one full sister was sitting by herself. Barkley went down to visit with her for a few moments and invited her to stay the night. She was pregnant and the baby was due. In the audience Barkley could see many former students including Mark Dunn, Sam Meredith, Damian Carpenter. The Air Force provided an honor guard. However, no one had claimed Glen's body.

He was Barkley's in spirit and now in reality. So it was that Barkley planned to lay Glenn to rest in his own family cemetery. Barkley thought back to the child in Iran that he had taken in to live with him. One day the little boy asked, "Could I be your son?" Barkley replied, "Looks like you already are". He could have buried him on the hill where Mark Sitz, another student was buried. But Glenn didn't have a family who would visit his grave. No, that wouldn't do. Barkley was "his" father. He knew that as long as there were Ponders and Moores the family cemetery would be lovingly attended—that there would be family coming to visit.

As the funeral came to a close, the casket was carried by the Honor Guard to the hearse. It moved away slowly, around the curve leaving Oneida. It followed the same road that had brought Glenn to him over nine years ago. However, this time a hearse carried Glenn away from Oneida. Barkley, his "adopted" father, and His Forever Father, God, though unseen, would be sitting beside his casket all the way. They would make a turn to the left a few miles down the road, go over a low water bride, and finally wind into the peaceful valley with mountain ranges in the distance. In this valley, in the most serene spot where Barkley's ancestors lay, their graves marked by granite tombstones; the open grave, right in front of little Babe (Barkley's younger brother) just ten feet away, was ready to receive Glenn. Glenn would be the same distance from Barkley's own grave when the time came! The honor guard fired a volley and Taps sounded on the lone bugle.

One could well ask, how could Barkley go back to all those healthy, robust, young people and give them hope? He was able to go forward, to step once again away from what would surely have been total despair, had he not known that death itself, of a sinner saved by grace, merely opened the door to eternal life; to the healing of every mortal flaw for his Glenn, who had heard the story of Christ' great love and received His gift of salvation. He knew—*He the Pearly Gates*

Would Open—for this child: hunted, haunted, horrified by some deep unknown tragedy of life.

He the Pearly Gates Would Open

Like a dove when hunted, frightened,
As a wounded fawn was I;
Brokenhearted, yet He healed me,
He will heed the sinner's cry.

Love divine, so great and wondrous,
Deep and mighty, pure, sublime!
Coming from the heart of Jesus,
Just the same through tests of time.

Love divine, so great and wondrous,
All my sins He then forgave!
I will sing His praise forever,
For His blood, His power to save.

He the pearly gates will open,
So that I may enter in;
For He purchased my redemption
And forgave me all my sin.
Frederick A. Blom, 1913

More than seventy years before, Oneida founder James Anderson Burns had written, "I sometimes wonder why some of us give our lives for Oneida Baptist Institute. I find the most concrete and conclusive answer when I attend chapel services. I look into hundreds of pairs of bright eyes and happy, hopeful faces. Oneida Institute exists for them, to bless their young lives and make a blessing to others. This is why we give our lives to such an Institution." Barkley would return because he had an even greater urgency in his heart to bless his young charges and win them to the Lord. Time was moving more quickly it seemed to him every day.

Working for the Love of It!

One Saturday afternoon a few days later, it was a sunny, almost spring-like day. This came in February, which is supposed to be cold, snowy and icy. I thanked God in my heart for the beauty of the day. But there was also other beauty, that of the human spirit.

I pleasantly was occupied getting things done in my office. I am always far behind with letter-writing, and there are always articles such as this waiting to be written. It was a wonderful to be able to do such work for even 30 minutes uninterrupted. That rarely happens, so when it does the time is doubly savored.

As I worked I realized there were many others working all around me. Not one of them was required or even expected to be doing what he or she was doing. Yet there were things to be done, and they were getting done. No one expected even a dollar for the extra effort, nor did they get it. Just doing it was its own reward.

Our business manager, Jerry Pierce now in his third year, is working at his desk. He took a cut in his salary 3-4 times what Oneida Baptist Institute can pay him. He shared with his church publicly a leading to serve with us even before I was aware of such a possibility.

Working near him on a computer problem were two staff members, one who has served faithfully for 17 years and another 1984 graduate who has worked with us several years. Working alongside them was a former staff member back for a two-day visit who had pitched in his expertise. On this day I learned that he could return shortly to serve again full time. Thank you, Lord.

Then our guidance counselor (Myrtle Cooke) was hard at work. Valedictorian of our 1960 class, she took a cut of $17,000 seven years ago to serve with us. Had she remained where she was she would be making about $30,000 more. But four weeks had ended in the nine-week quarter. There were "progress" reports to get out alerting parents that their child was making D-F average in that point in time in one or more subjects. Also some new students had come in during the week and requests for their records from their previous schools had to be prepared.

Just across the concrete wall from my desk, Kay Underwood, our admissions secretary was hard at work. This remarkable wife of one of the busiest men on campus, and mother of three in school, two here at OBI and one in college, regularly averages about a 13-hour day and has for seven years. On this Saturday afternoon she was doing last minute details preparatory to receive 12 new students.

Just across my desk a lady was hard at work helping me with correspondence. She has come for several weeks of volunteer service. She first visited our school graduation weekend last year and fell in love with Oneida's work. Very versatile in her abilities, she has been back several vacation times upholstering furniture and doing "Whatsoever thy hand findeth to do with all her might." Being nearly unable to see me for the mound of paperwork accumulated on my desk, this life-long secretary got a "make do" table, a typewriter and went to work. There she was even on a sunny February afternoon, typing away.

All the folks just mentioned were working within just a few feet of me, in our office area. But there were several score others working in other places about campus. It was the regular shift for a group of houseparent's, cooks, etc. But also many other teachers, farm workers, other staff were busy doing work related things on an afternoon when officially, all were "off" work. They were working because they wanted to, they love the boys and girls they serve. When you love what you are doing, when Gad has truly "called" you to serve, you can do so without watching the clock. The motivation of one's work makes all the difference. It is a joy to work.

Oneida cannot pay anything like a normal salary. Nor has it ever. Yet no one has ever starved or frozen to death. Nor has the Lord ever lacked for dedicated, able servants to carry forward his work, his work at Oneida.

The hymn by Ben Speer says it all:

Does the place you're called to labor
Seem so small and little known?
It is great if God is in it,
And He'll not forget his own.

Labor not for wealth or fame,
There's a crown and you can win it
If you'll go in Jesus name.

Western Recorder, March 12, 1991

March meant the third quarter ended. The seniors were off to Washington and Colonial Williamsburg and the rest of the campus was off for the ten-day spring break. Fourth quarter began. The boys' basketball team advanced from district to regional competition with a record of 21-9. Several others advanced to state competition academically. Both middle school and high school had done well. The drama team had worked for months and gave wonderful performances of *The Body and the Wheel*. There was activity all over campus and something going on somewhere all the time. According to Barkley, "There was never a dull day." Everyone was back and they were all fully engaged in the count down that would lead to graduation week end.

Our Guardian Angels

Tuesday, April 9. About 4:30 PM. The first hint of trouble was our office lights going out. My electric typewriter stopped. I walked outside. As I did so, someone ran by and said something about a radio report that a tornado-like cloud had been spotted near London, 40 miles away.

Glancing to my right, I could see our farm manger far across Goose Creek, plowing in the lower field near Red Bird Creek. Directly across the creek I could see activity around the two greenhouses where transplanting had been going on for days for the spring gardens. Farther to the right other boys could be seen near the shop buildings and the pig barn.

Directly below me our baseball team was in full uniform, warming up, waiting the arrival of Lee County. Far to the right our girls' and boys' tennis teams were practicing on the four new courts, waiting for Clay County to arrive for the match. Looking behind me, I could see students entering the dining area and our campus grill filled as the eight serving lines are open at 4:30 PM for the evening meal.

At that moment I noticed three of our younger boys accompanying a sixth grade boy from Pennsylvania with us only two weeks and still homesick. He looked frightened and matter-of-factly told me, "I'm afraid." He grasped my hand and hung on fiercely. He apparently had heard the word "tornado" and the sky was getting darker.

I reassured him and hand-in-hand we walked back toward the gym to find his shirt. With no warning there was a powerful surge of wind like I have never felt before, and large hailstones began to rain down with a staccato beat.

The hail lasted for several minutes. They seemed like hours. Objects weighing several hundred pounds were flying through the air or being tossed on the ground like they weighed ounces. Large trees came crashing down. Metal covering the wood dormer windows of our swimming pool building was stripped off like peeling an orange. Pieces were flying through the air with deadly speed. One third of the roof shingles and the underlying tarpaper were stripped off our middle school building. Many tree limbs broke off and blew hundreds of feet across Goose Creek as a bird might have flown.

Miraculously no one was killed. Many could have been. There were no injuries from the flying debris trees though several hundred people were caught outside. Truly Almighty God and guardian angels were about each individual during those critical minutes.

Many headed for the central dining room, which has no large windows to spray broken glass in such an emergency. The concrete and brick walls are several feet thick being underground on the east side. There was no panic. I was never so proud of our students and staff. Within minutes, due to the foresight of Dean "Bud" Underwood, gasoline powered generators provided electricity for the dining room, for the new gym where hundreds played later that evening.

Within 10 minutes, gasoline-powered pumps kept up the pressure of our water system. We were not without water during the next 24 hours as the electricity was off most of the time. Never has it been previously off more than about four hours.

315

With about three hours of daylight left, three of our staff and nine boys reroofed the middle school building with shingles in stock matching the remainder of the roof. In the meantime scores of other students picked up debris, sawed up trees and hauled it all away with tractors and wagons. One would have thought we had drilled for months. Each seemed to know just what to do.

There was nearly perfect order in all four dorms through the night. It was pitch-black darkness except for a few flashlights and gasoline generated glimmers of light in the hallways.

Miraculously, the large trees uprooted fell away from our buildings minimizing that type of damage. The total experience was unforgettable, terrible, yet inspirational.
Western Recorder, April 23, 1991

It was Homecoming weekend. April 27 was the big day! The dogwood and redbud were in full bloom. Hundreds gathered on the campus with gratitude in their hearts, gratitude that their dear OBI still stood. The campus looked even more beautiful to them, knowing its near miss by the tornado. Several old buildings sported new slanted roofs: the huge old gym, the swimming pool, Carnahan Hall, Marvin-Wheeler Hall, Hopwood House, Sanderson House, and several others. There were new bathrooms in Carnahan Hall and Marvin-Wheeler Hall as well. Barkley couldn't have Homecoming without progress to show everyone. The newest building was the 3,000-square-foot shop on the farm. It was dedicated along with the new tennis courts.

Of course, he always showed off what the students were doing with pride. This year was no exception. There were tennis meets, a big track & field day, and a baseball game for the day, along with a band field show and a choir concert.

There was just a slight hint to Tom Jenkin, a former teacher, that he was worried about anything. He had written him earlier on February 14, Valentines Day. In the letter he mentioned the new roof on the gym. He wrote, "The old gym has a new roof I've been assured will last for thirty years...at which time I expect I will have been dead many, many years."

It seemed like the weeks between Homecoming and graduation were mere days. In a flash May flowers were springing into blossom all over campus and on the hillsides as well. Old fashioned Sweet Williams and trilliums were growing on the hills, under the towering cedars and beeches. Their delicate fragrance and elegant patches of color caught the eye under the paw paws and giant tulip trees in full bloom, with their massive grapelike clusters of white hanging on every branch. It was a sight that nearly took the breath away. Tiny violets and yellow mounds of dandelions competed with the deep green grass for space on the freshly mowed lawns. The petals of daisies could be seen falling from the fingers of many a girl—*Love Me, Love Me Not, Love Me, Love Me Not, Love Me!*

A Big Day

Graduation day, 1991, dawned with sunshine and ended with a hard rain. The rain came as "showers of blessing" on a day filled with blessings, smiles and tears of joy mixed with sadness of parting.

All the baccalaureate services since 1949 have been held in the Oneida Baptist Church. We have that service on the same day as the graduation ceremony. Being a boarding school where most of the student families live quite some distance, it is more convenient to have these two important services on the same day for reasons of travel, lodging and other considerations.

It is fitting that the baccalaureate service is held where the seniors have worshiped Sunday after Sunday. With only one-third the seating capacity of our chapel where the commencement service is held in the afternoon, the morning service is for the class, members of their immediate families and some of our staff. It is always a rather personal service.

Our invocation this year was led by Byron Perrine, assistant principal for teacher supervision and evaluation. He has a doctorate and teaches our German classes. The past two summers he has gone to Germany for additional study. His wife is an outstanding OBI math teacher, and both their children are honor students.

The class and congregation sang, *I'll Go Where You Want Me to Go, Dear Lord, I'll Be What You Want Me to Be.* I breathed a silent prayer that such was the heart desire of at least a majority.

Pastor Joel Rackley led a prayer, followed by the collection of the morning offering. The congregation sang the Doxology. Truly we can and do 'praise God from whom all blessings flow'. Our graduating choir members, joined by a few selected underclassmen, sang *Out of the Depths.* Then followed a spine-tingling rendition of *Were You There?*

Evangelist Joe Mobley of London challenged the class with a powerful message on Gideon.

The graduating class came to the end of their last worship service in the night at church as they sang *Blest Be the Tie That Binds.* A graduate in the 1947 class, now an OBI teacher, Luther Burns, led the benediction and the class marched out to *Onward Christian Soldiers.*

In the afternoon, faculty and staff and some of our trustees, all in academic regalia, followed the flag-bearers into Melvin Davidson Chapel to the beat of the Grand March. Following were 66 graduates in their caps and gowns... blue for boys and white for girls.

A.B. Colvin's invocation was followed by salutatorian Ryan Weaver's welcoming address. With three of our trumpeters accompanying, the congregation sang *God of Our Fathers.*

Then followed the awarding of honors to the academically "top" student of each grade from the sixth grade up. Also, awards were given to the student of each grade having made the "most progress" by vote of the faculty. I gave the President's Award to 15 graduating seniors, and Oneidas to highest awards. The highest honor Oneida can give, by vote of the faculty, went to Angie Berry, the class valedictorian. She has been with us for seven years. Receiving the second highest honor, in a tie by secret ballot, was salutatorian Rian Weaver, here four years, and John Quakenbush, who first came in the eighth grade.

Fifteen staff members received special plaques recognizing their 15th, 10th and fifth years of service. John Sanderson received an award for 19 years of teaching and 16 years as senior sponsor. He has taken on a full-time church pastorate.

The congregation sang *Since Jesus Came Into My Heart* and the Oneida Choir responded with *Speak to One Another, Come Unto Me, Soon Ah Will Be Done* and *We Will Remember Thy Name*. Principal Larry Gritton presented the 22 seniors receiving the advanced diploma and the 46 receiving the standard diploma. As I spoke of each graduate individually, trustee Chairman Preston Baker awarded the diplomas.

The new graduates sang *Take My Life, Lead Me Lord* and Angie Berry said goodbye for the class.

The singing of *Oneida Fair* and the benediction by Dale Walker ended the service. A Methodist missionary to Indonesia for 28 years, he and his wife were with us to see son Andy, who came as a seventh grader, graduate.

Western Recorder, June 11, 1991

Like Mr. Chips

Summer school is over. It was a wonderful session. We had 227 enrolled at our maximum. That is the largest group we have had for a summer session which began with 40 in 1974. Amazingly, although we had the largest number, we had the fewest discipline problems by far ever. It was almost scary.

We have had many individuals, as usual, come and do volunteer work this summer. Many are "regulars" like Bill Cole who has averaged a week a month since 1980 doing carpentry. Hiram Campbell has been coming for about 12 years from Ohio. He, or men employed by him, have done literally several hundred thousand dollars worth of donated electrical work as our physical plant has increased five-fold.

Edna Meadors, widow of a former director of missions, has done a summer of volunteer work tutoring in our Special Help program. The year before last she was here the entire year.

Other summer tutoring volunteers have included Eleanor Casey Odle, who graduated in 1975, and is now the mother of five. Remembering her as a schoolgirl, seemingly only yesterday, and seeing her as wife and mother today is a thrill. In the meantime, two of her nephews and two nieces have attended here from Texas, and a niece will graduate this year.

Then Mike Showalter, who graduated from a Virginia college in May, has tutored all summer as a volunteer. He graduated from OBI four years ago having enrolled as a sophomore. Mike is a legend at Oneida. He ran away 24 hours after he enrolled, stole a bicycle to pedal to Louisville but discovered it had a flat tire. Continuing to walk, he was picked up 17 miles away and brought back to us. He was a delight to work with and accepted Christ the following year. In his senior year, he ranked fourth in the state in the academic "Sweet 16" in vocal music and got a full scholarship to college. He has continued to grow and mature wonderfully as a Christian.

Mary Ratliff is another who has done a summer of volunteer service with us. She also is an outstanding Christian young lady who accepted Christ during her seven years in middle and high school here. Active in BSU here and later, she has been a summer missionary several times and is now preparing for her senior year of college. For years, Mary sang in our choir traveling thousands of miles, played in the band, was active in so many ways. Yes, seeing Eleanor, Mike and Mary, who were just children when they first came here, and now who are mature Christian adults in love with the Lord, is a reaffirmation of what OBI is all about.

Terre Carrington Williams, with us all her high school years, was married in our chapel a few weeks after her 1979 graduation. Her husband, Bruce, had graduated here the year before. Both found the Lord at Oneida and theirs has been a Christian home from the first day. They have two beautiful daughters. Bruce is a sergeant in the Army military police. After several tours of duty in Germany, recruiting duty here in the U.S., Bruce is stationed in Korea for a year. Terre and the girls are here with us. Terre has supervised 19 other Special Help teachers this summer, doing a super job. We are so proud of her.

While I'm reminiscing, let me tell you about Stella. I hadn't seen her in 13 years. When she came to us in the mid '70s she was a gawky, not very pretty, mountain girl from a very poor family. Neither parent, nor aunts nor uncles, as I recall, had ever finished high school. During the years we worked with her, doing intensive tutoring, the family was able to pay a total of about $200. Imagine my surprise and delight when Stella came to see me several weeks ago. She is a fine looking woman today, and married a Christian man shortly after leaving Oneida. She had been trying to get him to come see her "Oneida" for 10 years she told me. They stayed hours. They showed me pictures of their beautiful daughter, two handsome sons. They are hardworking, doing well financially, made a $50 donation and pledged to give that much weekly so long as they are financially able to do so.

In a few days, I begin my 23rd year of service at Oneida, my 20th year as president. God has been good to me.

All the above are my children. Their children are like grandchildren. Like the famed Mr. Chips, I have thousands of children.

Western Recorder, July 30, 1991

A Coat from God

It was very cold one recent day. Our band director spotted one of our boys not wearing a coat. Concerned, he asked the young man if he forgot to put his coat on. "I don't have a coat," the boy said.

With many things on his mind, Mr. Burns mentally checked his situation as something needing attention. To himself he thought that perhaps there was an extra band coat in storage. Later that evening he found none. A coat must be found elsewhere.

The next morning Mr. Burns checked his mail following our daily chapel service. There was a package addressed simply "Band Director" with a Covington postmark. Inside was a used Oneida band jacket in excellent condition. There was no note. Mr. Burns came to share with me what had just happened. Neither then nor a day later has either of us been able to think who might have sent the coat. It really doesn't matter who God's instrument was.

The important fact is that God knew this young man's need before we did. He put it into some person's mind and heart to pack up the coat and send it to Oneida.

In *Isaiah* 65:24 we read, "And it shall come to pass, that before they call, I will answer; and while they are yet speaking, I will hear."

Our God, "the same yesterday, today and forever" has been meeting the needs of his own for many thousands of years. He is great enough to be concerned about one of his little ones at Oneida school.

I have been witness to countless similar evidences of God's provision in things great and small here at Oneida. I saw this as a child here 35 or 40 years ago, as a staff member 28 years ago and now for 19 years as president.

Richard Burns and I have just discussed the current episode again, with all and wonder and yet not with surprise. I mentioned that his great-great uncle, James Anderson Burns, founder of our school, had many such experiences. He replied, "Are you thinking about the fish?" Yes I was. Let me share that story with you as recorded in Darrell C. Richardson's biography of Burns titled *Mountain Rising*.

Burns constantly encouraged his teachers, and his never failing enthusiasm was contagious. "Having begun a good work in you, he will perform it until the day all is fulfilled," he would say to his coworkers. "We shall labor on until God wills that all be fulfilled."

For several years the average pay of the teachers was $14 a month. Somehow they managed to live. They worked with their hands at various tasks. They rented land and raised gardens and crops in summer. In addition to the fishing, they engaged in hunting, which placed a little meat on the table.

"One morning I ate breakfast with Dan Hacker," recalled Burns. "As we finished, Dan's wife Lucinda said, 'This is our last piece of meat.' Dan and I walked into the yard. He asked 'What will we do today?' I replied, 'Let's finish laying our corn crop.' Without another word, we crossed Goose Creek in a little boat, got our hoes and went to work. At 11 o'clock the last row had been hoed, and we started home. The crop was laid by. When we reached the river it was very muddy and swollen. There had been a heavy rain the night before on the headwaters. I paddled the boat. It struck something which had not been there when we crossed in the morning. I stopped paddling. Dan reached out into the muddy water and drew up a fish basket, a sort of trap. It had fourteen very large catfish in it, meat for several days. It had floated down the river from somewhere. We never knew from where."

"We didn't talk about it, but I saw a strange light in Dan's eyes. Coincidence? Yes, undoubtedly. But who controls all coincidences of life, even the very small and seemingly insignificant ones? Believe as you may, but let me believe as I may. It encourages my heart in troublous times to think that our heavenly Father knows and tempers every wind that blows."

Just this date a wonderful gift came with a precious note: "even as a Catholic, I well recognize the fine work Oneida Baptist is doing. Have a blessed Christmas and a wonderful new year."

And so we say to each of our readers.

Western Recorder, December 28, 1991

1992-93
Year 21

We ARE a FAITH work! A lot of people talk about that but we ARE.
We do those things commanded by Christ: share the Gospel which
we do DAILY with every teacher and student attending chapel; feed
the hungry, clothe the naked, give water to the thirsty, care for the
sick, take in the stranger. We do EACH of those things DAILY.
—Barkley Moore

Dear Friends:

1992! How time does go by! We pray for you and every loved one a good year.

We celebrated the new year in good style here at Oneida. Students and staff came back from Christmas vacation and we got in two days of school before New Year's eve. That night we had a three and one half hour movie, playing in the gym, and a "Watch Night Service" in our local church past the midnight hour. Then all students and staff assembled in the dining room to make sandwiches out of varying types of meats, a variety of toppings and bread. It was really a wonderful evening. Everyone slept in three hours later New Year's Day and then we had a half day of school including our Chapel service. Guests from Iowa, New York, Tennessee, Pennsylvania and Ohio, were with us to share in the service. Themes from Oneida's first Chapel service on New Year's Day, 1900 were a part of the 1992 service as well. Jesus Keep Me Near the Cross and "Except the Lord build the house, they labor in vain that build it..." (*Psalms* 127:1)

Staying near the cross, striving to be in obedience to God's will, is what has made it possible for Oneida to enter upon its 93rd year of ministry. Every day has been a miracle of God.

Of course, the most wonderful thing about our New Year's Eve and New Year's Day was the spirit of our students and staff. If we were not the only school in the United States having school, we were on of the very few. Folks unfamiliar with Oneida might imagine that we had a lot of down-in-the-mouth people through it all. No, it was a time of good fellowship, high spirits. I can honestly say I neither observed nor heard a negative attitude. That is very remarkable, even more so when one knows the very negative spirit of many of our girls and boys as they first come to stay with us. It was truly a wonder way to begin 1992. I cannot imagine that anyone, anywhere got off to any better start.

Forty-three of our young people spent the entire first week of the month practicing nightly for auditions to be in the musical Oklahoma, which will be presented here, April 23-24-25, at 8:00 PM. Mark your calendar! We are having academic meets, basketball games, wrestling and swim meets, the choir is here and there singing. Our pep band has a real workout every home varsity basketball game. Everyday the pigs and cows must be fed and much else done on the farm. Every room on campus in every building must be cleaned daily, dishes washed three times daily, grounds work to be done, trash barrels to be emptied… Second quarter ends, third quarter begins, examinations, grade reports, and 'calling' the 'Honor Roll' are all a part of the first month of a new calendar year.
Letters, 1992

There was so much to be thankful for as the new year began. The Kentucky Baptist Convention gave Oneida an extra $20,000 just before Christmas. On January 9 Barkley wrote Dr. Bill Marshall to express his gratitude. He had a great deal to say about how the money had been spent.

Dear Dr. Marshall:

It was wonderful to get the extra $20,000 just before Christmas. Please share our appreciation with ALL concerned. And a "thank you" to you personally for making the recommendation. Every dollar means a lot.

The money came just as we had the opportunity to purchase three choice pieces of property near our campus, which we have done. Two of the houses are two blocks from our main campus. Each of them are two of the finest houses of our village, one four-bedroom and full basement, the other a three-bedroom with adjoining land on which we could build at least three houses if we should choose to do so someday. Both these properties are above the flood plain. The third property adjoins three other lots, and three houses, that we have purchased in the past four years. These are located on the main highway as you enter the village of Oneida. We will eventually tear down the house. Again there is room to build four or five houses, and this area is also above the flood plain.

In the past eight months we have also made the following MAJOR improvements, all paid for:

Built a large room on three different staff houses. Some of this was done with the help of volunteers.
New roofs on our chapel building and also on McConnville Hall which includes our campus clinic...and apartments for three staff.
Were donated TV sets for every classroom in varying buildings.
Were donated many thousands of dollars of science equipment, much of it new.
Traded in six used pianos that were donated six years ago for six new pianos for our piano labs, where we have a total of 12 pianos.
Bought 21 new IBM computers, four times more powerful than what we had had before, for our lab. The old computers we placed in individual middle school classrooms and in our staff school.
Have been donated a very interesting and large Indian arrowhead and tomahawk collection, valued at $15,000. These are displayed in our library.
Bought all new typewriters for our business department...
Letters, 1992

The Kentucky Baptist Convention had helped make December 1991 the best month financially in the history of the school. Even with the purchase of over $100,000 dollars worth of property, the school was debt-free and all the bills were paid. With over $3,400,000 donated in the 1991 fiscal year, the years of long and arduous toil by Barkley and his staff had begun to really pay itself forward. At this point, he could have slowed down and worked more normal hours as most would have, but instead he pushed ahead to improve the school and its holdings even further. Did he think he wouldn't be around for many more years? He spoke of it more than once.

That Barkley was overweight, no one, even he, could deny. One dear lady was a little unhappy with the length of his talk before the "Tour", and prodded him in a terse letter. He shouldn't talk so much and he shouldn't eat so much: "You are fat." His response:

> You are quite right that I am 'fat' but I am happy to say no more so than the last time you were here...but not a lot less either. I 'wish' also that it weren't so, and I do try to lose and, like most, in similar situation fail to lose very much. I am quite active, put in about 18 hour days...and will be grateful for however MANY years I am allowed by the Lord. The Lord has blessed me with enough energy and opportunity to have lived already about 100 years in these first 50!

And in 1992 he would live at least five years rolled into one. The year would see more of everything happening: more students, more staff, more wins in academics and in sports, more trips for everyone associated with the school, more building, more donations, and perhaps an extra pound for him. How he enjoyed all that delicious food the Oneida cooks and Kentucky Baptists cooked up for him at every church where he and the choir went! He demonstrated such pleasure and gratitude, how could any of them have offered a mere salad? When you don't sleep or rest, food becomes both sleep and rest! He was on a mission his whole life, with no time for anything but that mission. Oneida was his work and he made no excuses for that. He was still telling the story of God's goodness and provisions in every letter. Because, as he said,

We ARE a FAITH work! A lot of people talk about that but we ARE. We do those things commanded by Christ: share the Gospel which we do DAILY with every teacher and student attending chapel; feed the hungry, clothe the naked, give water to the thirsty, care for the sick, take in the stranger. We do EACH of those things DAILY. We do ALL that we do in our understanding of HOW God wants His work carried forward...by FAITH and in LOVE. Doing so we believe ourselves to be IN God's will. Being in His will we look to HIM to do that which His Word promises: to PROVIDE our NEEDS. Not everything necessarily what we want or think we want but our needs...
Letters, 1992

In February he received a gift of $10,000 in the mail. He wrote the donor, thanking him, his heart filled with gratitude. And in the letter he talked about all the wonderful things going on at Oneida. There were nineteen buses lined up in a row ready to go to Lexington, Kentucky! And here's why.

Oneida won the 13th REGIONAL BASKETBALL CHAMPIONSHIP defeating Harlan 64-62. That was the first regional championship ever for us in basketball though we have won many such trophies in other sports. Therefore, our game in Rupp Arena was our very first state tournament in basketball. Although Green County beat us 64-59 in a closely fought game right down to the last minute, it was a tremendous day for Oneida. Of the eight schools that played in the opening day, Oneida was the only one the Lexington TV stations did a special segment about after the game. It was wonderfully done commenting how over 600 Oneida students and staff were present for the game and including scenes of our boys playing and our students cheering as well as interviews with our German teacher, one of our senior boys, and myself. Two different newscasters called Oneida students "winners". We certainly felt like winners despite the score.

There was excellent spirit among students and staff, and our students acted with wonderful discipline and grace going to and returning from the game as well as during the game. Many strangers approached varying staff members and myself to favorably comment on their spirit and behavior. We got every child to Lexington and back, never had to look for any of them a single time, no one was lost. Our transportation was wonderfully organized as was our feeding of the students after the game. The food was prepared here and taken to Lexington and was served in 21 minutes to our entire group of over 600. Think of that! There was never a day in Oneida history when we had reason to be prouder. So many of our alumni, former staff, and friends came from different states. Truly it was a wonderful day including beautiful weather. We thank God for His blessing, for traveling mercies, for protecting players and fans alike from injury of any sort.

Also our boys varsity wrestling team has won the STATE CHAMPIONSHIP in Class "A" for the second year in a row. In varying invitational tournaments and matches they have won more individual trophies and medals than in the previous five years combined Their state win was the 16th team or individual championship in a variety of sports that Oneida has won in the past 18 years. Our girls and boys have earned the right to compete in a total of 60 state tournaments during these years.

124 of our students were on the second quarter HONOR ROLL academically. We continue to do well in middle school and high school academic competitions. Our choir is singing in varying churches and our band playing at ballgames and preparing for spring performances and competition. Our drama group is hard at work on their musical *Oklahoma*, to be presented April 23, 24, 25. Keep our Oneida Family in your prayers.

Letters, 1992

The spring continued to be one of the busiest and most successful ever. The Academic Problem Solving Team won the Regional Championship; Mr. Drennan's chess team got seven of ten trophies in a contest with three different schools. The drafting team went to Louisville and took first place in a contest by the Kentucky Civil Engineering Society; the swimmers and divers were again in the state tournament. Mr. Coffey was voted "Coach of the Year" for the second time in five years.

On the old Keith Farm that had been given to the school, two of the staff were donating enough money to build a two-story three-bedroom, two-bath log cabin. The plans were set to get all the tillable land of the property into grass and run thirty to forty head of cattle there. Also, Barkley was making substantial additions to at least two more pieces of the staff housing that summer.

There were to be six weddings! It thrilled Barkley that his staff and "young 'uns" were finding mates at Oneida. He took the time to be at all the weddings. In the spring and summer and summer issues of the *Mountaineer*, hot off the press, there were so many honored, it appeared Oneida was taking all the trophies home; academically as well as in sports. He was personally honored by being asked to consider becoming a member of the SBC Education Commission. He was surprised and humbled to have his name brought up, but turned down the offer. He wrote back to Mr. Bill Haycraft:

> Events of the past several weeks since I last saw you led me to decline being considered. For 20 years I have worked night and day, seven days a week trying to fulfill my obligations to the Lord in the stewardship of Oneida...with 500 young lives to care for daily, and a staff of 125 to supervise. My recent illness and all are just a reminder that, if anything, I need to be letting up a little in my daily activity rather than adding more responsibilities. [He had suffered from a respiratory infection, near pneumonia, for several weeks at the beginning of the year, suffering extreme shortness of breath.] I will pray for you and the others involved as you seek to find those men and women that the Lord would have to help guide the varying programs as trustees.
>
> *Letters*, 1992

The highlight of every March was the senior trip to Washington. This year they would be making a side trip to Norfolk, Virginia to the Naval Yard. During the spring break Barkley would be off on a speaking engagement that would take him all the way to Pennsylvania. However, even with all that he was doing for his own students at Oneida, Barkley never buried his head in the sand, unaware of what was happening in the world of education outside Oneida. When he was opposed to something, he took a stand. The Kentucky Senate was about to vote on Education Reform. He was stirred up! For one thing, Oneida used paddling as one means of discipline. It was agreed upon by both the parent and student upon a students enrolling at Oneida; and that was threatened by the bill. Plus, the passage of Senator Karem's bill would take away a district's right to make the decision whether to be a part of the Whittle Educational Network or not. Oneida used the TV monitor for educational programming every day. He wrote:

> It is a real bargain for the Kentucky taxpayer as well as each child, who has the daily opportunity to watch these twelve minutes of programming...and then use the equipment for whatever other filmed material is desirable that day: copies of KET program, films of Shakespeare plays, whatever.
>
> Issue Number Two: I and hundreds of thousands of others (including parents, teachers in the classroom, (even students themselves) oppose ANY law designed to totally eliminate corporal punishment in the classroom...Where there is no DISCIPLINE, there is no learning, no matter how much money you throw at the situation. The United States of America already spends more on education than the rest of the world combined. If MONEY was the answer to our problems, we would have NO problem. A big part of the educational problem today in our country is the breakdown of classroom discipline, because too many districts have decided "no paddling". This is a situation again where districts should DECIDE FOR THEMSELVES—not an edict from the legislature. Yes, there are cases where the right to paddle is abused, as ANYTHING can be abused, but there are already recourse sufficient when that happens. When there is a problem, some folks try to solve the problem by throwing the baby out with the dirty bath water. To eliminate paddling as one of many tools of discipline (and one of the most

effective tools) is akin to that. Why don't we just throw out the dirty water and keep the baby—suspend without pay for a period of time, fire from their job if necessary, or other appropriate action for an ABUSER, but allow normal folks the exercise of a form of discipline that extends back to the most ancient times. Tried and tested. "To spare the rod is to spoil the child." No amount of philosophizing or pontificating changes the evidence to be seen all about us. Everybody in the state should not be forced to GOOSE-STEP in every matter. Let's allow for there to be a VARIETY of approaches. That is what DEMOCRACY is supposed to be about.

Letters, 1992

In April there was a tremendous Homecoming. The musical, *Oklahoma,* was outstanding. The big event on Saturday was the dedication service for the new carillon in the chapel tower. It was dedicated to Hugh L. Spurlock, Class of 1927, who was there celebrating his sixty-fifth anniversary. He had served as math teacher, coach, and principal of Oneida for fifteen years. The craft house brought in $2,500 in crafts made by the students. The marching band strutted their stuff in brand new uniforms which had arrived in time for the concert and annual parade in Knoxville. And now the spring crops were being planted. There were 531 girls and boys busy everywhere Barkley looked, and five additional teachers settling in to Oneida's busy days.

In May the Middle School did a 105-minute musical. Barkley was amazed by the memorization of the entire performance. That night the school hosted a dinner for over 500 athletes from the Conference. Then they all went to chapel, where the band played for thirty minutes. Barkley got to bed at 4:35 AM Saturday morning but was up and in the office at 8:00 AM where he signed letters for an hour and a half, before boarding the Greyhound with the choir. They were gone forty-one and a half hours and arrived back at Oneida at 2:57 AM Monday morning. During that time they had traveled 856 miles and given four major concerts, in which he spoke four times. They visited the Jefferson Davis Memorial, went over the Mississippi River, and were in Missouri and Illinois for a short time. They were warmly welcomed by receptive congregations. After chapel on Monday, Barkley left for Cedarmore, Kentucky, where he spoke to the Executive Board of Kentucky Baptists for nearly an hour, showing the new film about Oneida.

He arrived back at Oneida at 1:00 AM Tuesday. The activities of graduation week started in days. There were more seniors graduating who had received the Lord, as Savior, than ever. In a week-long series of award convocations, students were honored for being "good and outstanding workers", the most outstanding students in each class—right down to the students with the cleanest dorm rooms. They ate all the ice cream they could hold along with every type of topping one could imagine. It all ended with Commencement in the chapel with hundreds there while Barkley honored all seventy one of the seniors in a teary- eyed ceremony with parents crying the most!

Harold Holderman, one of his dearest friends and a longtime teacher at Oneida, and then at the Glendale Children's Home at Glendale, Kentucky, had been diagnosed with heart failure. He had been at Homecoming. On May 6 Barkley wrote a very tender letter to him, his last before Harold died on June 1.

Harold, you are in God's hands and, as Paul said, "to live is Christ, to die is gain". You are in our prayers. Always you will be a part of Oneida because of the many years you INVESTED in the lives of many. One of our 1939 graduates is in a similar condition to you…a bad heart The doctors told his wife that he might go at any moment. That was THREE years ago. I saw him recently. I have a letter in the school safe that a father gave me in 1973 when his son enrolled as a 9th grader at Oneida. It was his only son and the doctor had told him a few weeks before that he might die at any moment of a heart attack. That was 19 years ago and Marvin's letter is still in my safe because the father is very much alive. Marvin doesn't even know of the existence of the letter and I'm sure the father has forgotten ever writing it, but I will give it to Marvin someday. But, who knows, Marvin may go first or I might. We buried Mr. J.B. Henson six weeks ago at Danville. The doctors told him in 1948 that he had less than a year to live and he proceeded to sell his 300 acre

farm near Shelbyville. He lived another 43 years dying at the age of 100 years, three months, 12 days. He often told me had he not sold that farm he would have been a millionaire! We all must die...no one escapes that. Each of us has known that all our lives. It is all in <u>God's</u> TIMING. He is in charge as HE was <u>before</u> each of our births. I know you will continue living each day that God gives you...all of our days are a daily gift from HIM. As we prepared the house for you to stay in while you were at Homecoming, so God has prepared a far greater place for you and those you love, <u>all who have claimed Him by faith</u>. Think of what a HOMECOMING all of us will have THERE. Oneida's is fun but that will be GLORY!
Letters, 1992

On May 20, right after graduation, Barkley left the campus for a 1700-mile trip with his family to Washington. It was the first time that he had ever taken time off from Oneida for a trip with his family and he had it planned to the minute. He had invited every one of them, from aunts to cousins. They would take one of the Greyhounds. He would show them all the places the seniors had been going to those many years. Although he had never been along with them, he knew the places by heart! His Aunt Claire would be turning ninety during the trip and they would have a big celebration for her. Those long awaited hours, moments they would share, would live in their hearts and minds for a lifetime and beyond! Mr. and Mrs. Moore had their son to themselves after three decades of sharing him with others. If there were people any where in the world who deserved that trip it was the people that surrounded him on that bus.

It had been said by the *Christian Science Monitor*, way back in 1971, upon his return from Iran and the Peace Corps, that "Barkley was not built for bureaucracy. He was built for people." He had poured his life out for his girls and boys over the years even on holidays when his family could rightly have expected him to spend the time with them. They understood the cost. The *Chicago Times* had praised their son as well: "If the fabric of Barkley Moore's life could be ripped into a thousand pieces, each would be a good deed." Mrs. Moore had felt that ripping every time she looked into her son's tired eyes. She knew the price he had paid, for he was her gift to hurting people and she had paid for it as well with the knowing love and understanding only a mother's heart could feel when she looked into her son's eyes!

They lingered long under the cherry blossoms, gazed out upon the Potomac, stood reverently before Lincoln, walked the streets of Colonial Williamsburg, saw the Tomb of the Unknown Soldier and the eternal flame at John F. Kennedy's grave. Mr. Moore, would say, "Now, Evelyn, let Barkley lead the way," when he would suggest just one more site they must see. Even with family he was leading the "Tour", arms swinging, fingers pointing, descriptions firing at the speed of a bullet. They must see it all! And they did! Heading homeward with the breathtaking Blue Ridge Mountains in the distance, rising from the green valley floor to distances and peaks that could have rivaled his beloved Gonbad's, he surely took a trip down Memory Lane to his other land, his other family left behind in war torn Iran!

No sooner were they back than it was time for the Mountain Missions Conference. Dr. Bill Marshall, Executive Director of the Kentucky Baptist Convention, and his wife were guests of Barkley's mother at the house on the hill. He didn't sleep there very often himself, having years ago taken to sleeping in a single room in Anderson Hall, after he gave up Miss Wilson's tiny apartment in the boys' dorm. The Marshalls had the first level, with not only a parlor, but a kitchen, bath, and bedroom as well. They could walk out to the lovely lawn overlooking the campus. Mrs. Moore's peonies and irises were blooming just outside the door and the fragrance wafted over the deep green lawn in the dewy mountain air at nightfall.

It was on this visit that Barkley would have the time to show Dr. Marshall much of the campus not seen by guests on the walking tour. With Dr. Marshall driving, Barkley would show him more of the farm, the extended properties away from the main campus, up Bullskin, around to the Keith farm, and even take a trip to the Squire Hensley Cemetery, the cemetery where Barkley's ancestors are buried. There were now over 500 acres on the main campus and adjoining properties that the school owned. There were four new houses and two more under construction that Dr. Marshall had not seen, and the 12,000-square-foot shop and storage center were under construction. Barkley had found in Dr. Marshall another wonderful friend and supporter for Oneida. He spoke and wrote to others of Dr. Marshall's support for Oneida and his endearing kindness and eagerness to be of help. Barkley very much appreciated this support.

The busy days of the summer months; summer building, summer gardening, summer school session with the largest enrollment ever, gave way to an early fall. Barkley rarely left the campus after the hurried spring and trip to Washington, unless he was invited to speak or needed to travel with the choir. He was very content to oversee Oneida's own busy world on those 500-plus acres. He had only been outside the state of Kentucky a few times since 1980. However, the world had come to him on a daily basis with hundreds of visitors a week for years and he was still proffering the invitation. But it certainly was time for:

A Little Slower Pace

I gave myself three hours off this Wednesday morning. Knowing I had no scheduled appointments for the day, something that happens very rarely, I slept a bit extra and watched the Olympics.

Our summer school session was over last Friday. Several hundred students left for a three-week break preparatory to our new term beginning Aug. 16.

On Sunday morning, 23 students and staff traveled five hours to share in the wedding of two of our staff at Goshen Church in Breckenridge County. I watched the bride grow up from a sixth grade child in our dorm. She was with us seven years before going on to college.

The groom's oldest aunt came to be a student in our school 54 years ago at the age of 28. Living too far from a high school, she had been out of school for many years until she heard of Oneida. She was the valedictorian of our 1942 class and was back a few months ago for her 50th class reunion. There are many "ties that bind" our Oneida family together.

Many other Oneidians met us at the church, and the ladies had prepared a wonderful meal for us. Lightning struck the transformer near the church an hour before the ceremony, cutting off the lights and air-conditioning. But a candlelight ceremony had been planned anyway. The church was packed with people standing while the wedding was performed to the clap of thunder. The Lord's Supper was a beautiful part of the memorable service.

One of our 1992 graduates, a boy with us six years, was at the service. Learning it was his 19th birthday, two of our boys and I took him to a nearby state park lodge for a birthday dinner. We drove to Marshall County and spent the night...
Western Recorder, August 24, 1992

Recent Highlights

Standout events of the past few weeks have been made with scores of other things happening in between and more than 700 visitors to show around and eat with us. We love to have company, and growing numbers are coming to see the work here. I try to spend some time with every guest.

Thursday, Aug. 20, Pastor Rackley, OBI teacher Steve May and I left early in the morning to drive to Paducah. There we each spoke at the funeral of OBI volunteer Melvin Hopwood, saw some former OBI staff and students and renewed other acquaintances.

Sunday, Aug. 23, Jerry Smith was ordained to the gospel ministry. He is in his 28th year of OBI teaching, mainly Bible. Licensed, he has been a worker in the Crane Creek Baptist Church all these years but was recently called as pastor. He was the third of longtime staff members, with 59 years of cumulative OBI service, to be ordained as ministers in the past two years. Each is serving a nearby church.

Guests who traveled the farthest to see us recently were Leo and Ruby Pendleton of Yuma, Ariz. A neighbor boy enrolled at OBI 10 years ago, and that is how they first became acquainted with our work. They are frequent financial donors, among that host of small but frequent donors that make our work possible.

Thursday, Sept. 3, I made my annual report to the 122nd session of our local Booneville Association. Our student choir did two numbers and it was my first time to hear them this school year.

Sunday, Sept. 6, was an unforgettable day. Over 100 guests from many different places were on campus to see the school. Then at 3:00 PM was the 90-minute memorial service honoring Melvin Hopwood in which many present and former OBI staff took part, having been unable to attend the funeral several weeks before. This was scheduled after Mrs. Hopwood's return from Paducah.

At 6:20 PM the body of senior Rhonda Barger, one of our seniors, was brought to our chapel to lie in state. Over 300 outside guests were with us that evening and others came the next day for the funeral. We kept to our normal school schedule except for an earlier Sunday evening worship service and no morning chapel service on Monday.

Wednesday, Sept. 9, one of our staff and I traveled to Paris to have lunch with Mrs. Logan English whose family has lived in beautiful Wyndhurst for 104 years. It was an unforgettable meal and afternoon in that historic home whose two occupants have been supportive of OBI for decades. That evening I ate at a fish fry of Paris First Baptist Church and spoke at the evening service centered on state missions.

Friday-Saturday, Sept. 11-12, my mother, a staff member, two students and I traveled to Smith's Grove for the lying-in-state funeral the following morning of Mrs. Morman Kersey. She and her husband have been among our most faithful supporters the past 19 years. An ensemble of our choir arrived in time to sing at the service. For many years if our choir sang within 100 miles of Louisville and the Kerseys knew about it, they were there to hear our choir and pay for everyone's bountiful meal.

That same day 41 of our students were at MissionsFest at Immanuel in Lexington, scores of our cross-country team were in Covington for a large meet, 15 of our academic team were in Frankfort, and two soccer games were played at home.

Western Recorder, September 29, 1992

An Old Fashioned Bonnet and Long Dress

Oneida's third Family Day, held Saturday, Oct. 3, was a tremendous success. Our cooks prepared for 2,000 at the noon meal, and there wasn't much left over.

Unlike the two previous years when it was cold, and raining at times, we had a bright, sunny day with the temperature between 75-80 degrees.

Being a boarding school, we have some unique opportunities, and also some special problems. For years it was only with great effort and difficulty that a teacher and parents could meet with one another. Parents would be on campus the day they first brought their child, would dash in and out at homegoing times, and would then be here on graduation day. Or, sometimes, their last time here was when their child had been expelled. So for a parent and teacher to actually be able to meet and talk about the child, it was necessary for the parent to make a special trip here for that purpose.

Because of this, we got the idea three years ago to set aside a day two months into the school term and encourage our parents to come for the entire day. That allows them to see their child's classroom and meet and have a vonference with the teachers as necessary. This year each teacher was in the classroom for six and a half hours continuously meeting with parents.

Our teachers really enjoy getting to meet the parents, and the feedback from parents is equally positive. Each is able to give the other information and insight which will benefit the child.

From the opening day of school, we focus our students on preparing for the activities of Family Day, and their individual performances in cross-country, volleyball and soccer competitions with other schools that day. Also it is a target date for our first art exhibit, marching band field show, and a variety of other activities. Our senior class also has its Fall Festival on Family Day. They sponsor a variety of games and contests to raise money for their annual trip to Washington and Colonial Williamsburg. They also sell homemade cakes and such; after expenses, they cleared over $1,000 this year.

Family Day also is a big day for our Craft House. Nearly $2,300 worth of crafts were sold this year. This goes directly to our student aid fund.

A large crowd was already here by 9:00 AM. Twelve schools took part in six cross-country races. Oneida took first place in all three of the boys' races: middle school, junior varsity and varsity. Our girls also won the junior varsity and varsity races, but our middle school team came in third.

The Somerset soccer varsity team got revenge for our having given them their only defeat several weeks before. At this writing, our team has won half its games. Also our girls' volleyball team was defeated by Temple Christian Academy. We are proud of all our teams.

Another highlight of the day was our one room schoolhouse, Double Creek, being open all day. Our staff children, grades two-five, who study there daily were there during the afternoon. They were dressed in the style of 100 years ago in honor of the bicentennial. Their mothers had made each girl a long dress and bonnet, and the boys had on knee pants and long stockings. They sang several times listing all the American presidents from the first George to the last...
Western Recorder, October 13, 1992

How God Wonderfully Butters Our Bread

"Mr. Moore, I remember in 1972 my mother was dying of cancer. I was a student at Oneida and had to drop out to take care of her. My younger sister and older brother were also attending school there. It was the saddest and hardest time in a young girl's life, seeing life gradually leave my mother each day.

"You visited my mother, and after she died, you encouraged me to go back to school. I did, and graduated in 1974.

"It was hard to get back to the reality of school with the pressure of just losing my mother. But you encouraged me: 'You can do it Pat.' I had no money and wondered how I would even pay for school supplies. You encouraged me not to worry.

"Through you and your staff I began to pick up the pieces. Thank God I did. Today when I look at the educational problems facing students throughout the country, I often wonder if they had leadership like Oneida provides if more students might get motivated and want to be successful.

"Thank all the staff for helping me through a difficult time in my life. My mother died 20 years ago. I felt this letter was long overdue.

"My prayers will always be with this school I loved so well. It makes me so happy to hear of the great results. Just encourage your students to go on for educations, something for 'time and eternity'. God bless you and Oneida always."

The day after Thanksgiving, another 1974 graduate made contact. He came from another state to visit, and gave me a $1,500 donation.

Ali is happily married, teaching in a college, and his wife is a medical doctor. They have a daughter and two sons. I first knew him as a young blacksmith in Iran working 12-hour days for the American equivalent of $25 per month. That was in 1967. He dropped out of school after the sixth grade to help his family. He was the oldest child in a large impoverished family, and had to quit school when his father became too ill to work. He had been out of school for six years. He was very embittered because he had always been the top student of his class. He told me once that he cried every morning for two years as he saw his classmates passing by on their way to school, and he was too poor to go.

It was my privilege to encourage him. I got him interested in studying after his 12-hour workdays. I began to teach him English and hired a tutor to teach him other subjects in Persian. In this way, studying at night, he passed his seventh and eighth grades.

During two years of military service, with the help of fellow soldiers, he studied and passed special exams at freshman and sophomore levels. During this time I returned to America, after six and a half years of Peace Corps service.

A year a half later, I returned to Iran, visiting many former students, and made arrangement for Ali to come to America that fall for further study. He attended Oneida two years, graduating with honors in 1974, and then to college on a full scholarship. Today, he is a very productive American citizen.

One of my favorite passages of Scripture is the promise: "Cast your bread on the waters, and it will return after many days." And when it returns, often you see how wonderfully God has "buttered" it. *Western Recorder*, December 8, 1992

1993-94
Year 22

There are miracles today just as real as in Bible times. But many are unaware because there are no miracles in their own life experiences. There can be no miracles without faith. Nor can there be miracles where love is missing. But faith and love, active, sharing the good news of a risen Lord, ministering in his name to the needs of others, is blessed of our Lord who is the same yesterday, today and ever. All things are possible with him.
—Barkley Moore

I n 1993 the Oneida Baptist Institute opened with the largest enrollment ever. Over 600 students enrolled on a mild winter day in January—so many that every bed was filled and many were waiting. Barkley and the Trustees had for ten years limited enrollment to 518, with an extra fifteen to thirty beds empty for flexibility. Barkley said, "We are taking them 'first applied, first served'." There were ninety-two local students enrolled, almost double the number when he had become president twenty-one years before. Nothing made him happier. "As long as we have a bed, it doesn't matter how 'good' or 'bad' a child is supposed to be, we take them anyway because God made them and Jesus died for them."

There were so many courses for them to choose from and so many activities in which to participate, they were among the most fortunate students in Kentucky. In addition to all the standard academic courses, music, drama, art, and advanced studies in science, math, and three languages were offered. The music lab included all the instruments students needed individually, as well as a piano lab. (Most Oneida students wouldn't have had the funds for instruments had they been at home.) Students could also choose many vocational training programs: auto mechanics, welding, drafting, agriculture, printing, and photography. And there was the remedial reading department. Under Mrs. Floy Dejarnette's leadership, this special help department, with one-on-one support, had proven that students from any background, and with any handicap, could be coached and brought up to where they should be. Oneida was the one school in Kentucky where those special needs students were made into outstanding students, many in remarkable time.

There were enough sports programs—swimming, fencing, wrestling, track, baseball, basketball, soccer, tennis, and golf—that each student could participate in some sport. The latest equipment, equal to the best facilities in the state of Kentucky, was available, and the facilities were open to them evenings and weekends, including Sunday. Most of these programs would have been out of reach of even middle-class families.

Barkley had added six more staff, including three full-time teachers and two full-time substitute teachers, making the teacher-student ratio the best ever. Sadly, however, on the first day of school, the beloved swim coach and band director, Mr. Ed Koury, became ill and died of complications from diabetes. The news soon reached the many former students who had loved him and were scattered to the far corners of America. It was indeed a sad day, but hope rose in their hearts.

> *Death, be not proud, though some have called thee*
> *Mighty and dreadful, for thou art not so;*
> *For those, whom thou think'st thou dost overthrow,*
> *Die not, poor Death, nor yet canst thou kill me....*
> *One short sleep past, we wake eternally,*
> *And Death shall be no more;*
> *Death, thou shalt die.*
> John Donne

Living and dying were intertwined at Oneida, as everywhere. This lesson taught by life itself was one that Barkley wanted his students to understand, but he did not want them to be overwhelmed when death struck. While they certainly grieved the many loses, they sang the old victorious songs of the faith, leaning hard on the Scriptures and the promises of old! Faith was not seeing but *Standing on the Promises* of God. They would move forward in the victory of faith put into action.

Barkley was ever praising the students' academic performance. Just recently there had been more than 180 on the honor roll. Two students received invitations to President Clinton's inauguration. Returning to the campus, they had intriguing and exciting stories to tell. The drama team was busy practicing *Where the Lilies Bloom* for presentation in May. Barkley always felt there was room for improvement, so he never let the students at OBI settle for where they were. They would hear that lecture again!

The BSU and the Organization for Christian Athletes had seen many more participants, and they were leading the students in vespers and individual study of the Bible. In chapel and at church there were powerful messages being preached. The choir was out singing almost every weekend, and would be all spring.

They school was off to a good start in intermural sports. The boys' wrestling team won the state "Class A" championship for the third year. The swim team was outstanding; one of the boys, with the team five years, set a new school record. The basketball team was having a wonderful season.

Volunteers were busy working on Morman and Agnes Kersey Hall and on Harold Combs Hall, which would house four new two-story apartments for staff, each 1,400 square feet, including living and dining rooms, kitchen, three bedrooms, two baths. It was a major project and much needed. The new carpentry shop was equipped to completely build the cabinets needed.

Campers on Mission from several states had adopted Oneida some years before as a result of an appeal Barkley had made; they would be arriving soon. By now the idea of volunteerism had brought thousands of willing hands and hundreds of thousands of dollars worth of labor.

For the first time in years, the basketball season saw Oneida go down to defeat. Though tears fell, they were still proud. They would stand tall and walk with pride when they came home, because that was the Oneida spirit. Barkley may have actually been *more* proud of them for the great effort they put forth that last game. He wrote:

Quiet Pride Through Tears

Every basketball team in the state except one, no matter how outstanding their season, ends their year in defeat and sorrow. The exception is the state championship and glory.

Last night there were many tears in our dressing room at Bell County High as our varsity boys were defeated in the regional. Our four seniors had just played their last high school game.

There was strong emotion, a genuine feeling of sorrow and loss, yet a quiet pride showed through the tears. Each with bodies of men, and the four graduating seniors now legal age, yet their tears were not unmanly. So natural for ones who had shared and suffered much together, the thousands of hours of practice over the years, the several hundred games played, injuries suffered, pain endured, the thousands of miles travelled going to and from competition, the loss of sleep and other things sacrificed. But there had been the pure joy of play, so many more times the thrill of victory.

Many of this team had even gotten to play a year ago in Rupp Arena in the state class A tournament, having won the championship of the region. But last night bigger, stronger Corbin defeated us 118-95...

Larry Allen Gritton Jr., a 5'10" guard, made 59 points in his last two high school games for a career and Oneida record of 3,058 points in varsity competition. The previous record was 2,507 by a 6'5" center who graduated in 1980. In 13 years of school, Larry has had only one B...every other grade has been A. He claimed Christ at age 8 and has dedicated his life to full-time Christian service. He has always done a superb job teaching all of our sixth grade boys every week in Sunday school, and has helped lead many Bible studies in our dorms. The Sunday before district tournament he preached in a small country church in a neighboring county. Larry has been on mission trips playing basketball with the Kentucky Baptist Crusaders in Mexico and Argentina and is planning to go to mainland China this summer. [This is the Larry Gritton Jr. who is now the President of Oneida.]

Western Recorder, March 16, 1993

On the farm, it was spring planting time. While there had been fresh vegetables from the greenhouses all winter, now it was time once again to plant the big gardens, including those eight acres of famous Irish potatoes that Barkley bragged about. In fact, Dr. Jim Taylor, President of Cumberland College, would be bringing a banker to see the potatoes growing and get a taste of them as well. The banker fell in love with Oneida's farm without having seen it, through reading articles Barkley had written for the *Western Recorder*.

The Oneida Baptist Church had a new pastor, Brother Al Griffin. Each day in the week leading up to Easter, he or another staff member preached in chapel. On Easter morning just before daybreak, many were gathered on the mountain overlooking the chapel, the campus, the athletic field, the farm, and the village of Oneida. It was from there that they saw the first rays of daybreak and sang:

> *Up from the grave He arose,*
> *With a mighty triumph o'er His foes,*
> *He arose a Victor from the dark domain,*
> *And He lives forever, with His saints to reign.*
> *He arose! He Arose!*
> *Hallelujah, Christ arose!*
>
> *He lives! He lives! Christ Jesus lives today!*
> *He walks with me and talks with me along life's narrow way.*
> *He lives! He lives! Salvation to impart!*
> *You ask me how I know He lives? He lives within my heart.*

When we all get to heaven,
What a day of rejoicing that will be!
When we all see Jesus,
We'll sing and shout the victory!

Homecoming was set for April 17. There were so many returning that Barkley sent all the students home for a special Homegoing. There was never a larger or finer Homecoming. As daybreak dawned over the mountain of Little Bullskin, sending glittering golden beams through the morning haze, hundreds were already up making ready for the day. They had filled up all the motels in Manchester and most of those in London, forty miles away. Dozens had driven full-size motor homes and were already installed at Oneida's campground, which had all the amenities. Every space was filled. Barkley had bought 500 extra chairs. The students had made or renovated sixty-five more tables, and they were in place in the Sparks Gym. Meals would be served in both dining rooms and in Sparks Gym, and there would be a big picnic-style meal under the trees at noon.

Over 300 people would be back from the 40s, 50s, 60s, and there would be hundreds of others, making this the largest Homecoming ever. Many hadn't been back in years; many had never been back. In the past year, several hundred "lost" names had been added to the mailing list, and these people had been contacted. Folks arrived from all over the nation, including Alaska and Hawaii. In the chapel stood a new grand piano and a new organ, ready for the rousing annual hymn sing that had been part of Homecoming so long no one could remember just when it all started. The new book, *Beyond Goose Creek*, hot off the Institute's own press, sold out, and orders were placed for more.

After the visitors had all left, Barkley and many of the faculty sat for some time reflecting on it all. Guidance Counselor Myrtle Cooke was the most pleased of all, for it had been she who had helped Barkley with names and addresses, and with greeting old students and introducing them to each other; many didn't know each other after years of absence. All in all, tired though they were, a friendly game of Rook was in order when they finally sat down together, reminiscing, in the dining room after the evening meal on Sunday. Hadn't this just been the best Homecoming any of them had ever seen?

Arriving at the office the next morning relaxed and ready to have a productive day now that the events of Homecoming were over, Barkley did something he seldom did. He took the time to stroll over to the kitchen for an early lunch. Pinto beans and cornbread were already in the warming oven. It wasn't difficult to get Archie Couch, one of the cooks, to dish him up a big bowl of beans. Nothing pleased him more.

While he was gone the mail came, so that was the first order of business when he returned. Seeing a letter that he had been expecting, he opened it first. Barkley Moore was instantly hopping mad! The school had been turned down for matching funds from a would-be donor's company. Seems they only did such for colleges and universities. He wrote:

May I suggest <u>your company</u> like thousands of others is <u>contributing to a MISALLOCATION of EDUCATIONAL RESOURCES in the United States</u> and our country is INCREASINGLY suffering from this philosophy (attitude), whatever. We are steadily declining from our FIRST place educationally. 'HOW SO?'

<u>FAR TOO MANY BILLIONS OF DOLLARS IS DIVERTED TO COLLEGE AND GRADUATE SCHOOLS THAT SHOULD BE SPENT ON ELEMENTARY, MIDDLE AND HIGH SCHOOL EDUCATION.</u>

<u>NO ONE</u> is going to college or other higher education until, FIRST, they graduate from HIGH SCHOOL. It is NOT ENOUGH that one has a high school diploma, but THAT diploma represent genuine ACADEMIC skills.

MILLIONS of young people are graduating from U.S. high schools with less than an 8th grade educational level...often far less. <u>NEARLY ONE MILLION BOYS AND GIRLS ARE 'DROPPING OUT' EVERY YEAR before ever getting a high school diploma.</u>

There are <u>FAR TOO MANY RESOURCES PUT ON COLLEGE AND UNIVERSITY EDUCATION where there is a VAST DUPLICATION OF RESOURCES and FIERCE</u>

COMPETITION FOR STUDENTS COSTING LITERALLY MILLIONS IN RECRUITING COSTS. HUNDREDS OF MILLIONS...YEARLY...

Ever an advocate for every boy or girl getting a high school education, he was dumbfounded by the attitude of many who seemed to pay no attention to the dropout rates for high school students in America.

I'm Glad I Didn't Sleep In

It was very quiet this Sunday morning. Our seniors and six accompanying staff left Friday morning on the 43rd annual Oneida odyssey to Washington, D.C., and colonial Williamsburg. Most everyone else left Thursday afternoon for spring break.

I was tempted to sleep in but resisted the urge. In my Sunday best I walked about the campus, making sure all was OK, and started to church.

I spotted a van with a man and woman and two young boys driving slowly through the campus, looking somewhat anxiously about. The man had been on campus for a visit as a teenager 25 years ago. He told me his family had heard our choir sing three years ago and I spoke. He told me that we had never met. I learned he had never seen our little bimonthly school paper. However, he said they had long wanted to see OBI.

I invited them to our local church. Afterward, we went to our dining room. Our cooks had outdone themselves with both home-grown beef and ham, potatoes dug by our boys, peas, fresh baked rolls, a large salad bar with some of the vegetables from our winter greenhouse, and both peach and apple cobbler.

Again I apologized that all our students were away; they said they wanted to see everything anyway. I silently put my afternoon plans aside. It was not difficult because there are few things I enjoy more than introducing God's wonderful work at Oneida. I first did that as a child 40 years ago.

Five and one-half hours after first meeting the family, it was time to say "goodbye." It had been an exciting afternoon for they were so interested in everything. Their third- and fifth-grade sons did not once yawn, complain, act bored, say they were tired. I was really impressed with their obvious intelligence and self-discipline.

The father nonchalantly said he wanted to give me something. He handed me a folded check which I only glanced at…then shock! It was for $10,000! Very rarely do we ever receive a gift of such magnitude. I rise every morning not knowing from where most of our support will come.

Western Recorder, March 30, 1993

On May 24 Barkley wrote to W.R. Sphar about many changes that were going on at Oneida. One of the most exciting to him was a student of his who was returning:

Assisting Dr. Seymour at the high school level as a fulltime Assistant Principal for Discipline is David Robinson, one of our own boys…one of the true miracles of our school (came to us as an eight grader, on hard drugs, alcoholic, the youngest member of a Cincinnati gang)…graduated in 1982 as "Mr. Oneida", an excellent record at college, three magnificent years of teaching and coaching at Oneida (five years ago he coached our middle school boys to a 37-0 record), and then went on to the Southern Baptist Theological Seminary where he completed his seminary degree this past Christmas. He and his wife are jewels.

Bittersweet Days

The last days of our school year were bittersweet as always. So many wonderful events, the culmination of years of striving on the part of 65 girls and boys about to graduate. Yet each day a "last time" to do something, and eventually the final "goodbyes", knowing that one will never see many again in this world.

Saturday, May 8, was a beautiful, sunny spring day, neither hot nor cool, just a beautiful day. I accompanied our marching band on a picnic at Levi Jackson State Park in London. There several of our staff grilled hamburgers, and we all had a wonderful time. Then we took in a movie and came home.

Sunday morning we were off with the choir for our last concerts of the school year at Germantown Baptist Church in the morning after having breakfast in Winchester. After a wonderful lunch provided by the Germantown folk, we traveled to Butler. Then it was on to Campbellsburg Baptist Church, where our choir sang that evening and I spoke briefly. After they fed us, we got home about midnight... about 20 hours after we had risen to begin the day.

On Thursday, Friday and Saturday evenings, our Oneida Players performed nearly flawlessly their spring production of *Where the Lilies Bloom.*

Saturday was another beautiful day; we hosted a track and field meet that lasted the larger part of the day.

Graduation day was picture-perfect weather-wise. The morning sermon in our local church preached by our former pastor for 13 years, Joel Rackley, was excellent. That final service in the church is always very moving, as is the afternoon graduation ceremony...
Western Recorder, June 1, 1993

Summer had come. The buildings begun in the spring were nearing completion, and work began in earnest on three major new facilities. Two, the Hiram and Curtis Campbell Hall and the Denvis and Juanita Rush Hall, would be on campus. Contractors had been hired for these. Rush Hall would house a visitor reception center seating at least 125 people, and would be used daily, seven days a week, for greeting and receiving the many groups of visitors who came to Oneida by car and bus. With over 10,000 square feet of space, it would have a movie-size screen and a small platform, a kitchen, and, on the top floor, a small apartment for Barkley and a very large storage area for the many files Oneida kept on students. There would be a large covered porch, facing the campus, for guests and students alike to use, with old-fashioned rocking chairs. At night the building would be used by the Baptist Student Union and Fellowship of Christian

Athletes for their meetings. Two full-time counselors would have offices there as well.

Campbell Hall, also 10,000 square feet, would be built beside the first building, overlooking the athletic fields. It too would have a large covered porch, but this porch would look out over the athletic field. It would have three levels, four classrooms, and much-needed storage. The first level would have a car wash for the school's many vehicles: vans and cars, tractors, trucks, bulldozers, backhoe, and garbage trucks.

The third building would be a modern hog-raising building. It would later be named for farm manager Jack Tillman and his wife, Sherry. With all the construction started and the largest summer school session (over 267 enrolled) about to end, it was time for a weekend trip to Turkey Foot.

Miles of Mountain Hiking to Turkey Foot

Have you ever made a 32-mile hike with a 15- to 30-pound pack? Several OBI staff and 21 of our boys have just done so. For all involved it was an experience that will be remembered forever.

It was testing, tiring, a little painful and exhilarating. They had a lot of fun and are glad they did it. Boys' Dean Bud Underwood and wife, Kay, our admissions director, devoted many hours to planning, preparation and execution. Everything went off like clockwork.

On Monday they met to pack at 6:30 AM and went on one of our school buses to Lornero on the Laurel County line, where they began their hike on a trail laid out by the U.S. Forest Service. In each of their packs were changes of socks, an extra pair of shoes, swim trunks, two quarts of water, snacks of cookies and granola bars.

They walked 50 minutes and rested 10. At noon they swam for 25 minutes, then lunched on Vienna sausage, pork and beans, a cup of fruit cocktail and vanilla pudding.

That evening, having walked 10 miles, they camped at S-Tree, which has neither electricity or water. Mrs. Underwood and her daughter-in-law, OBI teacher Lori, met them with a van-load of their sleeping bags, fresh water and a change of clothing. Also they delivered fried chicken from the OBI kitchen, and heated corn and green beans over a fire. By 9:30, with campfires built, all settled down to sleep while the women returned to campus.

Tuesday morning the Underwood women, with OBI automotive repair and welding teacher Harold Underwood, left the campus at 5:30 with fresh water and the ingredients for breakfast. Dozens of eggs were scrambled over an open fire, along with pounds of bacon and sausage. Many loaves of bread were toasted in skillets.

Dirty clothes and bedrolls were put in the van as the support group returned to campus, and the hikers were off to walk 14 miles the second day.

Dean of Students Erma Smith, husband John, our drafting teacher, their youngest son, '82 OBI graduate Chuck, and myself jointed the three support persons in taking a fresh change of clothing, bedrolls and the ingredients for supper and met at the pre-arranged campsite called Turkey Foot.

Our hikers beat us there, and each had bathed in cold, rushing river water near their four campsites. They had wood fires going at each one. Soon hamburgers were being fried along with skillets full of raw onions. These, along with fresh tomatoes and pickles, made for wonderful hamburgers and cheeseburgers. Baked beans and potato salad satisfied even the hungriest. The 20th birthday of one of our seniors, and the 56th birthday of John Smith, who had served at OBI 18 years, were celebrated with homemade chocolate cake.

All the support group left near dark except myself. I settled down on a rubber mat with a pillow and cover. Soon everyone was sound asleep including Mr. Underwood's dog, Sunshine, who walked all 32 miles and had his own little sleeping pallet. Not having hiked all those miles, my sleep came later. It was beautiful looking up at the stars, a very bright moon, surrounded by trees 80 to 100 feet tall. It was delightfully cool and only the snap and crackle of the fire disturbed the silence.

Wednesday breakfast ingredients arrived from campus, campfires were doused, and the fellows began their eight miles of hiking while I returned with the sleeping bags to campus.
Western Recorder, July 6, 1993

Two Starlit Nights Thirty-One Years Apart

Last issue I told you about 21 of our students and several staff sharing in a three-day camping trip including 32 miles of hiking.

Looking at the stars while the campfire burned nearly out, getting down to one glowing coal, I remembered other similar experiences—both in OBI service and while serving for over six years in the Peace Corps near the border of the then Soviet Union in the Turkoman tribal area. Many memories flooded in.

I remembered helping lead a large group of Oneida schoolboys on a camping trip in the fall of 1962. Harold Combs, a 1945 OBI graduate, biology teacher, dean of boys, and principal, was the organizer of that trip. Those mountain trails leading over to the post office that still operates at Mistletoe are little changed these 30 years later.

On that long-ago camping and hiking trip was a senior boy named "Bud" Underwood. Raised in Dayton, Ohio, one who had been in 13 schools over 11 years, Bud had never had such an experience. Walking in the mountains, sleeping under the stars, cooking over a campfire. Later as a husband and father, he saw to it that his four children had many such experiences as a family, time to share, be together, and to later treasure.

Lying there remembering, I recalled that a fellow OBI classmate, Bill Smith and I, college completed, were back working at Oneida (under then President David Jackson) when "Bud" was a senior. We were on that hiking trip. In fact, we went back miles to the school's kitchen and had a tremendous amount of hot chocolate made, and surprised the weary and thirsty hikers with this treat late in the night. Just this very morning Bill and his wife, Peggy, surprised me with a visit from Florida.

So, on this starlit night, I think how things change, and how they remain the same. The organizer of that camping trip 31 years ago, Harold Combs, has been retired many years. But "Bud" Underwood is now the dean. His oldest son is named Harold, in honor of the man who was his dorm supervisor at a very critical and formative time of his life.

Young Harold, who grew up hearing his parents' stories of OBI, came to Oneida from college and began teaching on his 21st birthday. That was seven years ago, now married three years, young Harold teaches automotive repair and welding. He is also our soccer and baseball coach, and has coached three class A wrestling teams to state championships. He also has been a part of this 1993 camping trip.

Much has happened over the 31 years that separate two starlit nights. A few feet away "Bud" Underwood, who has had such a powerful influence on the lives of several thousand boys in the past nine years, lies quietly sleeping. All around us are teenagers, all but two having their first camping and hiking experience. It is hard work and a tremendous responsibility to walk 32 miles and shepherd nearly 20 teenage boys day and night for three days... cooking, teaching to build fires, referee disputes, doctor mosquito or chigger bites. Out of it and many other experiences, boys are learning to be men, lives are being salvaged for useful work on this earth and for eternity.

I wonder which of these sleeping boys may be leading another generation of Oneida boys hiking 31 more years from now? I probably won't live to see that. Who knows? I would be a mere 83.
Western Recorder, July 20, 1993

Back on campus, the trees were beginning to show that the season was soon to change. The "leaves on the branches hung down like bullfrogs drying on a clothes line" (an Oneida tale from the 1920s). The flowers, well watered, were still blooming in the summer heat. One might think this would have been a good time to be lazy, with everyone taking long naps in the afternoons. There were no such days at Oneida! The campers, including Barkley and the other staff, had barely returned to campus and gotten settled into the work schedule before it was time for hundreds of students to arrive for the opening of the fall term. They would be soon be fit to be hung out to dry!

No Water, No Lights!

At 4:00 AM the walkie-talkie that sits near my bed crackled into life. Our dorm house-parents, key maintenance men and several others of us have this means of instant communication.

Imagine my consternation to learn that, on our first day with everyone back to start our 94th academic year, we were without water anywhere on campus. Until one and a half years ago, we always processed and purified our own water. But now we are on a public system.

I made sure the proper public authorities were made aware of our desperate situation. Then we began to make "do" with the unexpected emergency.

Cooks were preparing breakfast for hundreds and they were notified to use paper plates and cups as we had no way of knowing when we would have water to wash dishes.

Over 600 boys, girls and adult staff would be waking up, using the toilets, taking showers, washing their faces, shaving, brushing their teeth, and we had no water. What would we do?

After brainstorming over our radios, some other key staff members were awakened, along with several of our senior and junior boys. We have thousands of feet of fire hose. Staff and students began unrolling the hoses near our indoor heated swimming pools which has thousands of gallons of water to a depth of nine feet. Gasoline-powered pumps were put in position to pump water through the hoses to the dorms.

We have 400- and 600-gallon capacity water tanks on wheels. Our boys wheeled these into position and water was pumped into them. Our girls have tubs, along with showers, so their tubs were filled. They then could carry water to flush the toilets, to take sponge baths, rinse their hair, *etc.*

We keep scores of five-gallon buckets in storage. Each had been washed out and kept for future use. Being good stewards and using our imagination, we are very good at stretching whatever resources come into our hands.

Soon those buckets were all in use. Each student needing to use a toilet was sent by a student monitor to carry a bucket of water for flushing. Boys came out to the water tanks and ran water to shampoo their hair, wash their faces, etc.

At 8:30 AM, with everyone already about the normal routine, our water came back on.

The very next night at dusk, we suddenly lost all electric power. This has happened before. Soon staff and students set up gasoline-powered generators kept in storage for just such emergencies to provide lights for three hours in our dorm stairwells and other critical places.

We still do not know why our water and power went out. But we made it through.

For the nearly 100 girls and boys here for the first time, many already homesick, no water, and then no electricity, added real grist to their normal homesick litany over the phone to family and friends.

Having detailed the above real...and many other imagined... woes, one girl was overheard telling her mother with a wail, "Would you believe, they have even made the gardener the principal!" This was said in reference to our new principal who has her earned doctorate and works in our flower beds for the love of it.

Western Recorder, July 27, 1993

By September, the students were all back for the third-quarter session. Oneida was off to a good start, with the soccer team winning their first five games—something they had never done before. The girls' track team swept their first meet, and the boys' track team won their first track meet too. The Band and the Choir each had opening performances in the Manchester town square as part of "Clay County Days". What a responsibility each person at Oneida had! There were more than 200 young people under the age of fourteen at Oneida that fall. Barkley thought being a private Christian school made all the difference in how these would be educated. He wrote:

Recent Highlights

Have you ever thought how much time a public school student spends waiting for and riding a school bus daily? A conservative figure would be two hours. That adds up to 10 hours weekly or 360 hours for the nine-month school year. That is equivalent to 45 standard eight-hour working days per school year! Multiply that amount of time by millions of school children and the wasted time is staggering.

One of the advantages of a boarding school is that the 10 hours most young people spend weekly waiting for and riding a bus can be spent in many more productive ways. Extra time for study, practicing a musical instrument, reading, participating in extra athletic practice, drama or academic team.

In a boarding school, all the waking hours can be a learning time whether in study, play or work. All of it is within a broad framework, and more integrated because it is being supervised day and night (even weekends) by the same staff.

It has been well said that "idle minds are the devil's workshop". One of the great strengths of Oneida is that we have a well-rounded program that keeps our young people usefully occupied from the time they awaken each morning until bedtime, and that includes weekends.

Having such an active program, and having our students all their waking hours, makes it possible for much more to be accomplished in a shorter period of time. The cumulative effect is often truly life-changing.

Another great advantage we have, being a Christina school (not relying on tax money) is that we are free to share Christ in the classroom and every situation. How can a teacher tell a girl or boy who they are, what they might do or be, if they cannot tell them about God, and what Christ has already done for them? Our teachers have the wonderful advantage.

Not every child accepts the message, but at least we are able to tell everyone many times. The great majority of them come to us spiritually lost. It naturally follows that many also are lost academically, socially and in every way. They have no sense of who they are, no self respect, and thus little or no respect for others.

But, praise God, the great majority who leave us, after being with us for a time, go away in a much different condition. They have the Lord in their lives. That does make a difference. It gives one an entirely different perspective on everything.

We teach our students that they are made in God's image, each one uniquely different. We are able to teach about love here. For God is love. Those who truly have God in their hearts have love in their life. If love is not in what we are doing, then Jesus is not in that activity.

It is so wonderful that when we are able to live by faith, doing in love that which God has commanded us to do, he blesses and multiplies. There are miracles today just as real as in Bible times. But many are unaware because there are no miracles in their own life experiences. There can be no miracles without faith. Nor can there be miracles where love is missing. But faith and love, active, sharing the good news of a risen Lord, ministering in his name to the needs of others, is blessed of our Lord who is the same yesterday, today and ever. All things are possible with Him.

Western Recorder, September 28, 1993

A fall term never went by more quickly. The falling leaves signified that Thanksgiving would arrive shortly. Every day the new buildings rose higher, and Barkley longed to have them done by Christmas. Every day, while he was leading the many "Tours", he shared the details of their progress. It was a beautiful fall, never more lovely to him. He often thought back to the trip to Turkey Foot. Who would God be sending to Oneida in the years ahead? Who was now there, perhaps unknown to him, who might be another Burns? He let his thoughts travel many years down the road, through the swirling clouds of that November sky; yes, he could see, through the eyes of faith, another youngster growing in strength and wisdom and honor!

Bubble Gum and Turkey

Miss Bottoms' sixth grade class is an above-average, highly motivated, imaginative group of four girls and five boys. They are well organized.

Some weeks ago they decided they were going to have a class Thanksgiving dinner. They each made donations from their weekly allowances toward a class fund to buy the turkey. Treasurer Brian, a young man from Louisville whose mother was one of my students for four years, dutifully deposited the money in the class account in our student bank.

The class then proceeded to draw up a menu. It was agreed that Miss Bottoms would bake the turkey and the class members would do the rest of the cooking themselves. Class President Jason, from Kettering, Ohio, has a culinary specialty...macaroni and cheese. So the class also agreed to buy the necessary ingredients so Jason could do his thing. Then the class came up with the more traditional foods such as mashed potatoes, green beans, corn, dressing, cranberries and bread.

But the class finances did not quite cover all these other items, so they decided to talk our kitchen folk out of the raw ingredients and were successful.

There was rising excitement. The guest list began to expand. Another of their teachers, Pat Rowe and family, were invited. They also asked me, our middle school principal and secretary to come.

We showed up with some trepidation. The principal whispered to me that he had overheard Miss Bottoms, his assistant coach for the high school varsity girls' basketball team, asking someone how to bake a turkey.

But bake it she had, and Jason's large bowl of macaroni and cheese looked most inviting, as did everything the young people had prepared. After the blessing, we each served ourselves and found turkey and all to be most delicious.

Being a perfect host, one of the boys came around about midway through the meal with a large sack of bubble gum which he enthusiastically pressed upon me and the principal. Being traditionalists, we both smiled but declined the proffered bubble gum between our turkey and mashed potato course.

The whole meal was topped off not only with the usual Thanksgiving pumpkin pie, but also with peach and apple pie. Then there was an absolutely delicious crumb-covered pie called Dutch apple.

Having eaten, I was informed there was $2.42 left in the class account...we like to stay in the "black" financially.

A special guest for the evening was Jorge who had just arrived from Miami a few hours before. Born in the Cuban community, his Spanish is more fluent than his English. Our newest sixth-grader, a handsome 12-year-old, he was obviously an exciting addition for our young ladies. In fact, he charmed all.

Another Jason, highest-ranking academically, is a mountain boy form Lee County. Nick from Corbin, Jamie from Detroit, Kammie from Cincinnati, Sarah from Oneida, Henry from Shepherdsville and Leslie from Floyd County completed the dinner party....

Thirty minutes after the meal our young friends were engrossed in the video Aladdin and Teen-age Mutant Ninja Turtles. At one point Henry had Jorge in a headlock. Later I overheard Henry telling the other boys that Jorge was the only one ever to get out of his headlock. Oh, to be 11 again!

Western Recorder, December 27, 1993

Oneida Christmas Roundup

The last thing we do each year before our more than 700 students and staff scatter for the 17-day Christmas break is to worship in our chapel.

Of course, we worship there every day, but the Christmas service is extra special. This year each one who had a part simply outdid themselves. Our students studying Russian read a part of the Christmas miracle in Russian and then in English, and sang several carols in Russian.

Not to be outdone was the German class singing *Silent Night* on the 175th anniversary of its first being sung in its original tongue. Then the Spanish classes all joined together on stage to sing.

Our band performed beautifully as a group, then a duet of instruments, and a solo performance by one of our younger band members. Our choir sang three carols.

But the ones that really stole the show were our 25 girls and boys in our staff school, kindergarten through grade five. One of our teachers for this age group grew up in three Arab countries where her parents served as foreign missionaries. She had taught the children several songs familiar to Arab Christians. The little ones did these beautifully as well as others in English.

Then came the benediction and the shout of "Home for Christmas" for all, many who live hundreds, even thousands, of miles away from home for the sake of a Christian education here at Oneida.

In the weeks of December there had been so many events. Our Oneida Players had brought Scrooge and the others of Dickens' *A Christmas Carol* to life on three memorable evenings before very appreciative audiences.

Our international students from nine countries had a memorable evening of eating and singing in their own languages.

Our dorm house-parents went all out in three dorm parties of fun and fellowship and a special treat for each girl and boy from the youngest to the oldest.

The Ensemble put up the chapel tree early in December and covered the great 6,500-pound beams with garlands as is their annual custom. The choir pianist, one of our elementary teachers, and her husband, our assistant farm manager, hosted all to a two-hour party in their home three miles from the main campus.

We also had trees, a contest for best-decorated classroom doors, windows and bulletin boards, all of which had their Christmas finery. Many of our staff were on our knees in the Oneida Baptist Church the last moments of the old year and the first of 1994. Then, as has become tradition in recent years, we encircled the auditorium holding hands, and impromptu we sang *Blessed Assurance, Jesus Is Mine*. *Western Recorder*, January 4, 1994

1994
Year 23

We all must die…no one escapes that. Each of us has known that all our lives. It is all in <u>God's</u> TIMING, "to live is Christ, to die is gain". "For I am persuaded that neither death, or life, nor angels, nor things to come, nor height, nor depth nor any other creature shall be able to separate us from the love of Christ, which is in Christ Jesus our Lord."
—Barkley Moore

January 24, 1994, Oneida, Kentucky. Rain had been drizzling over almost all of Kentucky for several hours. At Oneida, three small creeks, the Red Bird, Bullskin, and Goose Creeks, surrounding the quaint village and converging into the South Fork of the Kentucky River, were beginning to overflow their banks. As first light broke over the cold unrobed hills, silence filled the morning air. It had been just a few hours earlier that Gloria Bowling, Barkley's sister, had returned with Dr. Moore from Baptist Hospital in Corbin, Kentucky, where Dr. Moore had been hospitalized for several days with pneumonia. His doctors wanted him to stay in the hospital, but Barkley just had to get back to his boys and girls. Barkley's mother had come by to tidy up the room and lay out his clothes for the following day. Fussing over him was her deepest joy; tonight she would fuss *at* him, telling him to stay in bed the next day. She lovingly caressed the cool sheets and pressed the pillows smooth with her hands. Two dear women, both servants of the Lord at Oneida and dear sisters in the Lord to Barkley, Pat Hignite, the hostess of Anderson Hall, and Myrtle Cooke, Guidance Counselor, had bid him goodnight. He had told them he would be in chapel the next morning, wearing his oxygen mask. He planned to assure the students that he would be fine. It was A Time to Bid Farewell. With a final goodnight, Pat looked back. Dr. Moore gave her a final wave with his hand. No one knew that their beloved friend, beloved son, would be gone before morning came.

It was as if sorrow had waited for daybreak to come to make known its secret. As January 25 dawned, the body of a humble saint but a giant of a man, Barkley Moore, lay lifeless in the east room on the second floor of Anderson Hall, now the Guest House, but in former days the home of the presidents of the Oneida Baptist Institute, including James Anderson Burns. In the early morning hours, Barkley Moore had been called by a dispatch of Heaven to a new assignment. He had finished his race on earth. In the blink of an eye, he was standing in Paradise gazing into the eyes of his dear Savior!

Through the mist of time, I see another one of those presidents, an elegant lady, Sylvia W. Russell, standing at the window of Anderson Hall. She seems to be whispering the same eulogy she had spoken of one of those presidents, James Anderson Burns. The words were a whisper through the winter breeze: "There comes to me—the recollection of a legend I have heard sometime, somewhere—that if a living being be shut up in the walls of a building, the building will have a soul. So here, the life-blood of the man seems to speak out from each brick and stone in these buildings and from every blade of grass, from every twig and from every tree."

And so the lifeblood of a giant of the faith, Barkley Moore, had been poured out for the Divine call of God on his life—and His purpose and mission in the lives and minds of children; not just the children along the backwaters and hollows of Clay County, but the world! The Lord had led him over the mountains, around the back roads, to places where there were no roads, around treacherous ravines, where breathtaking beauty and pain and suffering abounded on every hand, to the far corners of the world. Mr. Burns had been led to begin a school, Oneida Institute—to love young people for their Master, to lead them to Christ, to give guidance, shelter from the storms of life, and a Christian education to needy young men and women. Nearly fifty years after Mr. Burns had passed that way, Barkley Moore had picked up the mantle of enduring love, and marched to the front to lead the charge in the battle for the minds and hearts of children, to love them in the Saviors' name—and now he was gone.

The hills had taken note! A gloom too deep for words hung in the mist shrouded air. It was A Time to Grieve.

Over eons of time, these verdant hills, rising around the lush valley floor with a fine knoll pushing upward like a diamond glittering in the sun, had stood to greet the dawn's sun rising over Little Bullskin's hills. The rain continued to pour down like teardrops the rest of the day and the next, until the rivers overflowed their banks and threatened to shut in every soul and shut out the world, while the grieving hills, every brown blade of grass, every twig, and every tree mourned. Tears fell freely down the cheeks of family, students, adopted children, and thousands of friends, not just all over Kentucky but around the world, as the news spread of the death of a noble servant, a loving father to thousands of students, a giant of the faith. Barkley Moore, fifty-two years old, whose damaged lungs had miraculously served him all those years, having been completely used up for the Lord, had taken his last breath. But, what rejoicing in Heaven that morn! A saint had been called home, freed from a sick mortal body to take on immortality.

He had gone to his Father's house, "where shadows never come, and genial summer never ends: where the roses never fade, and the fruits never decay; where disease never invades and death never divides; where there are no tears and no goodbyes; where there is no sin and no sorrow; no temptation and not a breath of impurity; where all is light and love and sinless ecstasy." (*The Other Side of Death*, J. Sidlow Baxter)

The raindrops stopped falling! In their place freezing snowflakes blanketed the hills and valleys in a new wardrobe of glittering white. It was as if angel wings swathed the snow on every unrobed tree and gave them new life. Spires became shrines, and buildings and trees silhouetted in white dared the soul to see more than the darkness—to feel the promise of peace and life everlasting. On campus and in the now "snowed in" village, soft as the voice of an angel, came, "whispering hope"!

It was the same hope that rose over the mountains in James Anderson Burns' day. It now echoed in the hearts of tens of thousands across Kentucky and around the world. With every ounce of his being, Barkley Moore had written the message of hope into the lives of thousands. Yes, because his passion for learning, loving, caring for that little mountain school in Clay County, Kentucky, which he called his Galilee, was based on the immutable, matchless love of the Nazarene, he had caught the vision of where he should give the Offering of his life—in his Galilee. He had triumphed over great obstacles, won great battles, and led an army of young soldiers to the Lord.

Barkley Moore, like Elisha, had picked up the mantle. His task: love the Lord's children as if they were his own—build up a home, an estate for them, and a school where they would be protected, nurtured, disciplined, where they could grow in knowledge and wisdom for the glory of the Lord. He had built, as his Father wanted him to build, a great learning center for the hungry of heart and spirit and mind, yearning to know what lies over the mountains of life; yearning, but perhaps not knowing their deepest desire and need was to know the Nazarene, who would be their dearest friend, who came from beyond the Sunrise and Sunset Mountains: He who made the Mountains!

Yes, he had carried the mission of God's love for his children forward. Burns wrote, "The work of Oneida Institute has scarcely begun. It shall be carried on into the ages, a heritage for generations yet unborn. Workers will live and love and labor till their tasks are done-others will rise up to take their places—to carry the banner still further to the front—whither we do not know. But when the end has come, and the sheaves are garnered, we'll cast our trophies at his feet."

Barkley Moore had, with the blood, sweat, tears, joy of his life, left a physical imprint on this little place he called his Galilee, in buildings raised, buildings restored, holdings in land and property. But more important to him were the boys and girls he had rescued from a broken world, been instrumental in leading to the Lord, given a home, a school, a special place where they would be protected, nourished, nurtured; a place where they would be led to his Savior, the Lord Jesus Christ. He had finished his part of the building of Oneida Baptist Institute into a fine academic institution, with the finest resources in the state of Kentucky. He had enlarged the boundaries, as had Jabez, who called on the God of Israel to bless him and extend his borders. "...Oh that thou wouldest bless me indeed, and enlarge my coast, and that thine hand might be with me..." (*I Chronicles* 4: 10) It was not for himself that Barkley cried to the Lord! He deliberately turned down advances in pay. He left no personal wealth, it was just as it had been when he had left Iran twenty-four years earlier. He left this life penniless, having given away every dime he had earned to someone who needed it more, even to the clothes on his back. His beloved Kentucky Baptists and friends of Oneida all over the world had given over $50,000,000 for his boys and girls during his time at the Oneida Baptist Institute. His work was done! The Oneida Baptist Institute he left to his children and the children to come through its doors in the future would be the inheritance he left; they would inherit the work of his life, his love gift!

His was **"THE OFFERING"** of **"Gift-love"**, as C.S. Lewis so beautifully wrote: "the love that moves a man to work and plan and save for the future well-being of his family which he will die without sharing or seeing—that which sends a lonely or frightened child to its mother's [or father's] arms." And no child who had been even one day under Barkley's care had failed to hear of the Father in Heaven who loved and gave His only Son for his or her salvation!

Postlude

Eulogy for
Glen Barkley Moore

Dr. Jim Taylor, President, Cumberland College
Melvin Davidson Chapel
Oneida Baptist Institute
January 28, 1994

A true, true giant has fallen. Dr. Barkley Moore, President of Oneida Baptist Institute, has gone on to be with our Lord. Our hearts are grieved and we mourn his passing because we loved him like a brother. And like the Apostle of old, I reckon that the present sufferings of this world are not to be compared to the glory which awaits us at heaven's portals.

At age 52, Barkley Moore had done more, seen more, traveled more and contributed more to others than most people do in a hundred life times.

If it's true that an institution can be measured by the length and breadth of one man, then this is true of Oneida and of Barkley Moore.

Today, Barkley Moore casts a shadow for good the length and breadth of our Kentucky Baptist Convention. Indeed, he casts a shadow for good across this nation and literally around the world for he has left unmistakable and indelible footprints in the sands of time.

Barkley Moore never had a wife because he didn't need one.

After all, he was married to Oneida Baptist Institute. He didn't need children because he had all of you students who are currently here, and those many who have attended and those who have graduated from Oneida.

He cared deeply about others and about each one of you. Barkley was totally committed. We recognized Barkley's commitment by awarding him an honorary degree at Cumberland College—the highest honor Cumberland College bestows. But this honorary degree was only one of the many recognitions Barkley received for his outstanding accomplishments.

And, as I thought about Barkley, I recalled that he was warm and tenderhearted, but tough minded, and he always extended a helping hand to anyone who needed help.

Surely no towering shaft of marble we could ever erect could possibly equal the monument already erected to Barkley and we know as Oneida Baptist Institute.

But Barkley's contribution wasn't limited to Oneida Baptist Institute. For instance, I'll never forget turning on a national network T.V. show years ago, and hearing Dr. Robert Schuler of the Crystal Cathedral spend the better part of his sermon on Barkley Moore and his outstanding and stellar service in the Peace Corps. He described Barkley as a person reaching out to the disfranchised, and reaching out to the under-represented. I heard of how Sergeant Shriver of Kennedy Fame recognized Barkley Moore for service—the longest of any Peace Corps volunteer in history (Six and one half years).

I thought of how Barkley had felt the heavy hand of God on his shoulder, leaving law school in his senior year to commit himself totally, completely and without reservation to others.

I recalled how Barkley had walked 12 miles each way one day to keep an Iranian student from dropping out of school. At about this time in our Nation's story, a national best-selling book had appeared known as *The Ugly American*. But in contrast, when the people wrote articles about Barkley, they called him "The Beautiful American", because he was not arrogant or condescending or cavalier. Rather, Barkley put service above self by building schools, kindergartens, libraries, and educational facilities. He simply rolled up his sleeves and went to work helping others.

I had to pinch myself when I heard that Barkley had been on the Today Show talking about the Peace Corps. And I read about his service to others in the *New York Times* and the *Los Angeles Times*. Barkley literally walked with the high and the mighty, but he never lost the common touch.

As I thought about Barkley, I recalled that he was always there for any boy or girl who needed him, for any youngster who arrived on Oneida's campus. Barkley quickly became that youngster's mother, father, sister, brother, friend. He was family.

He knew his students and he knew his staff well. He could call them by name and knew from where they had come, and if Barkley had his way, he knew where they were headed. Those of us who knew Barkley well loved him for his sincerity, for his devotion to duty and for his complete commitment to Oneida. Barkley was totally committed and devoted and at times, almost totally preoccupied with Oneida, with the boys and girls he meant to help.

We love Barkley because of his sincerity, because of his commitment to plain living, and because of his genuine concern for others. When Barkley talked about Oneida, his eyes flashed with intensity and you could sense his overwhelming enthusiasm for Oneida and for the students and staff. When Barkley talked, people listened. His speeches and his columns in the Western Recorder made things come alive as he energized us in animated detail. No one yawned when Barkley talked—but they may have looked at their watch after an hour or so.

And—let me say, that if you have never had a tour of Oneida by Barkley Moore, well—then—you've just NEVER had a tour!! Barkley could point to a building and tell you the most intricate details. He could tell you who constructed it, when it was constructed. Barkley could point to anyone on campus and recall that person's life history with precise detail and could tell of his hopes and dreams. In his eyes you could see the radiance of the light of learning. Barkley was infected with enthusiasm and his enthusiasm was personal, noticeable and contagious and all encompassing.

Barkley literally saved lives and changed lives for the good, and pointed them in the right direction. Only heaven will record the thousands and even tens of thousands of lives that have been changed for good. Because of Barkley, life is inextricably different from what it could have possibly been otherwise for so many. He changed time and eternity.

Barkley was unlike anyone else I've ever known. Combining the traits and characteristics of a person with a photographic memory. He was a genius, a candidate for sainthood, an entrepreneur, a tent evangelist, contractor, an architect. But most importantly, a servant and a Christian role model in word and deed.

His Christian beliefs could not be contained and literally spilled over into his daily actions. His singular mission was to promote Oneida Baptist Institute and he did this by sheer personal magnetism and the force of his personality. No task was too daunting. Barkley was not a could've, would've, should've, might've person. Rather, Barkley was a take charge "can do" person. If there was a student who needed help, he helped. If a building needed to be built, he built it. If more farm land was needed, Barkley acquired it.

Barkley was a man of complete integrity and remarkable genius. He combined so many endearing qualities. He was a Mark Hopkins, a school master, about whom it was said, "All you need is a teacher at one end of the log and a student at the other end of the log." Barkley was truly a Mark Hopkins. As Judy Rose said, "Barkley is a modern day Mother Theresa." Barkley Moore was also a regular "Mr. Chips". You will recall from literature, that Mr. Chips was also a school master, he was a bachelor, and he had no children. Mr. Chips once overheard someone saying that he had no children. Mr. Chips responded to what was said by saying: "No children! No children! How wrong could you be? You see, I have thousands of children, and they are the students and former students at my school." And so it was for Barkley, whose children were and are the students of Oneida. Barkley was not only a Mark Hopkins and a Mr. Chips, he was also a Father Flannigan. It was Flannigan who said, "There's no such thing as a bad boy or a bad girl, there is good in every boy and girl." And, Barkley looked deeply for that good in every boy and girl, every young man and woman. Barkley was like Will Rogers who said, "I never met a man I didn't like."

Barkley worked endlessly, tirelessly, burning the candle at both ends. Barkley was far too busy to be little or petty. He worked day and night. Barkley clearly put the emphasis on the student. His legacy of faith, hard work, integrity and character personified true greatness, and he never lost his humility. He was an uncommon man with a common touch.

Many times at 11:00 at night or later, the phone would ring and it would be Barkley working late in his office when everyone else had gone home. Barkley had "just one more student who needed help". Barkley then was totally devoted and totally committed and was thankful for his wonderful staff and those who worked with him. Barkley had enormous energy and contagious enthusiasm.

Barkley's work with the Peace Corps was but a prelude of greater things to come as he saw to it that Oneida's assets and facilities increased astronomically, and more importantly, as students came to know our Lord and Savior, His clear love and pure motive always showed through.

When our son, Jim, passed away, it was Barkley and Farhad, a former student of Oneida and Cumberland, who came to our home among others and who sat with my wife and me into the wee hours of the morning, helping us deal with our loss of our only child. We shall never forget Barkley for what he was and what Oneida is. Barkley was by any measure, an example of uncompromising standards from his days as a student at Oneida to his days in the Peace Corps and through his days as President at Oneida Baptist Institute.

So let me say that Barkley, no doubt, is looking down today from the portal of Heaven and he is smiling. "Well done, thou good and faithful servant." Barkley is where there is no more pain, no more sorrow, no more suffering. And like the Apostle of old, I reckon that the present sufferings of this world are not to be compared to the glory which awaits us. Barkley now has left us with the greatest challenge of all—that challenge which Barkley left for us is to carry on what he and his predecessors and colleagues have started. Barkley would want us to carry on! And we must carry on!

As I left Washington's International Airport early this morning in the ice and snow, I wondered how mere mortal man's clay lips could ever describe this single, solitary life of Barkley Moore. Thus, you have heard my feeble attempts to touch on some of the endearing traits and characteristics of Dr. Barkley Moore. My soul is subdued and my feelings tender toward Barkley. God bless you. God bless the Moore family, and God bless Oneida Baptist Institute.

A Tree Has Fallen

William W. Marshall, Executive Director
of the Kentucky Baptist Convention
Western Recorder, *February 8, 1994*

In a mountain area considered remote by most Kentucky "flatlanders", a mighty tree has fallen. And in its falling the earth around it trembled.

The president of Oneida Baptist Institute was no ordinary man, though he would deny he had any marks of greatness. Modesty characterized his life, and his lifestyle, to such an extent that it was somewhat uncomfortable to be in his presence.

Barkley Moore was a single-focused leader, and Oneida was his focus. A product of the institution, a descendent of its founders, and except for a few years of advanced academic preparation and Peace Corps service, it was the only life he knew.

His propensity for work, his driven-ness for the school and his body size ultimately merged as powerful streams into a flood that prematurely swept away his life. I expressed my personal concern for him over the years during visits there when we had quality time together, alone. He usually smiled and graciously accepted these concerns as from a friend.

Often our conversations were "after-hours", in his office; he in his chair behind his desk and I on the couch where he sometimes slept.

On one such occasion, he opened mail as we talked, glancing at letters, sometimes reading me a passage, sometimes telling me the amount of a check, though never by name. I think it was on this occasion that I realized those letters were sometimes reflected in his weekly columns in the Western Recorder. These letters were very personal to him, and in them, I think, he often found refuge and renewal.

With his untimely death, I considered providential our last time together, just a bit over a year ago. Alice had joined me, and we stayed in the old hand-cut stone house atop the hill which Barkley called home, though he rarely slept there. We slept in the room his mother has always provided me when I was there for an overnight and especially during the Mountain Missions Conferences.

Following an afternoon of touring the campus again, with special attention to the newest buildings, renovations and acquisitions, we had "supper" in the cafeteria. Later that evening, on up until nearly midnight, we sat in the Moore parlor while he walked us through photographs, artifacts and other memorabilia reflecting his seven-year Peace Corps experience, something I had long hoped he would tell me about. Before he let me drive him back to the campus, we set a time for our journey away from campus the next day.

The next afternoon, having agreed to "pass" on supper, we set out. Since Barkley did not drive, I was chauffeur. Although we would visit several Oneida properties well away from the campus, one lingers, now more poignantly.

On U.S. 11 a mile or so toward Manchester, he directed me onto a gravel and dirt road. Within a few minutes, we were in sight of a small family graveyard. We parked not far from the short fence gate which permitted us access, Barkley leading the way.

It has been a hot mid-summer's day, but the late afternoon sun had grown merciful, and neither we nor he were in a hurry to get somewhere else.

It is a pleasant place; unpretentious stones marking generations of Barkley's kin, now resting silently as a family. This, he said to us, would be his resting place, unaware that it would be soon, or that the rising waters along the road would delay his burial for a few days.

I suppose I had made more than 20 trips to Oneida in the past but only on this journey had he invited us here to this quiet place.

I will visit again that special place where he now rests. And I will remember that summer afternoon. But he will not be there. He will still be walking the campus of Oneida—in the lives of staff, faculty and friends of the school.

Most especially, Barkley Moore will be present in the several thousand graduates whom he knew by name.

Annual Session of the Kentucky Baptist Convention

November 1994

W hen Barkley Moore's brothers and sisters in the Lord convened for the annual session of the Kentucky Baptist Convention in November 1994, they had many issues to discuss, but one thing on their hearts was not an issue: they would give Barkley Moore the honor due his life of sacrificial love and service to the children of Kentucky Baptists and the world. The messengers from 2300 churches of the Kentucky Baptist Convention would rise in recognition of his **"Offering"**—what he had worked, pleaded for, laid down his very life for: the call of his Master to "Go and make disciples [of all children] in all the nations, baptizing them into the name of the Father and of the Son and of the Holy Spirit, and then teach these new disciples [children] to obey all the commands I have given you."

Barkley Moore had preached the message, never thinking he should stop even as he entered the hospital, even after he was there for several days, even as he was told he should stay longer for care. He had to get back home to his boys and girls. He no doubt had one more letter to write, one more phone call to make!

Every Kentucky Baptist had heard again and again the message of the real, desperate needs of the children of the world: the poor, the illiterate, the ones left behind in broken marriages, the ones left behind in the secular education system, the ones left behind in third world countries, in war-torn countries, in rich and poverty-stricken countries, the disenfranchised and the dropouts of the richest nation in the world, the ones who slept in cars, the ones who broke the law so they would be fed even if it meant jail, the wealthy parents who begged him to take their children so they could be freed from the temptations of drugs, alcohol, wild parties in the public education system.

They had heard his pleas for help. They had seen him work so hard it made them uncomfortable. They had heard him plead the cause so beautifully it made them cry. They had read his messages in the *Western Recorder* and the words made them long to become better Christians, better parents, better husbands, better wives, better people. They had seen his faith and it urged them to step out in faith themselves. They had seen and felt his passionate love for children, for the old, the helpless, and it made them want to love more. They had seen his optimism for every boy and girl and they were lifted up to see the greatness in their own children, in the future of mankind. They had seen him walk in the steps of the Savior, the humble Galilean, and seen the difference a dedicated follower could make in a very small place when he made it his Galilee.

The Kentucky Baptist Convention had heard the Macedonian Call. They recognized the need for boys and girls, the children of the world, to have a special place, a safe haven, a home, clothes, food, medicine— whatever they lacked. They had heard the call to support Christian educators, Christian farmers, Christian fathers, Christian mothers, as they taught, nourished, protected, guided, loved these children in the name of Jesus in this special place, the **Oneida Baptist Institute**.

As a child Barkley Moore had been taught in Sunbeams, "I'm a Little Sunbeam, Sunbeam, Sunbeam. I'm a Little Sunbeam of God's Love." He lived out his whole life being a Sunbeam of God's Love wherever he went: to Gonbad, Iran; to the homes up the hollows of Little Bullskin; to the halls of higher learning; to the rooms of the sick and infirm; to the deathbeds and funeral homes of Oneida's friends and family; to the smallest churches and the largest churches of the Kentucky Baptist Convention. He was a Sunbeam of Hope wherever he went. And everywhere he went boys and girls and common folk could walk faster, stand taller, love more nobly, appreciate their blessings more, study harder because for one brief moment they felt the Sunbeam of God's Love shine right into their souls and they knew they were special, knew they were great and good because

"God made no mistakes." When the messengers cast their ballot for the **Barkley Moore Father's Day Offering** for Oneida Institute, they saw and felt, for one brief moment, the Glory of the Lord's Mantle of Love, as it fell upon their own shoulders. They felt the SUNBEAM!

They felt compelled to sing in their hearts the great mission song, sung by every young person in the Southern Baptist Convention as he grew up in a mission environment:

We've a Story to Tell to the Nations

We've a story to tell to the nations,
That shall turn their hearts to the right,
A story of truth and mercy,
A story of peace and light,

For the darkness shall turn to dawning,
And the dawning to noonday bright;
And Christ's great kingdom shall come on earth,
The kingdom of love and light.

We've a song to be sung to the nations,
That shall lift their hearts to the Lord,
A song that shall conquer evil
And shatter the spear and sword.

We've a message to give to the nations,
That the Lord who reigns up above
Has sent us His Son to save us,
And show us that God is love.

We've a Savior to show to the nations,
Who the path of sorrow has trod,
That all of the world's great peoples
Might come to the truth of God.
H. Ernest Nichol, 1862-1928

Judy Ratliff Powell

The Barkley Moore Father's Day Offering for Oneida Institute is to this day one of only four special named offerings of the Kentucky Baptist Convention. (The others are **The Lottie Moon Christmas Offering** for Foreign Missions, **The Annie Armstrong Offering** for Home Missions, and **The Eliza Broadus Offering** for State Missions.)

380

Final Facts

D r. Barkley Moore had taken the Oneida Baptist Institute from almost certain closure in 1972, with heavy debt and an annual income of less than $200,000, with only one hundred students and twenty-five teachers and staff members, to an annual income of $4,000,000, with 600 students and over 150 teachers and staff members, and had increased the holdings of the school in lands and buildings to nearly $12,000,000 in gross value.

GOD SPEED THEE, NOBLE SERVANT

CPSIA information can be obtained at www.ICGtesting.com
Printed in the USA
LVOW01s0355100614

389257LV00001BA/1/P